THE ISLE OF WIGHT

An Illustrated History

Jack and Johanna Jones

Jack Jones   *Johanna Jones*

THE DOVECOTE PRESS

First published in 1987 by The Dovecote Press Ltd.
Stanbridge, Wimborne, Dorset BH21 4JD
ISBN 0 946159 44 0 (casebound)
ISBN 0 946159 49 1 (paperback)
© Jack and Johanna Jones
Photoset in Palatino by
Character Graphics, Taunton, Somerset
Printed and bound in Great Britain by
Biddles Ltd, Guildford and King's Lynn

Contents

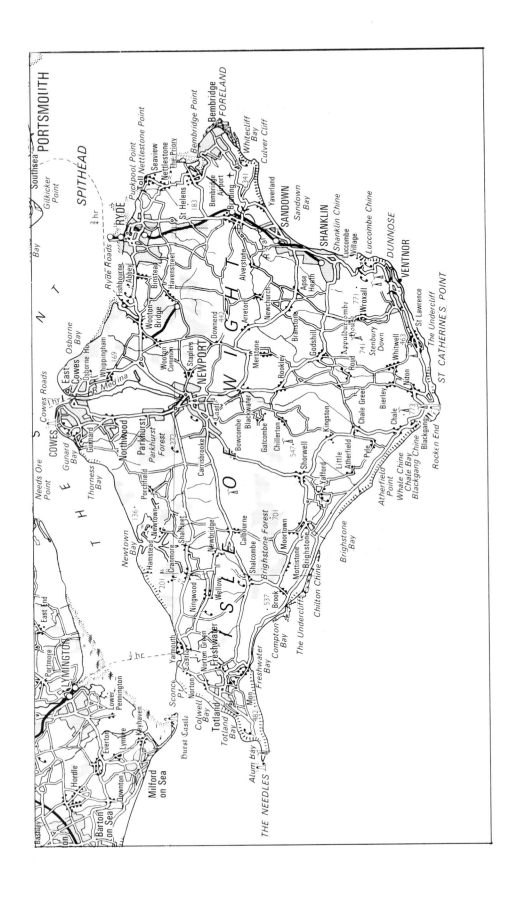

Introduction and Acknowledgements

Any attempt to condense the history of the Isle of Wight into one short volume will of necessity mean that it will be a highly selective document and one that reflects the particular interests of the writers. However, we have attempted to summarise the history of the Island from pre-historic times to our own day so that the reader may share with us our interest in and enthusiasm for the past which has shaped our present.

In preparing this book we have had information and generous assistance from the following organisations and individuals, to whom we offer our thanks; the Public Record Office; Staffordshire Record Office; The British Library; the Ordnance Survey for the map of the Island; Aerofilms Ltd; the British Hovercraft Corporation Ltd; Plessey Radar Ltd; the Isle of Wight County Press; Medina Borough Council; the following departments of the Isle of Wight County Council – Cultural Services for the use of their extensive collection of photographs; the County Record Office for generous and continuing help; the Archaeological Centre; Museums, Documentation and Collations department; Cowes Branch Library, marine section; the Trustees of Carisbrooke Castle Museum; the I W branch of the National Farmer's Union; the Women's Royal Voluntary Service; the British Red Cross; the Royal Yacht Squadron; Mr J Dearden, Ruskin Gallery, Bembridge School; Ryde School; Upper Chine School; Mr R Thompson, Unit Administration St Mary's Hospital; Mrs M Oglander; Mrs B Williamson; Mrs. C Caudwell; Mrs V Basford; Canon J Buckett, vicar of Newport; Mr C Webster, County Archivist; Dr R Prewer; Mr R H Buckett; Mr H B Pursley; Mr R H Smith; Mr John Fitzmaurice Mills; Mr D Stirman; Mr and Mrs D Attrill; Colonel and Mrs J A Aylmer. Particular thanks must go to the Revd Dom S F Hockey and Mr R Brinton for their help, and to our publisher David Burnett special thanks for struggling with two independent writers to achieve a single completed work.

ONE

The First Islanders

How old is the Isle of Wight? The oldest deposits still showing on the surface were laid down about 110 million years ago; but the dinosaurs whose fossil remains are found in these Wealden beds did not galumph around the Island as we know it. The scenery that they enjoyed consisted of the estuarine surroundings of a larger river, with the sea probably nowhere in sight. The horizon was punctuated by the gaunt shapes of tree-ferns whose herbage kept the iguanodons happily chomping, and whose trunks drifting down-river formed that glorious fossilised log-jam now known as the Pine Raft in Brook Bay.

Gradually over millions of years the land sank and came under a shallow cover of sea water depositing sediments that have given the Island its greensands and dark, slippery gault clays. Then, about 100 million years ago, the land subsided further and the sea deepened, forming a new series of deposits of calcium carbonate – the residue of the shells of tiny animals called foraminifera – interspersed with accretions of silica that formed clusters of flint nodules, to be gratefully used by prehistoric man for his tool-making millions of years later.

About 60 million years ago (dates are only approximate!) the chalk and limestone layers folded on an east-west axis like a rucked-up carpet, with a corresponding downward fold to the north, later to become the Solent. Between the hump and the dip – over what is now the northern part of the Island – warm temperatures and changing marine conditions deposited a sequence of sands and clays – which were to govern settlement patterns in historic times because they made for thicker vegetation cover and imposed the need for forest clearance before any cultivation.

There was another geological process, too, that would govern human settlement. Chalk being slowly soluble, millions of years of weathering gradually eroded the top of the chalk hump, exposing the older greensand layers far below. As the greensands are among the most cultivable soils, it is this eroded area that contained most of the building during the manor-house boom in the early 1600s, and which today encompasses nearly all the market gardens.

The heritage of geology to human setlement, then, was a very varied range of landscapes and soils, and this rich variety is part of the charm of the Island. Putting a date on the earliest appearance of man here is a horribly imprecise exercise because we can only study local finds of his (and her) flint tools and interpolate further information from similar tools found in a more datable context. There are indeed locally found core tools – such as hand-axes – dating from some 150,000 years ago. So slow was the evolution of these implements however that we cannot rule out a date as late as one of the milder phases of the last glaciation of the Ice Age – say about 50,000 years ago. Such a margin of error may seem less monstrous when seen against the vast scale of geological time in which the Island was created and life evolved. What can be said with

The mill pond at Alverstone, at the head of the eastern Yar, in about 1890.

9

The Longstone at Mottistone, the only megalithic monument in the Island. Behind the standing stone and the now recumbent stone is the low mound of a Neolithic long barrow associated with the burials of the first farming communities to settle in the Island during the third millennium BC.

more confidence is that core tools of this type were made by *homo sapiens*, for a similar flint equipment was found in connection with the Swanscombe skull – an unimpeachable relic from the Thames gravels, and not at all in the Piltdown league.

Other, flake tools, have been found in some quantity in the Island, and this type of industry is certainly referable to the final glaciation period, ending about 10,000 years ago. The makers of all these tools, though, were not exactly the first Islanders, for the Island had not yet been born. It was part of a great land mass, with higher ground to the south of us, giving way in turn to a large valley carved out by a main river where the English Channel now is. To the north of us·(if we identify with the modern Island) was a tributary river flowing south-eastwards out of the modern Southampton Water and through the modern Spithead, into the main 'Channel' river; and this Solent river in turn took tributary streams from the 'Island', which is the reason why the Island rivers and decayed rivers flow (or have flowed) from south to north.

The ice sheet at its fullest extent had not come farther south than the Thames valley, but certainly in the colder phases of the Ice Age the 'Island' would have presented a bleak, tundra type of landscape – a few stunted birches and little else in the way of vegetation. With the gradual improvement in climate temperate vegetation gratefully began to establish itself; and with the vegetation and the warmer temperature, the fish and the wildfowl; and following them, nomadic communities of hunters and fishermen, who used flint axes with 'tranchet' blades and made their hunting camps on river and lake banks and on the edge of forests.

Some of their camp sites now turn up below the limit of low tide; for with the melting of the great ice sheets the sea level was rising and making inroads on the coast. The sea flooded the Channel river and the Solent river, and finally.in about 6,000 B.C. (dates now are less wildly approximate) broke through the spine of chalk linking with 'England'; so now we meet the first. Islanders. They are mesolithic hunters still, but increasingly using small flint tools – arrowheads with chisel edges, and little flint blades with which to arm bone harpoons.

From now onwards practically every main cultural innovation associated with southern England proceeded to make its imprint on the Isle of Wight. Well before 3,000 B.C. the first communities of neolithic farmers appear in Britain, making the fundamental change from a hunting and gathering to a mainly settled economy. Their traces in the Island are not abundant, but fragments of their Peterborough-type decorated pottery have been found, and the survival of three long barrows is evidence of a degree of social organisation, suggesting a sizeable as well as a structured community. One of these, the Long Stone at Mottistone, fuses with the megalithic tradition in having a standing stone and a recumbent stone at its broad east end. A limited excavation of this barrow by Jacquetta Hawkes in September 1956 established that it was an artificial mound in association with neolithic pottery, but did not find trace of a burial chamber.

Metal-using, the next innovation, did not miss the Island. Several beaker burials are recorded, and flat copper axes – the type find of early Bronze Age metalwork – have turned up. Two classic hoards of early-middle Bronze Age metalwork – both about 1500 B.C. – are the Arreton

Down hoard (in the British Museum) and the Moons Hill hoard (in the Isle of Wight County Archaeological Centre), both including spearheads, flanged axes, and daggers. It is of the nature of prehistoric evidence that it tends to tell more about people's way of death rather than the way they lived; and the Island abounds in round barrows – 240 on record so far, and more turning up as crop marks every dry season – but many have been ploughed away, and others have been robbed in medieval and later periods, notably in the early 1800s when there was a frenzy of barrow-digging. One or two have had careful modern excavation, and one on Gallibury Down examined in 1979-80 gave radio-carbon dates, for organic material from the graves and pits below the mound, of between 1600 and 1400 B.C.

In general the grave-goods from these barrows are typical of the 'Wessex' culture; but pottery has been identified with affinities to Cornish ware – an interesting hint of prehistoric trade links, perhaps confirmed by the appearance in the Island of two polished stone axes from a factory site in Mount's Bay, Penzance.

Most of the features of the middle and later Bronze Age are among the Island finds: palstave axes, singly and in hoards; socketed bronze axes from Brittany; and urnfield sites.

Later Celtic settlement is reflected in a single-rampart promontory fort on Chillerton Down, and the remains of an occupation site at Knighton near Newchurch which produced, during excavation, some fragments of amphorae, indicating that the Islanders in about 100 B.C. were enjoying imported Italian wine, almost certainly reshipped through the prehistoric port at Hengistbury Head on the mainland.

How the Romans came to the Island in the course of Claudius's conquest of Britain in 43 A.D. is not clear either from historical or archaeological evidence – for the two sources now begin to overlap. The Island was annexed to Roman rule by the future Emperor Vespasian, whose

Some of the 'Five Barrows' on Brook Down, burials of the Bronze Age pastoralists who extended the use of metal weapons and tools, and had trading links as far afield as Scandinavia and the Mediterranean. These mounds date to about 1500 BC.

biographer Suetonius wrote: *Duas validissimas gentes superque viginti oppida et insulam Vectem Britanniae proximam in dicionem redegit.* ('He brought under our rule two of the strongest tribes, more than twenty towns, and the Isle of Wight near Britain'). The words *in dicionem redegit* are just ambiguous enough to cover either a skilful diplomatic annexation, or a military conquest. As Vespasian was at the head of a legion, and appears to have carved his way round much of central southern England, and was later given a triumph in celebration, one might infer that he took the Isle of Wight by force. There is a strange absence, though, of any Roman military material of the 1st century in the Island. This, being negative evidence, cannot be conclusive, so a slight mystery remains to add spice to future investigation.

The picture we get of the Island in Roman times is of quite intensive arable and stock farming based on the villas. Seven are known so far (though one was lost through coastal erosion in the 19th century) and there are signs of others. In three cases there are signs of a certain continuity of occupation on the site from the pre-Roman period. There are today substantial visible remains of two of the villas: a composite courtyard villa at Morton near Brading, with elaborate mosaic floors, and a corridor villa in Cypress Road, Newport, which has an exceptionally well-preserved bath block and hypocaust. As well as continuing and developing the Island farm production the new regime discovered and began to exploit the limestone deposits at Quarr near Binstead, which quarries indeed continued working during the medieval period and provided the stone for, among other buildings, Winchester and Chichester Cathedrals. As this quarry stone and the agricultural produce was traded out, various consumer goods came in to boost the standard of living: the omnipresent Samian table ware from the Gaulish factories, wine from Italy, even engraved glass bowls from Egypt. Where were these bought? The local farmers must have had somewhere for their shopping; but no sign of a town has yet been found.

The power vacuum caused by the disintegration of the Roman Empire at the beginning of the 5th century was filled by two waves of incomers: the pagan Jutes who moved in in the 6th century, and whose cemeteries with their interesting array of grave goods have been found at Bowcombe, Chessell, and even on the site of what was later to be Carisbrooke Castle; next, the Christian West Saxons who annexed the Island in the 7th century. Thus, as the historian Bede censoriously remarked, the Isle of Wight became the last place in Britain to receive Christianity.

Still the raids continued, the next being launched by the Vikings who from time to time made the Island their base camp for forays against the south of England in the late 10th and early 11th century. No archaeological trace of these Danish incursions has yet been found, but there are several notes of their visits in the Anglo-Saxon Chronicle. For the year 1001 it records:

> 'The went into the Isle of Wight, and there they roved about, even as they themselves would, and nothing withstood them... Then was it in every wise a heavy time, because they never ceased from their evil doings'.

It was one of history's ironies that, when something like settled rule at last came, it was brought by someone of Viking stock. His name was William of Normandy; and he came in 1066.

TWO

An Agricultural Island

The nature of our Island landscape was determined many millions of years before the first plough turned a furrow and began to make the land a servant of man. The character and vigour of the soil is settled by the rocks deep beneath the surface from which the farmer draws his harvest. The chalk downs, historic sheep runs of southern England, the clay lands on which grew the old forests, loamy fertile greensand, natural seedbeds for grain, all these land types can be found in the 94,146 acres of the Isle of Wight. They give to Island farming a diversity of soil which makes the whole area a miniature south of England.

Nearest to the mainland lie the clay lands. From Yarmouth to St Helens the flat fields and oak woods are a distinctive landscape. Here the forest of Parkhurst extended westward from near Newport to Newtown, closely wooded in earlier centuries but mostly heathland by the early nineteenth century. On these cold clay lands there was no prospect of easy agriculture and at the time of the Domesday survey only a few villages had been established, the population was only three to a square mile and just above one ox team could be found in the same area.

This heavy land with its low population contrasts with the sandy loams that outcrop at the foot of the central downs. From Brooke in the west this fertile belt crosses the centre of the Island, opening into the rich Arreton valley beyond Newport, continuing to Brading and extending southward to the coastal disticts of Shanklin and Bonchurch. The soil is perfectly adapted for easy cultivation and it is not surprising to find Domesday recording frequent villages under the downs and in the valleys. Here there were ten people and about three ox teams to a square mile.

The third land type comes in the chalk cliffs which dramatise the coastal scenery in both the west and east of the Island, from the splinter sharp Needles to the blocks of chalk at Whitecliff Bay in the east. And much of the interior beauty of the Island follows the ridges and valleys of the chalk downs from Freshwater through the centre of the Island to Sandown, with dominating hills outcropping at Niton and Bonchurch. These were the sheep walks, whose turf was cropped and manured for centuries by the flocks who were to be a staple part of agricultural life.

Farming is by its nature an occupation that defies rapid change but the continuity of crops grown in the Island is impressive. Although an early twelfth century writer spoke of the Island as 'but producing little corn' this must have been the last time such statement could be made. The granges or farmsteads of the Cistercian abbey at Quarr were growing corn as their main crop in the later twelfth century and in 1269 crops grown on the manors of Isabella de Fortibus, Lord of the Isle of Wight were, in order of yield, wheat, barley, oats, vetches, peas and beans. With the exception of vetches, these were the arable crops still being harvested in the late eighteenth century and into the nineteenth century,

Shepherds were elite farm workers and pride in his occupation is shown by this man who went to a Newport studio to be photographed in his work clothes with his sheep dog.

13

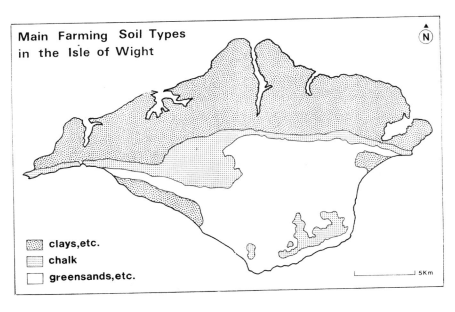

Main Farming Soil Types in the Isle of Wight

- clays,etc.
- chalk
- greensands,etc.

5 Km

N

Sheepwashing at Calbourne in 1976, the last year in which the sheepwash in Winkle Street was used. This was part of the common rights of farmers who had washed their sheep freely since medieval times.

with wheat being at all times the main crop.

The quantities of corn grown throughout the Island must have been considerable. When Edward I took his army to Scotland the royal bailiff of the Isle of Wight was ordered to supply corn for the soldiers. He sent off 250 quarters of corn on the *Blythe* in December 1303 and one month later another 450½ quarters went on the *La Mariote*. Here the term corn covers all the crops listed above with wheat and barley occupying most space. Other ships must have sailed, as receipts for a total of 850 quarters of wheat were issued in 1304.

As wheat provided flour for those able to afford it and barley made bread for the peasantry as well as ale so sheep complemented the local economy. Not only did they provide wool for clothing but also cheese and finally meat for eating, although mutton was a despised meat, not surprisingly, as it must have been a tough, stringy carcass that came into the kitchen. Island wool, however, was of good quality and was woven into kersey, a narrow rough cloth, for general use. By the end of the fourteenth century the Island was a chief centre of kersey making and there were six fulling mills working along inland streams.

The shepherds led an isolated life following their flocks as they slowly grazed over the downs. In 1400 the farmer at Rowborough had two hundred and fifty sheep in his flock. Around Calbourne there were many sheep and the stream that runs through Winkle Street in the village was for hundreds of years the common sheepwash for local farmers. But it was not only for their fleeces that sheep were valuable, their dung was essential to arable farming and the movable hurdles that folded them at night would be common sights on the great fields.

Sheep were most numerous, but medieval farms were completely mixed and they included all the animals that would still have a place on Island farms in the nineteenth century, oxen, horses, bullocks, heifers, pigs, geese and chickens. Milking cows would have been few in number, milk for cheese came from sheep. The cows were kept to produce oxen, those gentle, strong working beasts. Horses were mainly bred for the nobility, for they were expensive to keep. An unusual aspect of farming came from fishponds which could be included in leases, such as that of William Knyt in 1430 when he took on 200 acres including a fishpond at Claybrook (now Binfield Farm), Whippingham. Fish was a major food item, but not salmon, which shared the same low status as mutton. Some manors included among their profitable stock an animal less welcome on farms today. The first mention of the rabbit in the Island comes in 1225 when the wages of a coney keeper were included in the manorial accounts at Bowcombe, close to Carisbrooke Castle; there was a small grove of rabbits at Kern in 1398 and the tenant at Combley paid as part of his rent to Quarr Abbey in 1491, eight brace of rabbits.

Rabbits seem inevitably to attract poachers. At midnight on the 23rd November 1384 two warreners on Geoffrey Roucle's land at Brooke surprised a poaching party which would not have been out of place five hundred years later. Three men were caught laying out nets and using ferrets in the warren. They were armed with bows and arrows and opened fire on the warreners who returned it, wounding Thomas Smythe in the forehead. It was his subsequent death that ensured that this episode was recorded. Many other poachers must have slipped quietly home to improve the inevitable bean, cabbage and leak pottage with a taste of meat.

Farmers worked their arable land in the great open fields which were carefully divided by wide baulks of land separating one neighbour's holding from another. Tenants paid part of their rent in boon days working for their lord on tasks as varied as stacking manure or mending a wall. The annual ploughing meant days of heavy work plodding behind the slow but strong plough oxen and at the end of the farming year harvest called on all available hands to bring in the crops. Men who worked on Quarr Abbey lands at these two busy periods ended their labours with a cheerful feast at which barley bread, cheese and hundreds of herring, those abundant, cheap and protein rich fish, were consumed.

Paid casual labour was also employed. The hardworked harvesters got a penny a day and their food. At St Cross Priory a lad watching pigs and geese earned twopence. Children were out in the fields adding to the family income by scaring off crows as they were to do down the centuries, and older boys were provided with stout gloves and employed pulling up thistles.

Before the end of the fifteenth century boon work was gradually replaced by money rents. Intelligent farmers were conscious that stock and grain kept within enclosed fields improved significantly. Consequently, in 1489 'fields are dyked and made pasture for beasts and cattle'; in addition, too many farms were being 'taken into one man's hold' leaving a depopulated countryside, empty houses and decayed medieval manor houses.

Determined farmers continued enclosing their land and converting it into sheep pasture and as the sixteenth century advanced the countryside slowly evolved into one that would be recognisable today. A land 'full of egerowes' may have been an exaggeration, but in 1559 in St. Helens they were complaining of houses standing empty due to enclosure of common fields near towns and villages with loss of tillage to pasture for sheep.

It was only in the latter part of Queen Elizabeth I's reign that grain established itself as a staple crop. From 1560 corn could be exported

Fullingmills Farm at Calbourne is a unique example in the Island of a 'parlour wing' house added to an older building. A fine drawing room takes up the whole of the ground floor with two equally good sleeping chambers above. It is an early example of the wealth that came from corn and wool farming.

Style House, near Arreton Church, now two cottages, is a typical late 16th or early 17th century farmhouse. The revealing features are the central chimney stack with the entrance door in line with it. Modern windows have replaced earlier ones but their positions in the building show that this house had a parlour and hall on each side of the central fireplace and a service room at the top end.

from the Island without tax and this must have encouraged the move back to arable cultivation. In 1607 the collector of subsidy declared, 'the Comodities of this place are but corne and wooll' and so they were to be for the following three centuries. The high quality wool went to the West Country broadcloth weavers and to Rye for the Kent weavers, but kersies were still being made and exported from Newport in the 1560s. There must also have been a fairly good stock of cattle in Elizabeth's reign to sustain the Newport tanneries and leather trade and, when this declined, hides were exported, 209 being sent from Cowes in 1613.

The prosperity of farming in the seventeenth century shows in the number of manor houses that were built, or improved, and in the quantity and quality of the stone farmhouses of the period. Most stand on the fertile greensand where quite small holdings could provide a comfortable living. John Rawlins who lived at Style House, Arreton, in the early seventeenth century grew a small amount of wheat, barley and oats, kept four yearlings, two mares, four pigs, a cockerel, three hens, two geese as well as four stocks of bees. He was a typical small farmer and serves as a pattern for many other family farmers throughout the seventeenth and eighteenth centuries.

Having established a system based on corn and wool farmers were reluctant to change; they went on 'in the same beaten track which was trodden by their forefathers'. In 1771 an Islander was heard to say, 'two things will ruin the Isle of Wight – the building of the House of Industry and Sowing Turnips'. Neither was true but it was easier to build the new workhouse than to get turnips grown. This reluctance meant that few cattle or sheep could be overwintered and this held back soil improvement. It was only in the 1780s and 1790s that turnips were gradually introduced and with them came an increase in the flocks of Dorset ewes. Each year 40,000 sheep were shorn and their wool exported, while a profitable market in early fat lambs was established. In 1793 five thousand lambs went to London, in 1818 more than one thousand lambs a week went to markets on the mainland and in 1836 eight thousand went to London during the season. Just under a century later the Dorset Horn was still the favoured sheep and for a few weeks before Easter the Isle of Wight was 'the most important fat lamb supplier in England'.

Cattle brought into the yards for winter provided a concentrated manure which was used, with chalk and marl, for improving the land. At the end of the eighteenth century the pretty Channel Island cows were

Yaverland Manor in 1846, built by Jermyn Richards in about 1600. Richards lived in Brading where he had a brewing business and, 'by vending his beer to ships at St Helens … grew rich'.

This Audit House, or Town Hall, was built on the site of the present Newport Guildhall in 1638. It replaced an earlier building sited at the top of Holyrood Street. The open colonnade was used as a cheese market in the 18th century.

kept only as house cows while the red Devons took their places in the fields. Butter and cream were the dairy goods that sold well but their production left quantities of skimmed milk that was used to produce a less appetizing dairy product, Isle of Wight cheese. In 1795 Richard Warner wrote that it 'can scarcely be cut by a hatchet or saw; is to be masticated only by the firmest teeth, and digested only by the strongest stomachs'. This was Isle of Wight Rock, a cheese which against all reasonable expectations was still being made in the southern parts of the Island in the late nineteenth century.

It was in arable farming that significant improvements came at the end of the eighteenth century. In the centre and south of the Island the four year Norfolk rotation, or modifications of it, was used. All included turnips and clover and only the difficult northern clays continued with fallow in the cropping system. But beans grew well in clay; they were dibbled in and left to grow away in the weeds, producing substantial crops. Peas and beans were established at this time as a regular part of arable farming but the main crops were barley and, overwhelmingly, wheat. In the 1790s the Isle of Wight was 'the granary of the western counties' and 'the chief source of malt, salt, flour and biscuit for the navy'. Wheat yields were so great that eight times the local demand was harvested annually and extra men came regularly from the mainland for the harvest month. The four hundred West Country harvest men who came in 1793 were given official protection from the press gang so that the corn could be safely gathered in.

Just as happened in Tudor times, change and improvement was accompanied by more enclosure and ingrossings of holdings. Recent enclosures, many in the east of the Island, were easily recognized by their straight, quickthorn hedges, but at the back of the Island the fields were separated by 'narrow mounds, covered with brambles'. It was in the south that William Marshall reported in 1791 that 'within living memory...numerous small holdings...' had been 'laid out into those of larger

The only remaining example of the windmills that were found in many other parts of the Island is at Bembridge. This early 18th century cap mill was built from local stone, but ceased to work after the harvest of 1913.

17

size'. John Albin, a local writer described Brighstone in the same period as a parish where almost every house had a few acres of land attached, but now was landless. In other parts of the Island farms were absorbed into neighbouring units and the farm buildings abandoned. The dispossessed freeholders added to the landless poor who were to be an increasing problem as the years passed.

Even when land was added to land the result was still only to create a farming community with moderate holdings. Early in the nineteenth ccentury the average value of a farm was between £100 and £400 a year. The smallest farms were on the hard clay lands, the largest those that took in the chalk downland, while in the rich, loamy lands tiny holdings of only £50 pa value were neighbours to men living in seventeenth century stone houses with estates valued at £500. Many of these farms were freehold but all extended their acreage by renting land at prices varying from 12s (60p) per acre to 25s (£1.25).

For those established farmers the end of the eighteenth century was indeed a golden age. Wartime demands to feed and clothe the army and navy ensured good prices, and even when harvests were meagre rocketing prices for wheat still brought good returns. An average price of 45s (£2.25) a quarter in 1799 could be inflated to £8.00 in 1801 for those who got wheat to market. The exceptionally good living of the Napoleonic period had a sharp awakening in the post war period, although this was rather more delayed in the Isle of Wight than in other parts of the country. Although grain prices in the 1820s compared badly with those twenty five years earlier they still kept up an average of 56s (£2.80) per quarter for six years between 1819 and 1829. But the 'wheat and bean' farmers on the clay lands certainly had a hard time. They could no longer afford the four to six ploughings necessary for their grain cultivation, much land reverted to grass and their sheep flocks were badly affected by sheep rot in 1823-24, in 1828-29 and again in 1833 when 8,000 sheep were lost from the Island flock.

This devasting blow came at the beginning of the most serious agricultural depression which affected the whole Island. A period of drought began in 1834 and continued for several years, hay harvests were small, cattle brought to market obtained ludicrous prices. At Compton Farm, Freshwater, in 1835 three cows sold for one pound per head and a team of horses that might have realized £100 was knocked down for £26. The most telling indication of malaise came in rent reductions which landowners were forced to make; ten to twenty per cent reductions were made throughout the Island, but George Henry Ward of Cowes reduced his tenants' rents by forty five per cent between 1834-36, indicating the severe difficulties of the northern clay farmers.

There was little progress in agriculture for much of the nineteenth century. In 1861 the *Isle of Wight Observer* lamented that 'with few exceptions the State of Agriculture now is the same as it was in the year 1800.' The sour assessment is completely supported by an independent report made in the same year. Having adopted the four-fold system about 1800 and finding that it worked reasonably well Island farmers saw no reason for change. The crop returns were virtually the same as in the late eighteenth century; wheat 20 bushels per acre, barley 30 bushels and oats 35 bushels. Four horses were still needed to pull the high heavy plough with its cast iron share and the horses themselves were poorly

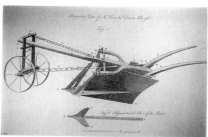

fed, eating nothing but barley straw during the winter with one bushel of oats a week when hard at work. Eighteenth century farmers would have recognized the Dorset horn sheep and the Channel Island cows, although shorthorns were kept on some farms by 1861.

This conservatism was perhaps inevitable in a county that was blessed with a mild climate, with good soil in many parts that gave little incentive for innovation, while in other areas money was needed to improve the heavy lands. The fact that many farms were freehold family holdings was also important. Major land improvements were more likely to come to tenant farmers on well run estates with money to spend.

Important developments in land drainage came in the 1860s. At Swainston Sir Richard Simeon began draining as deep as 4 feet; he introduced an improved rotation with an emphasis on turnips off which the sheep grazed, dunging the land as they went – all this seventy years after the Norfolk system was first introduced to the Island! The new system of keeping sheep and cattle on boarded gratings in covered stalls was used at Swainston, as it was in the more famous model farm at Osborne. Here, Prince Albert converted 800 acres of typical clay land into good fertile ground. Thorough drainage, enlarging fields to 15 – 20 acre size, and abandoning fallow once root crops thrived. Super phosphates, compost and guano were all used and a great deal of chalk – 30 tons per acre, brought to Barton Hard from Portsdown Hill for 2.9d (14p approx) a ton, one third cheaper than Arreton chalk and equally good. Chalk from Arreton Down cost 1.3d (7p) a waggon load and was hauled only up to six miles. Farmers in the Arreton valley used only 15-20 tons per acre and got excellent results with greater corn yields and ten turnips in place of one.

Royal patronage made mechanization possible at Osborne. A Burgess and Key reaper was employed and an 8-horse power Easton and Amos steam engine was used for all manner of work from threshing and cleaning wheat, cutting roots, crushing oil cake, to turning the saw mill.

Yet another improving gentleman was at work on West Ashey Farm. In 1857 George Young bought 730 acres of land 'almost in a state of

A steam plough demonstration in the 1850s.

Oxen were usually found only on gentlemen's estates or those of improving farmers. Here a working team is bringing home a load of hay in the 1850s. More usually oxen were fattened up for meat, especially on the rich water meadows around Brading Haven.

From the early 19th century threshing machines began to compete with hand threshers. Although not widely used, they contributed to an atmosphere of insecurity among labourers and led to outbreaks of arson.

B. WOODFORD,
MILLWRIGHT,
NODEHILL, NEWPORT,
Begs to inform the Agriculturists of the Isle of Wight, that he has three
PORTABLE
THRASHING MACHINES,
TO LET,
On the following reasonable Terms, viz.

	£	s.	d.
For one day, including man		10	0
Per hour extra		1	0
For three successive days	1	3	6
For six successive days	2	14	0

(Yelf, Newport.)

nature'. The improvements he undertook may still be seen today, an impressive collection of brick farm buildings with labourers' cottages, surrounded by large regular fields. The steading was built in 1859, two large yards, stalls and boxes for eighty cattle, a shed 84 feet long and 14 feet wide for feeding sheep on boards. Chalk, 40 tons per acre, and lime, 2½ tons, came from his own chalk pit, many of the bricks and pipes were made from clay on the land. For manure he bought Ryde town dung; carting away 1900 tons over a 2 year period. There was space in the buildings for a 10-horse power portable steam engine built by Clayton and Shuttleworth and this allowed a steam plough to be used in the large fields. There were also eight work oxen. These strong, docile animals were associated mainly with gentry estates and improving farmers from the early nineteenth century, although some imported oxen were also grazed on the rich pasture about Brading haven. The ox beef was sold for ship's meat and many cottagers enjoyed Christmas gifts of ox meat throughout the century.

Mechanization generally had to wait until the twentieth century but some farmers adopted new methods very early. Charles Vancouver, reviewing the agriculture of the Island in 1810 mentioned two threshing machines; in 1814 a boy at Heasley Farm had both hands mangled by a machine and in 1817 a farmer at Wroxall gathered his wheat and threshed it by machine the same day. By 1830 the threat implicit to labourers' winter work contributed to the serious disturbances at Newport in the autumn of that year. But with a supply of cheap labour most farmers continued with hand threshing and the beat of the flail in the barn remained a familiar winter sound throughout the century. The first self-binding reaper was used at Afton Farm, Freshwater, in August 1885. But the Isle of Wight County Press which gave this news had only a week previously printed the much more significant statement that farm-

20

ing had 'lost much of its dignity of late years through the pinch of poverty.'

First signs of the long decline in farming fortunes came in a clutch of farm sales advertised in September 1874. They included Merston Farm, Arreton; West Chale Farm; Heathfield Farm, Whippingham, and Mill House Farm, Ryde, the last three being only part of the complete holding of each seller. This retrenchment was forced by the first real impact of Free Trade. Cheap grain imports from the North American prairies brought tumbling home prices and later in the century frozen meats came from Australia and New Zealand and butter and bacon from Denmark. By 1895 the local paper described farmers selling up 'because they find themselves utterly unable under present conditions to make a living out of them.' Five years later the autumn editions of the County Press confirmed this continuing decline, twelve farms were offered for sale with the frequent addition of the sombre word, 'quitting'.

The one hope of hanging on in mixed farms lay with the dairy herd. Fresh milk had to be home produced; the towns demanded increased supplies and the railways were there to transport it. Milk became the basis on which mixed farming continued in the Island from the 1920s as arable was converted to grass. In a complete reversal from earlier times large landowners were splitting their arable into small dairy farms as they too sought to retrench. This information comes from an interesting survey of Island agriculture made in 1929 by a party of visiting schoolboys. The project was designed by the Department of Agriculture at Reading University, the first of its kind to involve schoolchildren aged between 12-14 years. Ninety three farmers, one fifth of the total farming community, were visited in West Wight, a few in the east and nineteen farmers in the north returned questionnaires. A majority were dairy farms, ninety per cent with Guernsey or Guernsey crosses and with average herds of twenty cows; the remainder were mixed farms growing corn. This survey exposed the isolation which still continued to mark the south and west just as it had in earlier times. In the twentieth century this determined that their milk output was converted into butter – the Island had one of the largest outputs per acre in the country.

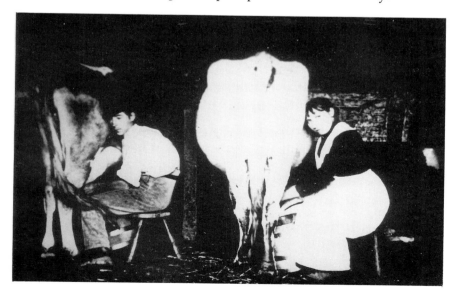

Morning and evening milking regulated the day on dairy or mixed farms.

21

Northern farmers with easier access to rail and ferry points were well placed to supply Portsmouth and in 1929 over 50,000 gallons went from Ryde. Out of this there grew an uncomfortable relationship with the Portsmouth Dairymen's Association. The Dairymen usually had the advantage and were ever ready to cut prices paid to Island farmers. Churns were another point of controversy. 'Like the poor' loss of churns in transit was 'always with us', complained the Island branch of the National Farmers' Union in 1935. Moreover, the Dairymen refused to supply churns to the Island as they did for mainland producers; and in May 1941 they were sending Island churns to follow Portsmouth evacuees instead of returning them to the farmers.

There was strong opposition to every attempt to centralize the dairy industry. In 1937 this provoked language which would have been familiar a hundred years earlier. At a special meeting of the NFU to discuss a Milk Reorganization Committee there was strong opposition and one of the members spoke of an attack 'on our liberties' and demanded the restoration of 'individual rights of free born British subjects'. But this was already a lost battle and the Milk Industry Bill became law.

In the 1930s the progress of farming in the Island can be followed through the additional committees appointed by the NFU. In 1930 a Sugar Beet committee was formed and arrangements made with a factory in Selby, Yorkshire, to take the beets. This worked satisfactorily and the acreage increased until war-time restrictions ended production, but within months of the war ending the committee was reformed and quickly re-established production.

The minutes of the NFU in the 1930s show the increasing importance of education in agricultural life. In September 1930 the County Council appointed Mr Basil Jenkins as Agricultural Adviser and Organizer, a post the Branch had been urging on the County for many years. The NFU itself had arranged educational lectures but a full time Adviser was able to push forward with evening classes and day courses. In 1935 the first steps were taken towards forming a Young Farmers' Club, which the Women's Institute supported with a five guinea donation. The project had to wait however, and it was only in the 1937 annual meeting that the branch secretary could report that this important part of farming education had been established.

It is surprising how late in Island farming history that potatoes came to be treated as a cash crop. They have, of course, always been associated with the poor. In 1795 Richard Warner saw that they were planted only by 'little farmers' and labourers, although the returns were reasonable, 60-80 sacks per acre. He wondered why farmers did not see the market Portsmouth offered. Caution probably supplied the answer. Potatoes were a notably unreliable crop, easily succumbing to disease. The most disastrous infection of the nineteenth century was first observed in the Isle of Wight when in July 1845 disease was already affecting the crop. This was the first record of potato blight, an invasion from North America that was to devastate the Irish peasantry. Potatoes continued to be grown by cottagers, but in 1930 they were still not commercial when the NFU discussed a proposed national potato marketing scheme. The branch could offer no opinion as 'so little potato growing is carried out in the island'. But four years later a Potato Advisory Committee was formed by the NFU, a certain indicator of an expanding crop, although many

A milk float leaving New Barn Farm, Apse Heath in the 1890s. Householders' jugs were filled from standard measures.

producers grew under one acre. Blight remained a recurring problem but during the 1939-45 war compensation of £10 per acre was paid to growers so that the acreage under crop was kept up.

Pigs, like potatoes, were for centuries the poor man's friend, easy to feed and giving good returns. In the late eighteenth century a particular Island type was bred, large and tall with black spots, an excellent bacon producer. By 1860 improving farmers were stocking Berkshire and Sussex breeds and the pig went on to be a major part of the farming economy. In 1929 the pig population was assessed as the largest in proportion to acreage in England. Fifty was the average number on a farm and these dairy fed animals produced high quality meat. There were two small bacon factories in the Island, but the big pork industry at Calne, Wiltshire attracted many farmers. Pigs were essential to farming in the pre-war years. A lecture on 'Pigs that Pay' in 1937 brought the comment, 'We hope they will … the pig is very often the "gentleman who pays the rent"'.

The Isle of Wight has been known as 'The Garden of England' since the eighteenth century, but market gardening was slow in establishing itself. Geographic isolation and difficulty in reaching large areas of population contributed to this, but shortage of labour was a major factor. Work was most pressing during the high summer season, but this was also the period when visitors were filling hotels and guest houses, providing more attractive and higher paid work. It was only the wartime demand for home grown food that established market gardening as a permanent part of the Island economy. Farmers started growing new crops such as tomatoes to replace the lost production of the Channel Islands, since when this aspect of commercial growing has continued to expand.

Wartime necessity as always revived farming although the long depression had left a chronic shortage of basic equipment. This problem was taken in hand during the months between Munich and Poland by the War Agricultural Executive Committee with Mr. A.A.H. Wykeham as Chairman and Mr S. A. Watson as Executive Officer. At the outbreak of war, because of this planning, results quickly appeared and by early October 1939 the first supplies of new machinery started to come in: Fordson tractors, Canadian ploughs, English harrows and sunshine drills from Australia and Canada. This minor industrial revolution was not without its teething troubles. One of the worst problems was with the drills. Designed for the wide open spaces of the Commonwealth, they were geared to sow about a third of the normal density of seed corn for

Haymaking in about 1870 in the fields above Carisbrooke mill pond with the castle in the background. The man on the right is preparing to sharpen his blade with a scythe stone. Mowers usually cut a breadth of 6ft at each stroke and a sharp blade was essential.

English agriculture. New gear wheels for the drills were soon made, enabling them to sow 1½. 2. or 2½ bushels per acre. This did not entirely solve the problem of insufficient equipment. In April 1940 the NFU reported shortages of disc harrows, drills and manure distributors, those for use with horses as well as tractors, as farmers still depended on horse power, although one man had driven a tractor in the First World War.

Shortage of labour, casual as well as permanent was a problem especially at haymaking and harvest, just as it had been in the Napoleonic Wars. County Council workmen were called in, the army helped and Irish labour was employed but not much liked. When the harvest was carried there was a shortage of threshers and thatchers to cover the ricks. In 1942 binder twine was in short supply and in August 1943 farmers were forbidden to use it for tying straw. Finally, there were too few sacks for the grain that was harvested. One wonders how anything was achieved at all.

In fact there was a fundamental spirit of self-help among farmers. This had been observed in the 1929 survey, which saw 'A good deal of informal co-operation between the small family farmers', who helped each other at busy periods. In 1943 a structured scheme of co-operation was established. The Island was divided into small districts each with a leader to whom farmers could apply for help. Schedules of work and payment were agreed and the National Agricultural Workers' Union was asked to support the trial. The scheme worked well and ended the ill feeling that some farmers had aroused by enticing workers away from their usual employment.

Rationing brought its problems. In 1941 a farmer complained that he had to give up clothing coupons for butter muslin. In 1942 when rubber was at a premium a cross memo was sent from the NFU to the Womens Land Army at Newport asking that girls should be instructed to wear rubber boots only when necessary and, 'particularly not in Newport on a Saturday afternoon'. On the other hand when the NFU learned that girls at Shalfleet Hostel were underfed, being sent to harvest with only 7½oz of cake to share between two at mid-day, the matter was immediately taken up with the WLA.

The innovations of wartime farming did not cease in 1945. There was no agricultural depression as had happened in earlier post war periods, and security of tenure for tenant farmers and guaranteed prices ensured that farming did not slip into recession. During the 1950s a number of farms were given up and the land was bought or leased by incomers from the mainland. The County Council, too, moved into agriculture as part of its smallholding policy. Bathingbourne is one example of a large holding which was divided into smaller units, giving an opportunity for those with small means to farm independently. Today most farms are independently owned family farms.

Gradually large scale mechanization was introduced. The horse as a work animal disappeared and tractors became an everyday part of the farm. As machinery grew in size so the fields had to expand to contain them. Many hedges disappeared as fields were thrown together but this was no more than the latest stage in a process that stretched back to Tudor times. On the northern clays modern drainage and deep ploughing made some impression on the hard lands and the effort was justified

In 1960 Mr Martin Boswell at Mersley Farm, Newchurch grew an experimental crop of sweet corn which suceeded well and advanced the horticultural varieties in the Arreton valley. Now asparagus and garlic are grown commerically as the industry adapts to modern demands. A modest development in viticulture and wine production has also developed, a very late descendant of the vineyard looked after by Sir Richard Worsley's gardener in the eighteenth century.

Increased grain and milk yields brought prosperity to farming in the 1960s and 1970s but the long term consequences of guaranteed sales have brought their own problems. Now political decisions seem likely to change once again the nature of farming in the future.

as new strains of cereal gave increasingly good harvests. Two innovations produced this result; stiffed strawed strains of wheat, barley and oats were raised which could, literally, stand up to the heavy use of nitrogenous fertilizers. Together these increased returns by up to 30%. And they were more quickly harvested as combines cut through the standing corn pouring out cataracts of grain.

The cattle herd also changed. Guernseys and Guernsey crosses had been the typical Island cow but in the 1950s and 1960s the black and white Friesians gradually replaced them. Artificial insemination allowed the quality of cattle to be upgraded relatively quickly and with semen from a good bull it was possible to transform the dairy herd within a few generations.

An itinerant team of threshers with their steam engine visiting Merrie Gardens Farm, Lake, in the 1920s.

In 1792 Sir Richard Worsley planted the first vineyard in the Island. Seven hundred vines grew on three acres of land at his 'cottage' in St. Lawrence and a Breton gardener was employed to manage them, shown here in this delightful drawing by John Nixon.

25

THREE

Church, Manors and People

When we look at the open landscape of the Island today it is hard to imagine its appearance nine hundred years ago when man had made little impression on the primeval forest and heath. Parkhurst Forest covered much of the north, extending from the rising ground to the north of Newport westward to Newtown. This great woodland was an unenclosed hunting ground but not a deer park in the true sense. This distinction was reserved for the 'King's Park' next to Watchingwell, 350 acres situated at the south-west corner of Parkhurst Forest where today Great Park Farm reminds us of the early enclosure. A bank and fence protected the breeding hinds and from here the deer were released into the forest to live at liberty until the huntsmen came to take their toll. When the young Henry III needed to replenish his venison stocks he sent three huntsmen to the Island and they, with twenty hounds and twelve greyhounds, stayed for eighteen days before they had caught the hundred deer required, seen them salted and prepared for the carriage back to London.

By the end of the fifteenth century there was another enclosed park at Wootton and on the south coast the whole area between Bonchurch and Niton – the Undercliff – was known as St Lawrence Park in the sixteenth century. This rough ground made an ideal chase, enclosed between the sea and the inland cliffs it must have provided great sport, attracting the greatest families in the Island. The de Aulas of Yaverland had a residence there as did the Russells from the same manor. At Old Park the de Esturs of Whitwell and Gatcombe had free warren and the de Insula family, or de L'Isle's of Wootton held the manor of Bonchurch. The de Wolvertons of Shorwell also held land here and what may have been their small hall still remains as a shell at St Lawrence. More land was certainly used in this way; Kingston and Shalfleet had deer parks and the name 'Park' can sometimes be associated with places where hunting grounds have long since disappeared.

The Saxon and Jutish invaders had cut clearings in the forests and scrub and many village names are reminders of their early origins. Near to navigable water Whippingham was settled, the homestead of Wippa's people; at Brading the little community on the eastern slope of the down became known as the people who live on, or by, the hill – Brerdinges; Calbourne and Carisbrooke are sited on fresh water streams; and Shalfleet's name derives from the shallow creek or stream at the head of the mud flats creeping in from the Solent.

In these small communities wood, cob and thatch were the common materials and in the first years of the Island's late conversion to Christianity this would probably have been true of the first small churches. The mother churches of the Island were those at Carisbrooke, Calbourne, Shalfleet, Arreton, Freshwater, Godshill, Newchurch, Niton, Whippingham. Arreton still has substantial remains of its pre-Conquest origins.

The west wall with its round-headed doorway and narrow round-headed window are part of the Saxon church.

For most of the churches, however, it was the twelfth century renaissance in spiritual and cultural life that was to be the stone building and re-building period. With an abundance of limestone quarries in Quarr, Binstead and Bembridge the masons can never have been without work. Appuldurcombe and St Cross Priory at Newport were founded before 1120, the stone chapel at St Nicholas-in-Castro was built about 1130 and it was probably in 1132 that Baldwin de Redvers, Lord of the Isle of Wight, founded the Cistercian Abbey at Quarr, the most important religious foundation in the Island. A group of about twelve monks was sent from Savigny Abbey in Normandy led by Gervase, who was to become the first abbot of the new foundation, dedicated to St Mary the Virgin and St John the Evangelist. They came to forested land that ran down to the shore on the coast between Fishbourne and Binstead, near the great quarries that had provided stone for the building of both Winchester and Chichester Cathedrals, and which gave them the name we still use today, Quarr. The small band of brothers cut into the oak forest to make space for their buildings and cleared about 50 acres for cultivation. From that time the daily life of the monastery was devoted to the divine office, a sequence of services that continued throughout the twenty-four hours and was the province of the choir monks. Lay brothers, usually drawn from the peasantry, undertook practical work, not least in agriculture, which expanded beyond the Abbey precincts. The granges, or larger farmsteads, that belonged to Quarr, were scattered about the Island, including Shate and Hamstead in the west, Luccombe on the south coast, with Combley and Haesley on the rich greensands near Arreton, the important manor which Baldwin had granted to Quarr in the foundation charter of the Abbey.

Across the valley from Baldwin's castle at Carisbrooke a priory church was being built in the 1150s, a foundation of the abbey of Lyre in northern France. Farther west at Shalfleet an immensely strong squat tower was added to the church, a symbol of the strength of Christianity and a protection from temporal foes. The original dedication of this church is lost and its present title is not related to the foundation.

Quarr Abbey: a detail from a manuscript map of about 1590, showing the Cistercian abbey dissolved by Henry VIII in 1536.

St George's Church, Shalfleet, with its dominating Norman tower. The tiny spire was added in the 18th century and inspired the rhyme
Shalfleet poor and simple people
Sold their bells to build a steeple

St John the Baptist Church, Yaverland with the manor house showing the close proximity of Norman churches with the lord's house. The 12th century doorway is now protected by a 19th century porch.

Newport had no town graveyard (all burials were at Carisbrooke) until 1582 when an outbreak of plague made a new cemetery necessary, here is the surviving gateway of the Elizabethan cemetery, Church Litten.

Medieval churches could not sustain themselves simply by being there. Income was needed to build them, to support the priests, to provide for the religious communities who prayed for the whole society as part of their daily office. The income came from land and the land to found a church or monastic house came from the landowners. Their reasons for doing so can be found in the foundation charter of Quarr Abbey, granted to God by Baldwin de Redvers – 'transitory goods are bestowed on us as a gift from the divine bounty precisely that we may ... through the exercise of charity purchase the good that is truly eternal and permanent.' To give to the church was 'a kind of contribution towards our ascent to the heights of contemplation.' The greatest lords could give most and it is not surprising to find William Fitz Osbern, lord of the Island donating three of the mother churches, Freshwater, Carisbrooke and Newchurch to his family foundation at Lyre.

Lesser lords, too, wished to serve God and daughter parishes evolved from chapels built within manorial estates so that the family could more easily attend the daily services. At Yaverland we see how close this physical relation between the house and church was. Only a few yards separate the house from the Norman doorway that leads into the church of St John the Baptist and, although the present house is sixteenth century in origin, it almost certainly contains within it part of the medieval building, and that in the end nearest to the church.

The parishes in which the growing number of churches stood were related in shape and distribution to the lands which provided tithe income to the church. This explains detached portions of parishes, the most easily observed today being Castlehold in the middle of Newport, a detached part of the parish of St Nicholas in the castle at Carisbrooke. Parish boundaries were scrupulously confirmed each year by 'beating the bounds' during Rogation-tide in May. The original parishes stretched north-south from shore to shore and were many miles in extent. Carisbrooke ran for twelve miles from what was later to be Cowes to the south coast at St. Catherine's. The long attenuated parish of Newchurch with its church at the centre stretched from present day Ryde to where Ventnor would evolve in the nineteenth century. The Norman church at Northwood evolved as a daughter church to Carisbrooke, Chale church was founded by Hugh Gendon in 1114, Newport church dedicated to Thomas Becket was built about 1180 and Shorwell church was founded about 1200. When such chapels were taken out of the original parish the mother church had to be protected from losing income. Baptisms and burials normally remained with the founder church and burials especially were carefully guarded. Newport did not have its own graveyard until the plague year of 1582 made it imperative to take up land in the town to create its own Church Litten.

Some of the obligations that linked daughter and mother churches were joyful occasions. Given good summer weather on the 15 August, the feast of the Assumption, a cheerful crowd of parishioners carrying their banners must have enjoyed the walk to Carisbrooke from Shorwell to pay tribute to the senior parish, take part in the festival service and share a social gathering with their neighbours. Newchurch did not have such occasions to celebrate; no daughter churches were created until the nineteenth century and the long distances that had to be walked from north and south were a burden for many generations.

Parish churches were the main centres of public worship but other buildings also served God. There were private oratories and chapels such as the one at Stenbury that belonged to the de Heyno family; at Limerstone was the chapel of the Holy Spirit; the little leper hospital and chapel of St Augustine was isolated between Parkhurst and Newport and was served by the monks at St Mary's Priory. Although it was a 'maladeria' this hospital would have taken patients with a variety of skin complaints, for, the term 'leper' embraced many unsightly diseases at that time. At Bembridge the chapel of St Urian was served by a monk from Quarr who attended each week to say mass. The most dramatically situated was St Catherine's oratory high on the downs above Chale where a chapel and lighthouse were built early in the fourteenth century. In Newport the chantry founded by John Garston and John White provided an additional priest to say mass for the growing population of Newport in the middle of the fifteenth century.

The regular income that sustained parish churches came from tithes, one tenth of 'whatever the sun shines upon, the dew falls upon and the wind blows upon.' The division of this tenth was shared between the minister, the upkeep of the church fabric and charity to the poor, one third being allotted to each. There was, too the important distinction between the great tithe of corn and the lesser tithe which could include almost every item produced in the countryside. The quantity of harvested crops can be judged by the size of the tithe barns, the most notable standing at Arreton, now only a stone shell but within living memory a noble and lofty building.

In practice it was the bishop who determined the allocation of the tithe between rectors who received the great tithe and vicars who had the lesser. Variations from the norm evolved and at St Nicholas-in-Castro corn and hay were the traditional crops of the great tithe. The bishop of Winchester determined the lesser tithe received by vicars and this could be more valuable in content than that of rectors. In 1257-58 the vicar of Shorwell had two thirds of seventeen lambs, six piglets, fifty six fleeces, two sheepskins, twenty eight cheeses – enough to keep him warm and fed in comfort. At Arreton in 1431 the vicar had a house and a dovecot with the tithe from the mill and hay from four tenements of rich grassland. There was also the tithe from calves, foals, geese, pigs, eggs, cheese, milk hemp, flax, songbirds, doves, honey and wax.

If the church was a major part of the life of medieval people – and we cannot begin to understand the period if we do not recognize this – their daily lives were lived among the woods and fields of the manor and village. Each had a separate but overlapping role in their society. The manors were landholdings which carried obligations to superior lords who in turn owed service to the king. Within their manors the lords maintained their own courts and these were occasionally remembered in the name of a farm such as Waytes Court in Brighstone. It is impossible to generalise about the local manors. Each would include the demesne land of the lord and the land held from him by tenants within the manor, but the value of the manors depended greatly on the quality of the land. At Domesday Bonchurch was mostly down and woodland and had only enough arable to support half a plough. Gatcombe was sufficiently prosperous in 1086 to have three ploughs at work on the desmene and four on other arable land; there were twenty acres of

Newchurch in the 19th century showing the well standing prominently in the village street.

The chapel and tower of St. Catherine's oratory were already in being before 1312. A priest lit the light, but mist made it unreliable and by the end of the 18th century only the tower remained. In 1785 Trinity House began to build a lighthouse near-by but it was not completed as the problem of fog remained.

Interior of the medieval barn at Arreton showing the aisled structure and elaborate roof timbers. Only the walls now remain of this outstanding building.

meadow for hay and a useful wood. But at Calbourne, the very valuable manor held by the bishop of Winchester, there was cultivated land to work twenty five ploughs. It was valued at £40 compared with Gatcombe at £6 and Bonchurch at only 20 shillings. Here the bishop had a substantial manor house built at Swainston for the occasions when he visited the Island. Edward I stayed in it for six days in 1285, since it had passed into royal hands the previous year and he was its new lord.

We do not know the preparations that must have been made for the royal visit but the detailed accounts of Isabella de Fortibus kept fourteen years earlier provide a fascinating insight into the way in which manors were pressed into service when the lord was at home. Countess Isabella, who held the lordship of the Island from 1262-1293, made Carisbrooke Castle her main residence and many of her manors were directly involved in providing for the large household. Each manor was represented by a reeve who was responsible to the Countess's officers. At the large manor of Bowcombe there were two, whilst at Wootton Henry Moche held office in 1269-70, supplanting William Norman who had been six pounds in arrears of payment and was now a fugitive keeping well away from his formidable lord.

During the year the reeves were responsible for keeping the castle provided with food and forage. The horses made great demands on nearby manors, at Chillerton all the hay went to the castle while Bowcombe was so hard pressed that hay and forage had to be bought in for their own animals. Of the 192 cheeses made in Niton, two-thirds went to Isabella, while Wootton supplied mutton, beef and bacon during the year.

Special occasions brought their own demands. When Isabella's daughter Aveline was to be married to Edmund, earl of Lancaster, the customary aid for marrying the lord's daughter had to be raised and was being collected three years before the twelve year old girl was married to the king's son in 1270. All who held land from the Countess by knight service – the obligation to support an armed man – had to pay, the amount being assessed on their land holdings. In Bowcombe the free tenants between them paid twenty shillings, a whole fee, for their parcels of land and they must have been thankful that there was only one daughter to marry.

While manors were units of land the villages were communities of people with inherited traditions that had within them the substance of local democracy. The working life of a village with shared ox-teams and communal labour at periods such as harvest ensured that joint decision-making and responsibility were part of village life. The natural growth of the community would tend to be near the church and manor house and some present day villages still retain this nucleated pattern. Mottistone, with its church, manor house and cottages around the green is one, whilst the core of Arreton is tucked beside the church. Freshwater is remarkable in having several little settlements established some distance from the cottages near the church. The hamlet of Norton is easily recognisable today but Middleton, Weston Manor and Easton survived as names on maps. Some churches, however, stand among fields, their original community lost or moved away. Northwood church is now isolated and St. Edmund at Wootton stands on the fringe of a village that has moved to the east. Both were built next to manor houses that have since disappeared.

Some communities were surprisingly large. In 1334 Mottistone had sixty taxpayers; Bowcombe, today no more than a farm and a few houses also had sixty while Carisbrooke had only twenty nine. The Poll Tax of 1378 listed seventy two taxpayers in Roud, sixty one in Knighton and sixty two at Week, all places that have to be sought out today, hidden among country lanes, but which once supported merchants, weavers, spinsters and tailors. Roud, which in this taxation included Appleford and Appuldurcombe, two small settlements, included a smith and a furrier, whilst Knighton had two butchers and a cooper, altogether enough occupations to show how self-sufficient these isolated communities were.

Villages grew but the medieval towns in the Isle of Wight were planned. All had easy access to the sea and were laid out on open ground. Newport at the head of the navigable river Medina was founded by Richard de Redvers well before the first charter granted by Richard de Redvers III about 1190 and Yarmouth is also a twelfth century town laid out on land held by Baldwin de Redvers. Brading, which was planted on the manor of Whitefield, also had its origins in the twelfth century when it, too had a harbour. In the thirteenth century another coastal town appeared. Francheville, later Newtown on the north coast, came out of manorial lands held by Aymer, bishop of Winchester, who sealed the charter of the new settlement at Swainston in 1256.

Each town followed a grid pattern and in Newport we still walk along streets whose lines were set in the twelfth century. At Newtown the streets have been hidden beneath grass for centuries but evocative names remain in Gold and Silver Streets, both indicating hope rather than achievement, since Newtown was never a successful experiment. There were advantages to both sides when a town was created. The lord lost legal jurisdiction over the men who settled there but he received a regular annual income from leases as the plots of land were taken up and from market tolls. In Newport the annual rental for a single plot was one shilling, a not inconsiderable amount in the twelfth century, but those who paid bought a freedom they could not hope to experience on manorial lands. There were more opportunities for trade and each town was granted a weekly market and an annual fair, both of which brought in income. In the thirteenth century Newport extended its liberties when Isabella de Fortibus granted a second charter giving the burgesses the right to hold their own court within the borough, keeping the money raised by fines. They were also able to exact tolls in the harbour, which extended down river to where it met the Solent. They also received a useful privilege of pasturing their cattle in Parkhurst Forest. In return the town paid annually eighteen marks to the countess and two marks to the Prior of Carisbrooke.

By the fourteenth century the little town had four butchers, a skinner and three tanners, two fishmongers, three merchants and two tinkers, a shoemaker and two spinsters. They were included in the tax return of 1357-58 as were two farmers and a shepherd, a reminder that these early medieval towns were still very like the village communities.

All these separate communities and individuals were bound by feudal obligations to the pinnacle of this pyramidal society, the crown, and in the Island the crown materialised in the castle at Carisbrooke, standing

This aerial view of Newtown shows the proximity of the town to the sea. The medieval grid street plan is mostly hidden below the present fields. Broad Street in which the Town Hall stands was bisected by High Street. Gold Street on the left runs parallel to the High Street. Just below the church Church Street crossed High Street and the route on this road continued to the marsh on the left of the view. The width of this street can be judged by Marsh Farm House which was built within its width at a later date.

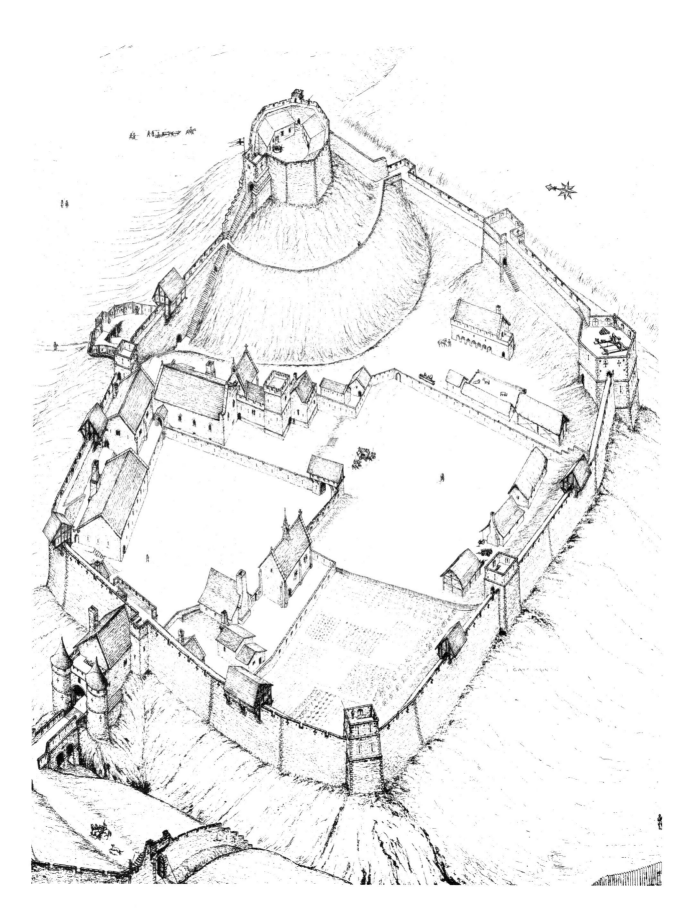

on its chalk hill above the village. It was to be the symbol, or residence of the ruler of the Island from the Norman period to the twentieth century and was already in existence in its earliest form before Domesday noted a castle standing in Alvington manor. When William I came to reward his supporters he granted lands scattered through out the kingdom, with the exception of the Welsh borders and the northern marches. Here great tracts of land were presented to a small number of noblemen to act as a first line of defence in the areas that separated the kingdom from potential enemies. The Isle of Wight was regarded in the same way. Situated in a strategic position on the south coast it, too, was a defence against any attack on the south of England. William gave it to William Fitz Osbern, a kinsman and trusted companion since their childhood and a staunch supporter of William's claim to the English throne. Fitz Osbern held the Island 'as freely as the King himself held the realm of England', but the constancy of an intimate adviser could not be guaranteed in his descendants and the treason of his son resulted in the Fitz Osbern lands being taken back into the king's hands.

Family ties were no guarantee of fidelity in these early years of Norman rule. Bishop Odo of Bayeux, who had fought at William's side, was prepared to put his own interests in claiming the papacy before his loyalty to William and in 1082 he assembled a fleet in the Solent, coming himself to the castle at Carisbrooke. When news reached William in Normandy he returned in fury to confront Odo, one of the most dramatic incidents in the castle's history. The bishop and king faced each other, one secure in the protection of his religious office, the other determined to secure his position against ambitious barons. Not one of William's knights would dare to arrest a servant of God but the king's political acumen did not fail him. He himself arrested his half-brother, not as a bishop, but as earl of Kent, a secular baron who had sworn allegiance to his king.

In the opening years of the twelfth century the lordship of the Island was granted to a Norman family related by marriage to the Fitz Osberns. Richard de Redvers was the first of the family to live at Carisbrooke; he was followed by his son Baldwin, earl of Devon, who built the stone castle during the troubled reign of King Stephen. The lordship remained with the family for several generations until in 1262 an outstanding personality emerged, Isabella de Fortibus, Countess of Devon and Aumale, Lady of the Isle of Wight. She was then twenty-six-years old, already a wealthy widow, endowed with extensive estates in Holderness, held by her late husband, the count of Aumale. When her brother Baldwin died Isabella inherited all his Devon lands together with the Isle of Wight and became the richest single woman in the kingdom. An immensely wealthy widow holding a strategic island was an anachronism in feudal society, but this strongwilled woman remained unmarried and independent until her death in 1293.

She made Carisbrook Castle her home and the administrative centre of her southern estates, transforming it from a military stronghold into a domestic building of comfort and beauty. Her building works were comprehensive; St. Peter's chapel was built, connnecting with the hall, the Great Chamber was rebuilt and for herself a new chamber on the north side of the castle was made, with a high window seat from where she could look over the valley to the village and Priory. Both these rooms

Carisbrooke Castle as it might have been during the Middle Ages.

These medieval gates guarding the entrance to Carisbrooke Castle remained in place until 1965 when they were removed to allow space for the car which brought the Queen to the Investiture of Earl Mountbatten of Burma as Governor of the Isle of Wight.

33

The 13th century window in the north wall of Carisbrooke Castle, made for Countess Isabella's new chamber. It was concealed for many centuries but re-opened in the Victorian restoration of the castle.

Isabella de Fortibus, Countess of Devon and Albermarle and Lord of the Isle of Wight from 1262-1293; a corbel in Christchurch Priory.

had leaded glass windows, a luxury reserved for the very rich. The old kitchen was pulled down and a great new one constructed, with a covered way leading to the hall.

Lavish expenditure on domestic building was one display of superiority, but more revealing of a tough determined nature was Isabella's lifelong absorption in litigation. She was prepared to action against the Newport town bailiffs, against monastic houses and against her own family, including her mother. There was a determination to lose nothing, including the Island itself as she successfully staved off attempts to sell her lands to the crown.

In 1293 Isabella made a pilgrimage to Canterbury and on the way back to London she was taken seriously ill. She was carried to her manor at Stockwell from where news quickly reached Edward I. He immediately sent William Langton, his treasurer, and the bishop of Durham to settle the matter of the Isle of Wight and early on the morning of the 9 November, in the garden of the manor house, the charter of sale was drawn up. It was witnessed and sealed with the countess's consent and the crown at last retrieved the Island, paying £4000 from the king's treasury on the 11 November. It was a paltry sum but the charter seems to have been entirely valid and it was certainly Isabella's intention to sell her holdings in the Island as she had no close relatives to whom she could leave them. She died between midnight and dawn on the 10 November and among her executors she named the Abbott of Quarr, a sturdy adversary in the many legal battles she had fought with the Abbey. By any standards Isabella de Fortibus was a remarkable woman, and a hint of her formidable character can still be detected in the likeness carved on a corbell in Christchurch Priory, Hampshire.

From 1269 the castle again became a military centre and was kept firmly under royal control. This was all too necessary, as the fourteenth century was marked by increased tension between England and France. The Island was periously situated and many landed families removed themselves to the mainland in 1338-39, earning strong condemnation from the king. When a similar exodus took place in the 1370s sterner measures were taken and the emigrants were warned that their lands would be taken by the crown if they did not return. Those who stayed were allowed to fortify their houses and some such as King's Manor, Freshwater, close to the river Yar, and Quarr Abbey on the northern shore did crenellate their buildings.

Almost nothing remains of these medieval manor houses, most of which would have been wood framed, but at Wolverton, Shorwell, the moat and platform on which the house was built is still visible near the seventeenth century house. Only in stone buildings do fragments survive. At Wolverton, St. Laurence, the remains of a hall stands near the later house and at Chale Abbey farm a fourteenth century window can be seen. Not surprisingly the finest work is at Swainston where medieval work survives in the cellars and medieval stonework is hidden beneath later plastering in the main house. A twelfth century double light window, comparable with the Norman window in the hall at Carisbrooke Castle can be seen, together with a thirteenth century upper hall.

The homes of lesser men have utterly disappeared but an agreement made between Quarr Abbey and John Hardynge of Shorwell in 1400 describes a small hall and upper room used by the family whilst most of the lower part of the building was taken up with stabling. At Shate in Brighstone the Jakeman family had rather more accommodation, a hall of three bays and a bakehouse half the size, but the barn was also the same length as the hall. The important structures in these tenant farms remained the working buildings of barn and byre.

Opportunities for small farmers to lease land and buildings from landowners such as Quarr Abbey indicate the changed economy in the later years of the fourteenth century. By then the effects of two devastating experiences were being felt. In 1349 the Black Death crept in and when the uncontainable sickness passed it had taken with it perhaps 40% of the population. The plague was at its worst in the Island during the early months of the year, sparing neither poor nor rich. John de Heyno of Stenbury died as did William de Montacute's wife. Reginald Oglander of Nunwell fell victim, whilst his wife also lost her father Robert Urry and her brother-in-law John Oglander. The great could be remembered, the poor died and their records are lost. But those who survived found their value as workers at a premium and it was they who had the opportunity to rent the empty lands from the church and nobility.

The other local occurrence was part of the long drawn out insecurity that accompanied the Hundred Years War. From 1337 the Island was always at risk from invasion. Three years later the French attacked St Helens and at the end of the day Theobald Russell, who had led the defence, was brought home to die of his wounds at Knighton. In the following year island men were called out for training and there were regular prohibitions on them leaving for the mainland.

The summer of 1377 finally brought a long feared invasion in force. On 21 August men and horses were landed on the north coast and from there they ravaged as far inland as Arreton. The three towns, Yarmouth, Newtown and Newport were devastated. Newtown was never to recover as a port and Newport was so badly burned that excavations below the streets still show a layer of charcoal, the last remnants of the wooden buildings destroyed in the raid. The town was said to have been uninhabited for two years and many house plots were still vacant many years later. St Cross Priory near the river, together with its mill, were burnt out. Ford Mill was also burned and not re-built until 1437.

The Island economy was slow to recover and landowners had to adapt to meet changed circumstances. It is at this period that some began to let out land on long leases. In 1498 Quarr Abbey leased Appuldurcombe to Sir John Lygh for thirty five years. Six years later he took on the lands of Carisbrooke Priory for twenty five years and in 1523 he leased the manor of Arreton for seventy years. Sir John was a rich man who invested shrewdly as did all those who could afford long term leases for additional land. The national economy was moving into an inflationary period when stability in rent payments was a security against the upward rise in prices.

Detail of the two light 12th century window at Swainston Manor, Calbourne.

FOUR

Embattled Puritans

Not all social and economic changes make an immediate impact on the landscape, but any observer of the Island towards the close of the 15th century would have spotted that something was brewing.

The centuries-old open landscape, almost prairie-like with its wide horizons, was beginning to close in. Much of the old pattern remained, of course. The focus of settlement was still the area centred round the parish church. There were 25 of these, their towers or spires serving as the most prominent landscape markers; and the land being farmed round them kept much of its medieval pattern of long, unfenced cultivated strips.

These open fields were giving way, though, to fenced and hedged enclosures; and these new fields were used sometimes for arable farming, sometimes for cattle, and increasingly for sheep.

The impact of the expansion of sheep farming in the 16th century was not unlike that of the micro-chip in the 20th century: neither of them made for a labour-intensive economy. The Tudor enclosures were themselves, of course, a product of a labour shortage. In the Isle of Wight, as elsewhere in the south of England, the combination of the Black Death and the French wars had made inroads on population. These culminated in a disastrous expedition to Brittany by Sir Edward Woodville in 1488 with a force variously reported as comprising between 400 and 700 men from the Isle of Wight. At the battle of St Aubin he and virtually the whole force were killed. Acccording to one later account only one young man returned to the Island to tell the tale.

An underpopulated Island was one vulnerable to attack, and the government responded promptly with an Act (4 Henry VII, cap. 16) in 1489 which stated that the Isle of Wight:

> 'is late decayed of people by reason that many towns and villages have been let down, and the fields dyked and made pasture for beasts and cattle, and also many dwelling-places, farms, and farmholds have of late time been used to be taken into one man's hold and hands, that of old time were wont to be in many several persons' hold and hands, and many several households kept in them; and thereby much people multiplied, and the same Isle thereby well inhabited, which now by the occasion aforesaid, is desolate and not inhabited, but occupied with beasts and cattle, so that if hasty remedy be not provided, that Isle cannot long be kept and defended, but open and ready to the hands of the king's enemies'.

The Act accordingly went on to forbid multiple holding or leasing of farms. It did little though to arrest the progress of field enclosure. At the time of the French landings on the Island in 1545 the English commander Sir Edward Bellingham complained that the country was unfit for moving artillery or for marching, being 'fowle, full of egerowse, lans, dyks, wods, yll and dale, and in sum placys marys'.

Further evidence that this enclosure process was linked with rural depopulation came in a complete survey of the Island in 1559. Of the detailed returns made to the Government commission by the eleven centons or parish clusters that made up the administrative framework of the Island, four survive. One of these was for the capital town of Newport, and another – for the centon of Mottistone – is incomplete and also contains returns from the little town of Yarmouth. The returns for the centons of Arreton and of St Helens, relating to nearly all the northern part of East Medine (the half of the Island east of the central Medina River) are complete, giving information not only for clay land of the extreme north but also for the arable country farther south on the chalk and greensand. Of 92 dwellings in St. Helens centon 16 (17.4%) were empty; and of 170 in Arreton 43 (25.3%) were empty – including the mill at Horringford, itself eloquent support for the general complaints made to the commission about the unprofitability of cereal cropping.

The church buildings echoed this tale of decay. The inquiry commission in 1559 found the small chapel at Standen, between Newport and Arreton, still with its font but empty and derelict, no service having been held there for thirty years. The parish church of St Helens was 'almost utterly decayed, so that oon may look in at oon end and owt at the other'. Of the Yarmouth churches, said formerly to have numbered three, there 'remained onlie the ruinated Chancell of one of the said Churches'. Newport parish church was so rickety that, according to the town court records in 1578, carts were prohibited from passing near its east end 'to avoide the daunger of shakinge the Churche'. Even with an improving economy in the 1600s the tale of decay continued. In 1610 Carisbrooke church had to have its north wall shored up with a wooden buttress; and in 1638 the parishioners of Gatcombe complained that their church 'is verie ruinous & in such decay as the Minister in stormy weather cannot read divine service in his seat'.

While the parish churches were not well maintained, the various monastic buildings and churches soon disappeared from the landscape after their suppression by Henry VIII, as the new owners made liberal use of them as stone quarries. From Chale on 15 June 1562 the College bailiff wrote to the Warden of Winchester College about the little oratory chapel attached to the 14th century lighthouse on Chale Down: 'yf hit shall plise youer worship the stones of the chapyll cared away styll and douthe no plesere there yf hit shall plise you to geve me leyve to fech them doun I wollde ocapy them about youre tenemente'. Just fifteen years later the ruins of the chapel were serving as a shepherd's bothy.

The most substantial monastic ruin of the Island was Quarr Abbey, dissolved in 1536. Most of the Quarr property was bought by George Mill of Southampton, and there is every indication that the partial demolition of the Abbey quickly followed the dissolution. According to the local diarist Sir John Oglander the position of the Abbey church was untraceable in 1607.

Dispersed over this changing landscape was a population, in 1559, of 8,767, made up of 1,880 'able men for the warres', and 6,887 'aged men, women and children'. As always, the historical record of this society is patchy. The non-literate majority leave not much historical trace; and, since the sale of the de Redvers estates to the Crown in 1293, there was no resident nobility, their place being taken by the non-hereditary ap-

Yarmouth church, opened in 1626 (the upper part of the tower is Victorian).

Sir John Oglander.

pointments to the Island lordship which was a defensive and administrative office.

The Lords of the Island – known later, in the 1500s, as Captains – came and went. Meanwhile the ordinary administration of the Island was effectively in the hands of the gentry, the occupants of the increasingly prosperous manor houses dotted around the countryside. Who were the gentry? They were mostly prosperous farmers, merchants, entrepreneurs, occasionally professional people, occasionally former servants of great households seeking to convert their savings into land. Different people would draw up different lists. Queen Elizabeth's Lord Treasurer Lord Burghley in the 1590s jotted down on a manuscript map of the Island in an atlas of his, the names of ten families he evidently considered noteworthy, each name neatly written over the name of the village or manor where they lived. In the 1620s a local gentleman Sir John Oglander (whose family had lived at Nunwell since Norman times) listed in his commonplace book the names of sixteen families, ending with the comment: 'The Gentlemans names ar these and no others'.

We shall hear more of John Oglander. Born in 1585 at Nunwell near Brading, at the age of four he went from the Island with his family to live across the Solent at Beaulieu. After school at Winchester he spent three years at Balliol College, Oxford; and it was while spending a further three years reading law at the Middle Temple that he met his future wife Frances More, youngest daughter of Sir George More of Loseley in Surrey. Within a few months John and Frances were married, and in 1607 they set up house at Nunwell, which John now received as a wedding gift. He was knighted in 1615, made Lieutenant-Governor of Portsmouth from 1620-23 Deputy-Lieutenant of the Isle of Wight from 1624-43, and sheriff of Hampshire. Surrounded by Parliamentarians in the Island he had a rough time during the Civil War, as we shall see later; and he died in 1655 without seeing the monarchy restored.

His importance for Island history lies not so much in the part he played in local administration, but rather in the copious notes he kept on spare pages and margins of his daily account books – notes both on past history and on current society and politics. These remain a major source of information about the Island at this time.

The numbers of gentry tending to increase in the 1600s though; and for good reason. Since the de Redvers sale of the Island in 1293 the Crown had been a main landowner. With the suppression of the monasteries in 1530s, even after the immediate dispersals of much of the monastic property, many farms and manors remained to swell the size of the royal holding. Elizabeth I as a matter of policy blocked the sale of manors on the Island because of the risk of them passing to absentee owners who would not then be so ready to contribute to local defence. The accession of James I in 1603, eager for money and having made peace with Spain, was good for manor sales, which sometimes found buyers in the City of London; thus the numbers of Island gentry were increased.

In character they ranged from oafish to scholarly, from sociable to morose, from misers to spendthrifts; and they had an elastic sense of ethics. In 1605 (the year of the Gunpowder Plot) Thomas Bowerman of Brook went into partnership with a 'curious Artist in London' for the counterfeiting of French coins and their subsequent circulation abroad. The coining was actually done at Brook. The goldsmith provided the

skill while Bowerman put up the capital and agreed to arrange access to outlets for the completed forgeries. It was on this last enterprise that the scheme broke down. A local sailor John Burley, the captain of Yarmouth Castle, happened to be courting one of the Bowerman daughters at the time, and she guilelessly invited him to help in shipping their products across the Channel. Burley was horrified, and went off to inform the authorities. On this occasion, though, crime paid. According to Oglander Bowerman received a pardon, and 'Bourley the Discredite'.

The houses of the gentry varied from elaborate farms to larger manor houses such as Wolverton at Shorwell, and Appuldurcombe near Wroxall. Their furnishing and internal decoration seems to have been modest rather than conspiciously lavish. Appuldurcombe in 1566 had several elaborate tapestries, but such wall decoration does not seem to have been general. The guest room over the hall at Knighton Gorges had its wall painted with historical scenes, and the parlour at Shalfleet Farm was painted with a representation of the Sibyls' prophecy about the birth of Christ. In 1633 a portrait painter named Cottington visited the Island and apparently found many customers for his pictures; and another painter, John Hoskyns, visiting Freshwater in the 1640s inspired the young Robert Hooke (the future scientist) to grind and mix his own paints, and copy the paintings on the walls of the parlour in his father's rectory house there.

Where did the money come from for all this building? Much of it, unspectacularly, simply by good and consistent farming. Cereal prices were notoriously erratic of course, and when the price did rise there were often restrictions on its export from the Island; but wool, the Island's

39

staple crop, held its price reasonably steady, and there was a regular market in the 1500s with the clothiers from Cranbrook in Kent often loading several ships at Newport with the entire summer shearing. There were other ways to fortune, of course; like marriage, in the case of Emmanuel Badd a former shoemaker's apprentice who 'by gods blessinge, and the losse of 5 wyfes…grewe very rytch'; and Barnaby Leigh of North Court at Shorwell who, wrote Oglander, augmented his estate 'by his good housebandrie and by his 3 wyfes'.

Yet another way to fortune was by sheer thrift, and in the days before banking this allowed the misers to count their hoards. These were people like Robert Brackley who occupied a house called Coppid Hall on the south side of South Street in Newport, next to the town archery butts. Finding himself stranded one night on the mainland, with no ferry boats for the Island to be found, he slept in a church porch to save the expense of an inn, caught pneumonia, and died worth a small fortune, the richest man in town. Then there was Robert Dillington of Knighton, son of a younger brother and with his fortune all to make, who when expecting visitors could sometimes be found in the stables raking all the hay out of the manger. By such careful financial practice he piled up a fortune, bought Mottistone manor in 1623, and five years later bought a baronetcy to go with it. For sheer coin-counting perhaps the champion miser was Richard Garde of Binstead, who so distrusted his household staff that in the 1630s he buried his store of money out in one of his fields. The story that now unfolded was uncannily like that of Harpagon's moneybox in Moliere's *L'Avare* (written 30 years later). Garde's obvious fretting over the secret hiding place effectively advertised its location. Inevitably there came the day when Garde found an empty hole in his field, and all the money gone. When the first panic had abated he called in his brother Peter for a council of war, the result of which was that Peter was sent to consult a witch at Ringwood in the New Forest. It was a long way, but the journey was worth the trouble. A day or two later, in the early morning, a neighbour of Richard Garde's – a man named Smith – was found injured and semi-conscious on Brading Down. When he recovered enough to talk he explained that he had been returning over the down from Newport the previous night, when he had been attacked suddenly by the Devil. Then, as he still lay ill, he was overcome by remorse and admitted to the theft of Garde's buried money. So Smith, probably one of the non-literate majority of Islanders, found his way into history.

*   *   *

At the beginning of the 16th century the Island had four towns: Yarmouth, Newtown, Newport, and Brading. Their position was clearly determined by geography. All four town sites lay at the limit of tidal access, and consequently all had an interest in maritime traffic. Their size and status at the end of the medieval period was, however, far from equal. Newtown now made no pretence of corporate urban existence. It does not, for instance, accompany the other three towns in a list of royal fee-farms in 1507, and the Island survey of 1559 reported that 'ther is now nother market nor almost no good howse standing'.

The returns made to the same commission of inquiry in 1559 stated that 'ther is not past a dosen hosis in yermothe', and the commissioners' own summary remarked that 'the Towne of Yarnemouth is in grete decay'. The detailed return for the area including Brading at this time does not survive, but some index of its commercial activity is suggested by its annual fee-farm rent of £2.13.4d compared with the Yarmouth fee-farm of £1.0.0d; and the Brading town papers show that this sum was assembled by an annual levy on tradesmen, ranging from victuallers at 3s.4d and tanners at 2s.0d, down to glovers, weavers, coopers, chandlers, tailors, carpenters, barbers, collar-makers, and pewterers, all at 4d.

It seems, then, that Brading was small and active; and, by comparison, Newport was large and metropolitan, with a fee-farm rent of £24.2.2d, and with a population, in 1559, of 1,175 in 240 houses – 13.4% of the entire Island population.

What did Newport look like? There is an interesting sketch of the early modern town inset to John Speed's map of the Island in 1611 showing clearly the compact layout, the neatness of the street grid betraying its origin as a 12th-century planted town.

The medieval town and church of Brading, formerly accessible by sea before the draining of Brading Haven in the 19th century.

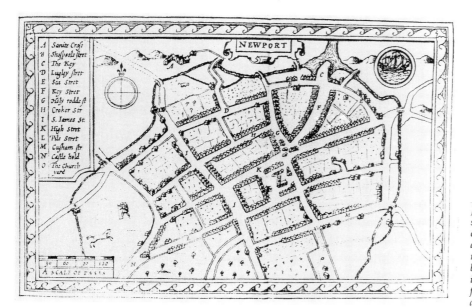

John Speed's plan of Newport in 1611 shows the town in the middle of a period of rapid growth through mercantile activity. The fairly regular street plan is a relic of the medieval town. A new feature by the beginning of James I's reign (1603) is the extent of the built-up street frontages replacing the open meadows and gardens of the medieval town.

Newport lies in a hollow at a point where the valley of the River Medina slices through the east-west chalk ridge. Most of the town area is quite level, but the streets start dipping towards the river at the eastern end of the town, this contour feature and the bend of the river explaining the less regular pattern of the streets at this end. Basically the town plan comprises four main streets aligned south-west to north-east: Crocker Street, Lugley Street, High Street, and Pyle Street, with their connecting cross-streets.

In Speed's 1611 plan much of the grid of streets is fringed with houses and shops, 476 buildings in all, and this is in broad agreement with the documentary evidence of the town terriers. The town by this date is shown as substantially built up along the main street frontages, but its appearance in the early 1500s would have been more open. Writing in 1633 Sir John Oglander (born in 1585) observes: 'Since my Memory it was a very poore Towne the Houses most Thatched, the streets unpaved, and in the Highstrete where now be fayre Houses weare Garden Plottes'.

Newport seems never to have been a walled town, though the town records in the 1500s do indicate two main gates. One, shown on the Speed plan of 1611, was the 'Town Gate' at the foot of Hunnyhill on the road to Cowes; and the other was at the Carisbrooke end of the town, a few yards west of the junction of Pyle Street and High Street. The purpose of these gates was for trade control, access of country carts to the town market being strictly regulated.

Of the public buildings in the early 1500s the central one was the 12th century church of St Thomas (finally demolished in 1854 for the building of the present church). Then there was the town hall, the seat of civil government. At the point where Holyrood Street widened at its junction with High Street there was a little island of houses called the Falcon. In 1405 the bailiffs let a piece of waste ground just to the east of this for the building of two shops with a first-floor large room for a new court house in which the bailiffs and commonalty were to hold their courts. It became known as the Audit House. The only surviving representation of it is the little sketch on Speed's plan, but some idea of its appearance may be retrieved from an inventory of its salvaged building materials at its demolition in 1638. These show that the roof was of 'slatts', the building was of Flemish brick, and the interior was wood-panelled.

There were hardly any other public buildings in Newport, even by the middle of the 16th century. The harbour was yet little developed, and the quay was muddy and unpaved. The archery butts were in one of the open spaces on the south side of South Street (then called Cosham Street). There was a market house in the main square, just opposite the west end of the church. There was a solitary alms house on the east side of Sea Street, near the Quay; and there was a cattle pound at the western junction of High Street and Pyle Street, just inside the gate on the road to Carisbrooke.

As for shops, those of the butchers were concentrated in a little row along the south side of High Street to the north of the church. The fishmongers were close to them, and the whole area of the church square was known as the flesh shambles and market. The town bull ring, for bull-baiting, was on the west side of this square.

The Newport of, say, 1558 – the year of Elizabeth's accession to the throne – was of a piece with the medieval town. The next century was to see striking developments, with many of the signs of modern urban life, and with the population growing from 1,175 in 1559 to 3,000 in 1641. Administrative changes reflected the new economic activity. Up to 1584 Newport was governed by two bailiffs, but in that year the two were reduced to one, thus clearing the ground for the next change, to borough status in 1608 when the then bailiff continued in office as mayor. New civic buildings were called for, and after many attempts to patch up the old Audit House this was demolished in 1637 and replaced on the same site with a new town hall in Purbeck stone (itself replaced by the present Nash building in 1816).

The town got its first school in 1562, in rather slummy accommodation at the back of the butchers' shambles; but it was a start. The building of a new school, on the corner of Lugley Street and the main road out to Cowes, was started in 1614 and completed in 1619, and that building still survives.

In the later 1500s the first attempts were made at the stone paving of the streets; and it was not very long before the same streets were being dug up again, in unsuccessful attempts to lay elm-trunk water mains in 1618 and again in 1623. The pipes were laid, and remains of them still turn up in excavations, but the system of wooden water mains never worked, and Newport had to wait until the 19th century for its first serviceable mains water system. The town was a pioneer, though, in the early building of public conveniences. The town assembly in 1591 concluded 'we do finde there is a greate inconvenience in the Toune for want of a Privie' and ordered one to be built by midsummer that year.

As the town became more closely packed with inhabitants, the threat of fire was never far away. There was continual concern about fire prevention, and much town legislation to ensure adequate chimneys and flues. In 1613 the town enacted a building regulation that chimneys 'shalbe made three foote above the topp of the howse'. There were frequent complaints about carrying open fire in the street – and one can understand the temptation to do so before the days of convenient matches. In 1587 each householder was ordered to keep a tub of water by the front door. In the event of a fire however the most effective treatment was often the removal of the burning roof – for which long-handled hooks called crooms were kept – or even the demolition of walls and buildings to limit the spread. There are occasional references in the town records to the necessary equipment: the purchase in 1676 of 'a good new rope for a grapple now made to be used in case of fire'; and, even more drastic, after a fire at a baker's shop in 1690, payments for barrels of gunpowder and beer 'expended and delivered at the late fire'. The town at least had a pump appliance by this time, for in 1687 the town assembly decided that 'the engine standing in the Church to be used in time of Fire in this toune shall from time to time be repaired and kept in good order for that purpose by the overseer of the poore of this toun'. In 1709, at the time of another abortive project for mains water supply, the town gave permission for the north end of the beast market (now St Jame's Square) to be dug up for construction of a cistern to supply river water 'by pipes into the principall streets and Lands of this Borough to the end that the Inhabitants may at easy rates be supplied with River water in their houses upon all occasions, and may be supplied with a present remedy in case of any accidentall calamitous fire.

Edward Horsey the Island Captain, at Carisbrooke Castle swearing in the two incoming town bailiffs William Porter and John Serle in 1567 (from a drawing in the town Ligger Book).

Newport's first school in 1562 was an unpretentious slum among the butchers' shambles. This much more impressive school was built between 1614 and 1619 and can still be seen. This drawing shows it in the 1930s.

Newport was late in getting a workable mains water supply, and this drawing of the water carrier's cart filling up from the Lukely stream at Hunnyhill shows how rough and ready the water service was even in the early 1800s.

The first attempt at a water main system in Newport was with bored-out elm trunks laid in the early 1600s. These two pipes found in High Street in 1980 show how one end was tapered like a pencil for the joint with the next pipe.

Another feature of urban life more usually associated with later centuries was Newport's first municipal library, set up in 1680 with an initial book purchase fund of £50, by no means a negligible sum.

Again we have to ask what factors economically fuelled the expansion of Newport in later Tudor and Stuart times. The main town industries in the 16th century were brewing and leather production (two of the Island's six tanneries were in the town, and there were extensive associated leather trades). The leather industry faded in the 17th century but brewing, if anything, increased and was joined by the baking of biscuits on an almost industrial scale. This, and the heavy investment in the development of the harbour from the 1580s onwards, is another pointer to the source of wealth. The town had always been to some extent a market and commercial centre; but the sharp increase in shipping traffic around the Island, linked with the building particularly of Cowes Castle in the 1530s and the rapid rise of the town of Cowes in the century following, added the new economic factor of maritime provisioning; and this was to be a growth industry.

*   *   *

'After Ireland, the island that was formerly called Vette, and is now called the Isle of Wight, excels all the others both in size and riches, and they glory in this above all other nations, that on their island there are no monks, no lawyers, and no foxes'.

So reported George Rainsford in 1556 to Philip II of Spain (now also co-regent of England) in his *Ritratto d'Ingliterra* (Portrait of England).

Certainly the protestant reformation found a ready foothold in the Island, at almost every level of society, and not least in the town of Newport. In 1552, when there was a general purge of church vestments, ornaments, and items of plate, 89 items had been sold from Newport church and only 25 were still in the hands of the churchwardens. By 1643, when the churchwardens received a parliamentary order 'for the demolishing of Monuments of superstition or Idolatry' there was evidently little left to throw away. 'There is taken away', they reported, 'the resemblance of a dove on the font and another on the pulpitt and a Crosse on the outside of the church and every other thing of that

44

nature that we can finde in and about the Church'. Indeed the most striking item of furniture in the church was a splendid pulpit (still to be seen in the present church) dating to the 1630s. It is of very elaborate design – even without 'the resemblance of a dove' – and carries in bold letters the text from Isaiah chapter 58, verse 1: 'Cry aloud and spare not: lift up thy voice like a trumpet'. These words were taken seriously, for in 1653 the Corporation sacked the minister William Martin because of 'the lowenes and weaknes of his voice by meanes whereof very fewe of the Congregacion could heare his Doctrine or receave benefitt by his publique Ministery'.

The life of the town was dominated by the Sunday service and the week-day lecture. Newport innkeepers in 1574 were forbidden to 'kepe anie victualinge or Drinkinge in their houses in the tyme of Common praier' and on Sunday mornings they were allowed to open only after the church service was over. Shops that dealt in perishable wares such as meat were allowed to open on Sunday morning but were required to close 'after the seconde peale'. Other shopkeepes such as drapers or artificers observed a quaint ritual. They were required to have their doors closed and their window shutters up on Sunday, but could open to serve customers if any specially called, on condition that they closed up again after serving. If any townspeople were 'found Idle in the streates at the tyme of the devine service' it would cost them a shilling. The same penalty applied to the master of any house where any 'tailor, showe maker, glovier or anie other Artifficer…is taken at worke on the Sondaie'.

The magnificent pulpit and headboard in Newport church date to the 1630s and show the importance attached to preaching in this rather Puritan community. In 1653 one minister was dismissed because of his feeble voice.

After the end of evening prayer on Sunday shopkeepers were allowed then to open their doors, but not their windows. Carts were not allowed through the town streets 'upon the Sondayes and holie dayes', and by 1580 there was an embargo on carts moving anywhere to 'carrie or Recarrie…nor millers to fetche anie gristes nor to grynde' during the Sunday service. By 1588 the town had turned its attention to the fruiterers, who were now prohibited from trading on the Sabbath; and soon afterwards it was ordered 'that none of the Inhabitaunts of this Towne shall play at any unlawfull games or tables cardes dice bowles or keeles' (i.e. ninepins or skittles) 'upon the Sundayes'. Guided perhaps by Exodus chapter 20, verse 10, town merchants were forbidden 'to send their servauntes into the country on the Sabath day'. The town government in James I's reign was equally strict. Various people were fined quite heavily in 1613 and 1614 for fishing on Sunday, and again in 1613 it was forbidden for idle persons or 'boyes of the age of discretion' to play or loiter in the streets on Sunday.

Sunday was only a part of the story. There was the matter of the weekly lecture, which confronted local tradesmen with the stark choice of deserting their weekly ration of Calvinism or else losing some commerical income. The town government tried to contrive as little choice as possible. In 1580, observing some thin attendances of both masters and servants at the Wednesday morning lecture, the town assembly ordained that 'no artifficer merchant or draper do suffer their folkes to woorke covertly in their houses in tyme of the sermon'. In 1586 a different technique was used to fill the church: an order 'that one of everie house within the toune shall every Wensdaye at the tyme of the sermon or lecture come to the churche to here the same'. By 1613 the lecture had moved to Saturday morning, the congregation being summoned by the town bell being rung for half an hour at nine o'clock. These weekly lectures, in various parts of the Island, drew support from all sections of the community. Their patrons included Sir George Carey (captain of the Island 1583-1603) and his successor Henry, Earl of Southampton (captain 1603-1625), and in the 1620s Sir John Oglander at Nunwell recorded in his account books payments to his local lecturer. As for Sir Edward Horsey, Carey's predecessor as captain (1565-1583) the inscription on his tomb in Newport church describes him as 'fautor evangelii', a promotor of the gospel; and he earlier in his career had had to abscond to the continent because of his involvement in the Dudley conspiracy against Mary Tudor in 1556. So his Puritan credentials should have satisfied even the Island.

*   *   *

The only substantial fortification during the medieval period was the Norman castle at Carisbrooke in the centre of the Island, and the shortcomings of its site from the point of view of coastal defence were underlined by the several French landings during the wars of the 14th century. Though not protecting the neighbouring countryside from foreign pillage, Carisbrook Castle resisted attack and reacted also to the introduction of gunpowder into European warfare by the introduction of small loopholes for handguns in the upper stage of the drum towers at the entrance, thus extended in the 1380s.

Gunpowder was indeed the first factor preparing the way for the next main phase of fortification. The technology of the 1300s was not able to generate any artillery threat to fortifications; but the greater size and effectiveness of guns by the 16th century posed a major threat to medieval defences with their high and not over-thick walls presenting inviting targets for gunnery.

As well as the threat there was an opportunity. The range of field covered by artillery now gave the theoretical basis for an organised system of coastal defence with forts and blockhouses covering navigable approach channels and potential landing beaches. The missing element needed to convert theory into practice was the matter of resources in masonry, labour and money.

The conditions were favourable at last in the 1530s with the suppression of the monasteries by Henry VIII, and his adventurous foreign policy made the need more acute. An ambitious plan of coastal works was begun in the south-east, and the Island's share of the building programme comprised two blockhouses on opposite shores of the Medina estuary, at East and West Cowes, using stone from the abbeys at Quarr, and at Beaulieu on the neighbouring mainland.

The blockhouse at East Cowes was dismantled within a few years of building, and no plan is known to survive. The West Cowes fort – which survives in a much altered form and now houses the Royal Yacht Squadron – was in the shape of a capital D with a double upright, and with its rounded segment facing north out towards the Solent. Midway along the inner upright of the D was a thick-walled round tower of two storeys and a gun-platform above, with a spiral stair within the thickness of the tower wall on the north-east. It was to be the only Island fort to fire a gun in anger (at the outbreak of the Civil War in 1642) but it was certainly among the most rickety in construction. By 1576 serious settlement cracks had put parts of the half-moon bastion out of alignment, and the Island captain Edward Horsey had to devise an emergency plan to patch up the bastion and to reduce the height of the central tower. In spite of these measures, trouble persisted; and when the Duke of Leinster made an inspection on 16 May 1692 he reported: 'The walls of Cows castle are rent from top to bottom and is in great danger of falling to the ground with every cannons fireing'.

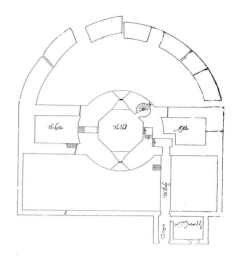

This survey of 1576 shows that West Cowes castle, built less than 40 years before, had subsiding foundations and bad cracks in its demilune bastion (top of survey).

More forts followed in the 1540s, their design profiting to some extent from the experience of Cowes. The fort at Cowes, apart from the provision of some gun embrasures on the landward side, was overlooked by some higher ground to the south and had to be amended to give better cover to the central gun platform. In the forts now being built at Yarmouth and Sandown a single arrowhead bastion in the Italian style was introduced into the design to give flanking cover on the landward side. In some respects, though, the plans inherited some of the defects of medieval design, with the walls being too high and not thick enough, and a major reworking of the design at Yarmouth was necessary in the 1560s to strengthen the work on the coastal side. Smaller blockhouses, and adaptations of earlier Tudor blockhouses, were sited at Sharpnode (at Sconce Point, west of Yarmouth), Worsley's Tower (between Sconce Point and Cliff End), and St Helens on the western lip of Brading Haven.

They were to have a mixed history. East Cowes, as we have seen, was soon dismantled. The fort at St Helens had disappeared without trace by the 1690s, while the one at Sandown was eaten up by the sea within a century of building, and was replaced by a new fort of square design with arrowhead bastions at the four corners, built between 1632 and 1636.

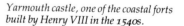

Yarmouth castle, one of the coastal forts built by Henry VIII in the 1540s.

Building work was still in progress at some of the forts at the time of the French incursion into the Solent in 1545 (when the *Mary Rose* foundered) and this may explain why two of the three French landings on the Island on 19 July do not seem to have been unduly hampered by the forts in the vicinity – at St Helens and Sandown (the other landing was at Bonchurch). The Islanders and the neighbouring Hampshire militia defending the Island seem to have reacted with some liveliness to the burning of some of their farms and cottages by the French (really an attempt by the invaders to smoke Henry VIII and his fleet out of Portsmouth harbour). The Bishop of Ajaccio later reported to a correspondent that 'in the Isle of Wight certain women fought and shot their arrows so swiftly that they did incredible hurt, and they ran like hares; and this because they hold these men here in no estimation, and every Englishman boasts that he can fight three Frenchmen'.

In the course of those landings in 1545 the French had debated the possibility of consolidating their hold on the Island and making it a military base. The main argument in favour was that 'having it under our control, we would then dominate Portsmouth, one of the best harbours in England, and so put the enemy to extraordinary expense in maintaining a standing army and fleet to contain us; also we would be on the shipping route between Spain and Flanders, which we could control as we wished, and in time the Island could be cultivated and produce food for the maintenance of the garrison that the King would keep there'. After some discussion the project was abandoned because the French fleet did not carry enough logistic support, especially engineers for fortification construction.

It was not only French eyes that were fixed covetously on the Isle of Wight. Significantly Philip II of Spain during his brief joint tenure of the English throne in the 1550s, placed great importance on the Island's defence. The scene was set for the next main phase of Island fortification.

With the accession of Elizabeth I in 1558 and the progressive worsenings of relations between England and Spain, a series of plans for the invasion of England came under scrutiny at Philip's new palace at the Escorial; and the Isle of Wight figured as a target in several. Things were becoming very tense when, after the death from plague of Sir Edward Horsey, Sir George Carey was appointed captain of the Island in 1583. Carey was the son of the Queen's cousin Lord Hunsdon, the Lord Chamberlain, and he brought to his new rural retreat at Carisbrooke the full flavour of the Court. A surveyor was brought in to plan the renovarion of the crumbling domestic quarters at Carisbrooke Castle, long since abandoned by his predecessors, and on the site of an old hall adjoining the north curtain wall Carey built what was in effect a Tudor country house with a central staircase leading to a long gallery, and two storeys of flanking rooms lit by splendid bay windows. There he moved his renaissance library of books on classical literature, history, theology, geography, languages, music, and natural science; and with them came his household musicians who played at all his meals and especially at the monthly banquets he gave for the Island gentlemen and their wives – from which, it is recorded, they usually went away with a hangover after the lavish hospitality. He was a patron of poets (Thomas Nashe stayed some months at Carisbrooke Castle in the winter of 1593/94, and liked the Island: 'O, it is a purified Continent, & a fertil plot fit to seat another Paradice, where, or in no place, the image of the ancient hospitalitie is to be found'); he was a patron too of musicians, and John Dowland dedicated to him in fulsome terms his 'First Book of Ayres' in 1597. He was a fount of political influence also. His house guests at the castle included Robert Dudley, Earl of Leicester; Robert Devereux, Earl of Essex; Ferdinando Stanley, Earl of Derby; Charles Blount, Lord Mountjoy; Henry Wriothesley, Earl of Southampton; and Sir John Norris – all of whom might today be classified as 'hawks' in terms of foreign policy. For the parliament of 1584/5 Carey secured six M.P.s for the Island – two each from the towns of Yarmouth, Newtown, and Newport – and the extent of his patronage may be seen that these six new franchises were among only 62 for whole country in the whole of Elizabeth's reign. Of course the three grateful towns accorded Carey the privilege of nominating at least one of the two members for each town.

Apart from his cultural and political pursuits Carey enjoyed the life of a country gentleman. He established a horse-breeding stud at Ningwood, from which he was reputed to have sold horses for as much as £100 each. He organised duck shoots on the marshes, and deer hunts in the forest, and one of these nearly put a premature end to his life when his sister, having been placed in cover with a crossbow, accidentally fired it towards Carey, whose horse reared at that moment and took the bolt in its own head.

He expanded his title from captain (which was in his warrant) to governor (which was not) and encouraged the minister at the weekly lecture to pray for 'our noble captain and governor'. A local gentleman who told Carey that, if he wanted to be a governor, he had better go to the West Indies among the base people, found himself promptly immured in the Fleet Prison. 'Your frynde, if fryndlie used', Carey described himself in reply to the resulting petition from the local gentry.

It was this bundle of political energy who now addressed himself to the imminent threat of invasion from Spain, and one of his first measures as captain, in 1584, was to tune up the Island defences. He had inherited the medieval beacon system, and he now gave orders for it to be brought into a state of readiness, with clear and comprehensive instruction to the watchers at each station. The number of Island beacon sites varied over the centuries, between twenty and thirty. The beacons – talls masts crowned with a metal fire bucket, and with an access ladder propped at an angle – were grouped in pairs to allow some flexibility about the gravity of the alarm. The two key sites were at the East and West Forelands which each had three beacons, and these passed messages to and from the mainland chain. When a full alarm was shown on the Solent coast, the militia could be on stand-by as far inland as Berkshire. Integral to the beacon system was the plan for moving reinforcements to the Island from the mainland. This was continually kept under review. In 1572 for example 1,264 men from throughout Hampshire were appointed to come to the relief of the Island in the event of invasion, and for their transport there were 47 boats capable of carrying 1,344 men.

The Island militia meanwhile was organised in eleven divisions or centons, each under an officer called a centoner. To bring these forces up to the required pitch of readiness Carey had the idea of instituting annual military games, with handsome prizes for the best pikeman, the best arquebus shot, and similar exercises.

It was now only a matter of time before the Spaniards launched their great Enterprise, as the projected invasion of England was known, and the game now was to guess where and when the attack would come. The Privy Council was using a mixture of intelligent speculation and of reports from secret agents; in fact some of the latter were uncannily accurate, though only the wisdom of hindsight would show it. The main Spanish plan, designed by their admiral Santa Cruz, was in fact to seize the Isle of Wight and use that as a base for occupation of the mainland. This broke down however when the logistics and cost were examined, and the amended plan was for a large fleet to sail up-Channel, take aboard some of the crack Spanish troops from Flanders, and then go for the Thames and London.

However, Philip's reserve instructions for the commander Medina Sidonia – who had reluctantly taken command after the death of Santa

Elizabethan signal beacon (detail from a manuscript map of about 1590). The Island had a chain of these beacons on its hills, and two stations at the east and west Forelands relayed signals to the mainland.

Cruz – were that if anything prevented this vital link-up he should then consider capturing the Isle of Wight which, wrote Philip, 'is apparently not so strong as to be able to resist, and may be defended if we gain it'. Indeed when on 25 July 1588 the great crescent of the Armada came within sight of the Island, Medina Sidonia – full of misgivings at having no news from the Flanders army – had already given orders that the fleet was to stay off the Isle of Wight to leave him the option of using the reserve instructions.

Events worked out differently: closely engaged at last by the English western fleet, the Spaniards were driven farther up the Channel and missed their chance of taking the Island. With relief the watching militia on the Island hills broke up their camps and dispersed, leaving only the handsome victualling bills 'for bere which was carryed out in to the feild when the Spannyards made their attempt for Ingeland'. Five Island ships saw service in that action – the *Elizabeth, Merget, Raphael, Flyboat,* and *Rat.*

It had been a narrow escape, but this was not the end of the alarms. Throughout the last decade of the 16th century the Spaniards continued to prepare invasion fleets, some of which went to join a current Spanish adventure in Brittany, and some of which sailed for England but were broken up by the weather. It was in the middle of one of these alarms, in the autumn of 1596, that Carey (who had now succeeded to his father's title of Lord Hunsdon) put up a scheme to the Privy Council for a major refortification of Carisbrooke Castle.

Hunsdon usually got what he asked for. The government agreed to find the money subject to a survey, and early in 1597 Federigo Gianibelli, a talented military engineer, came to Carisbrooke to prepare a scheme that would transform this ancient Norman castle into a piece of modern artillery defence. His plan was to construct a large defensive trace – nearly a mile in circuit – completely enclosing the medieval castle, resistant to artillery fire, and with flanking arrowhead bastions to give covering fire over the whole circuit.

The laborious scheme got underway in the summer of 1597 and there were some anxious moments, with the work only partly done, when confident reports announced an imminent Spanish attack on the Island. None came; the vast fortification was completed in 1602; in 1603 both Hunsdon and the Queen died; and in 1604 the new king, James I, made peace with Spain at the Somerset House conference in London. The Armada days at last were over.

The Spanish delegation at the 1604 conference, incidentally, had considered the possibility of demanding the cession of the Isle of Wight to Spain. The new king Philip III was advised by his minister Olivares that the English 'should make no difficulty in ceding to your Majesty the Isle of Wight, and your Majesty should be satisfied with this...If we possess the Isle of Wight we shall have all we need, without so much as ruffling their feelings'. Such was the advice. If the Spaniards ever asked, presumably the answer was 'no'.

Peace with Spain did not of course mean the end of threatened invasions of the Island. When on Sunday morning 4 November 1688 the great fleet of William of Orange appeared off the Island, the clifftops filled with interested and generally welcoming spectators. At a conventicle meeting at Chale Green the minister Thomas Newnham – a man who was described as 'in his sermons a Boanerges' – rose to the occasion.

We are told that he 'set aside the subject which he had intended to have preached on, and gave his people a discourse suited to such a circumstance of providence, with which many were much affected'.

Out in the Channel, among the Dutch fleet, attention was concentrated on the coming and going of pinnaces between William of Orange's frigate *Brill* and Admiral Herbert's ship the *Leyden*. All eyes were watching the masthead of the *Brill* for the plain red flag, flown under the English colours, which would signal a landing. This was, after all, a special day: William's birthday, and the anniversary of his wedding. After advice from the pilots however it was decided to continue to take advantage of the easterly wind and to proceed farther down-Channel; and the force duly made its landing the next day at Torbay.

One of the most elaborate invasion plans was prepared by the French in the winter of 1777-78. Its author Charles Francois Dumouriez (1739-1823) had observed the particular vulnerability of England with 50,000 men and many of its ships involved in war with the American colonies, leaving less than 10,000 troops at home, and with no militia organisation. In Portsmouth there was only one battalion of infantry, a few marines in addition awaiting drafting to ship fitting out there. A second-rate guardship was moored at Spithead. The Isle of Wight at this time, as well as providing a military hospital, was a temptingly well-stocked supply depot. At Brading and St Helens were stores of corn and other provisions for the Portsmouth squadrons, and at Cowes there were extensive timber supplies for the naval construction yards there that had developed from their modest beginnings in the 1630s. The only effective coastal defence was the fort in Sandown bay which had a garrison of 150.

Charles Francois Dumouriez, the French politician and soldier of fortune (1739-1823) who in 1777-8 prepared an elaborate plan for the invasion of the Isle of Wight by the French.

It happened that construction of the harbour works at Cherbourg was in progress at this time, offering a pretext for quartering in the vicinity 24 battalions of infantry, one regiment of dragoons, and eight artillery companies – a force considered large enough for the complete occupation of the Isle of Wight and for the building of new coastal defences there. The Island was indeed to be turned into a fortress, and its agriculture would be organised to sustain a large garrison independently of supply convoys from France. Of the 18,000 existing population, all except those needed for work in the fields were to be transported to the mainland of Hampshire.

The plan pivoted on an element of inspired improvisation, and the absence of any obvious invasion fleet. Embarkation of the army was to take place in Cherbourg harbour and roads, in two hundred of the local oyster-ketches – very manoeuvrable, shallow-draught boats. Thirty of these would be converted into gun-ships by shoring up the bows to allow the mounting of a 24-pounder; and they were to be fitted with two false keels to allow them to be beached upright. Ten of these gun-boats would sail ahead of the invasion fleet, and ten on either flank; with further naval protection from such French warships as were available.

The assembly of the ships was simple: one waited for the oyster-fishing season in the Bay of Cancale, and commandeered the ketches as they put out of harbour. Each ship would then be ballasted with a dismantled piece of ordnance and a hundred pounds of shot. Construction tools would be added, and the dragoons would take with them their saddles, bridles, and pistols; horses would come free, in the Isle of Wight! The

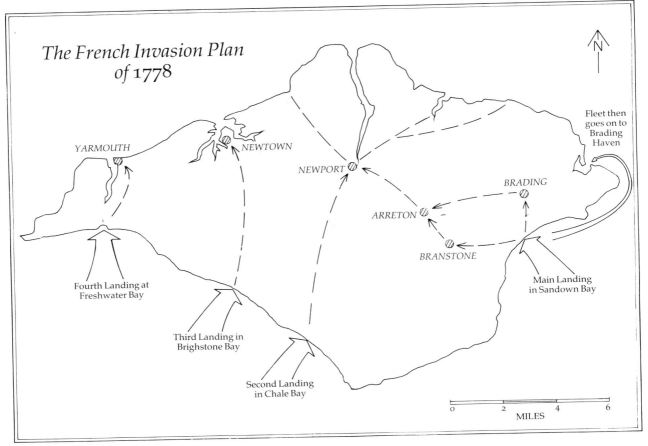

The French Invasion Plan of 1778

Fleet then goes on to Brading Haven

YARMOUTH

NEWTOWN

NEWPORT

BRADING

ARRETON

BRANSTONE

Fourth Landing at Freshwater Bay

Main Landing in Sandown Bay

Third Landing in Brighstone Bay

Second Landing in Chale Bay

0   2   4   6
MILES

embarkation time, as rehearsed, was two hours, and each ketch would be loaded with sixty men, each carrying a hundred cartridges and twenty pounds of biscuits.

The sixty-mile crossing to the Island was timed for November, leaving on the evening ebb tide and reaching the Isle of Wight on the morning flood tide. Pilots had already been recruited from among English and French smugglers.

The army was to be landed along the south coast of the Island, with the main force going ashore in Sandown Bay, and others then landing in Chale Bay, Brighstone Bay, and Freshwater Bay. The naval vessels and the thirty adapted gunboats would then go round and occupy Brading Harbour, also sending some ships farther along the north coast, to Ryde.

The main force in Sandown Bay was then to march inland in two columns: one through Brading and Arreton, and a left-hand column through Branstone to Arreton; both converging on Newport. The division landed at Chale Bay would also aim towards Newport through Kingston and Chillerton Down. Those landed at Brighstone Bay were to go over Brighstone Down and make for Newtown on the north-west coast; and the Freshwater Bay division were to make for Yarmouth, through Afton and Thorley.

While the ships in Brading Harbour were unloading the heavy ordnance and munitions, the force that had captured Newport would, after an hour's rest, fan out northwards to take full control of the Solent coast. Now the unarmed ketches would return to Cancale – presumably still in good time for the oyster season – while consolidation of the landings proceeded. A force of shipwrights, caulkers, sailmakers, and sailors brought over with the invasion force would be settled at Cowes and Yarmouth and begin construction of gun-sloops for shallow-water operations within the gunnery protection of Island coastal batteries. Thus the French could achieve a severe nuisance, if not a complete stoppage, to the naval base at Portmouth; and all at a fairly modest expense.

Such was the first phase of the plan, affecting the Isle of Wight. There were projected sequels for an extension of the action later with a larger force. Preparations of the first phase duly began, but soon ran into budget trouble – not because of any inherent defect of the plan but because of drastic emedations to it. The assembly port for the attack was changed from Cherbourge to le Havre; then Portsmouth was included in the invasion zone, without any increase in the attacking force; finally the stylish notion of using adapted oyster-ketches was abandoned in favour of a more orthodox naval force. Costs rose, and chances of success plummeted. By the time the scheme was abandoned, some 80 million francs had been spent on the military preparations alone. Philip II of Spain, who several times saw his nation go bankrupt, would have sympathised.

The plans remained on the shelf, and though taken out and dusted by Napoleon, they were never put into effect. Still other foreign leaders were to be tempted to invade the Isle of Wight, as we shall find when we come to the story of Hitler's war.

FIVE

Cavaliers and Roundheads

When the English Civil War began in August 1642 the Isle of Wight passed, without much effort it seemed, into the control of Parliament. There were, though, some anxious moments on the way.

On the Island the two sides had their own geographical centres of polarity, uncomfortably near to each other: the Royalists at Carisbrooke Castle, and the Parliamentarians in the town of Newport just a mile away.

With Colonel Goring at Portsmouth, after a summer of wavering, finally declaring for the King, the local issue was forced. A Parliamentary fleet closed in on the Solent and for the Island Royalists the task was clear: to break the blockade.

If the task was clear it was still not very practicable, and for the small knot of Royalists embattled at Carisbrooke the outlook was not cheerful. The Island captain was not there. Jerome, 2nd Earl of Portland, was in London having problems with Parliament (an earlier attempt by the Commons to depose him as Island Captain had been blocked by the Lords), and on 4 August he was put in the custody of the Sheriff of London 'lest he should comply with Colonell Goring, and command the Isle of Wight against the Parliament'. Two days later Philip, Earl of Pembroke, was appointed by Parliament to replace him.

That same Saturday at York the King had just had news of Portland's arrest, and he at once took steps to plug the gap by giving Jerome Brett, Portland's deputy, full authority to act as 'Lieutenant Governor of that our Isle', correctly anticipating Parliament's next move of trying to install a nominee of their own in place of Portland.

The week that followed was one of growing tension. On Monday 8 August the blockading ships moved into position in the Solent, and on Tuesday the first manifesto of the Island campaign appeared. It was a Royalist document, albeit a discreetly worded one. Issued by 'the deputy Lieutennants and Justices the Knights and gentlemen of the Isle of Wight' and declared:

1. That wee will with our lives and estates be assistant to each other in the defence of the true protestant Religeon established in the church of England against all papists or other ill affected persons whatsoever.
2. That wee will unanimously Joyne the uttermost of our endeavoures for the peace of this Island by protecting it by those forces already legally substituted amongst us and will admitt noe forraigne power or forces or newe government except his Majesty by advise of his Parliament uppon occasions that may arise shall thinke it necessary to alter it in any particuliers for the good and safety of the Kingdome.

It was signed by two dozen local gentlemen headed by Sir John Oglander and including all the fort commanders and three of the six Island M.P.s It seemed to be innocently drafted, but a Parliamentarian news letter commented that it 'might receive the construction of another sence'. Moses Read the Mayor of Newport had no doubt about its meaning: he sent a copy up to the Commons along with an urgent request for twenty or thirty barrels of gunpowder. The Commons' reaction when they debated the declaration on 15 August was that the three offending M.P.s – John Meux, Nicholas Weston, and John Leigh – 'be summoned forthwith to attend the Service of this House' and that Sir Robert Dillington and Captain Humphrey Turney (captain of Cowes Castle) be sent for as Delinquents.

The Mayor of Newport's anxiety about gunpowder was understandable because the Royalists were sitting on the entire Island stock. Since the 1540s most of the Island parishes kept their own bronze gun, usually in a shed built for the purpose against the wall of the local church tower. These were of course useless without the gunpowder from the main magazine at Carisbrooke Castle – an expensive commodity, only sparingly issued for militia exercises in the 1600s. To make doubly sure, the Island Royalists attempted some sabotage. 'The Touch hole of the feild peice of Brading neere Sandham Fort was soe artificially spiked upp with hardened steele that it is ympossible to gett yt out againe and supposed more would have ben soe served had yt not ben soe timely discovered', complained a memo among the Newport town records.

Moreover Captain Turney at Cowes had shrewdly managed to call some of the local militia weapons back into store. 'He had inveagled the Countrey round about, and by faire glozing speeches had perswaded them to bring in their Arms into the said Castle, telling them that they would be there kept in safety from the Cavaliers'. He had anticipated the August tension more acutely than the militia did. When the troops came in to ask for re-issue of the weapons, they found the Captain obdurate.

The Parliamentarians, then, may have had the overwhelming advantage of numbers, but they were lamentably under-provided with weapons. To make matters worse 'rumors were spredd in the Island that Collonel Brett had mounted and charged the ordinance of Carisbrooke Castle against Newport and had vaunted hee would beate downe the Towne and the Mayors house should be first. Which rumor did much terrify and affright the Inhabitants'. This note in the town records is confirmed by a news letter reported on Monday 15 August that 'there

The first gun fired on the Island in the English Civil War was from Cowes Castle (shown in this 18th century engraving) on 12 August 1642 when the small Royalist garrison fired at the Parliamentary warships blockading Portsmouth.

is in the Island much fear of the Captains of the Castles'.

On Friday 12 August the first shots were fired in anger. One of the Parliamentary blockading ships in the Solent, the *Lion* of Leith stationed off Cowes, hailed two boats bound for Portsmouth carrying a cargo of salt and a chest of money. As they ignored an order to heave to, Captain Ramsey the commander of the *Lion* fired a shot across their bows, and promptly came under fire himself from the guns at Cowes Castle, which were being fired by no less than Captain Turney, 'in a furie, with his owne hand'.

Meanwhile the Island Justices of the Peace were busy about their various partisan projects. Bulkley, a Parliamentarian, was going round showing a warrant from Parliament forbidding the sending of supplies to Portsmouth; while Sir John Oglander and Sir Robert Dillington were trying to neutralise the militia by persuading the companies to stand down from duty.

It was on Sunday 14 August that the royal courier got through to Carisbrooke Castle with the King's warrant appointing Brett as Lieutenant Governor. Brett needed this warrant to restore his morale because the royal courier had come hard on the heels of a messenger from Colonel Goring at Portsmouth appealing for men and supplies. In a revealing reply Brett wrote: 'For the present I cannot answere your desire for men both by reason of the boatemans unwillingnesse to undertake the Carrying of any, alsoe being Sunday I could have noe oppertunyty. To morrowe I shall not fayle to Indeavor my uttermost'.

This and a batch of letters from others of the Carisbrooke garrison went off to Portsmouth that same Sunday afternoon, and Brett was left to plan his campaign for the next morning when he would present his warrant to the consternation of the Mayor of Newport.

The visit to town was in fact a disaster. When Brett, accompanied by Captain Turney of Cowes, Captain Buck of Sandham Castle, Oglander, Dillington, and several other Royalists, reached Newport on Monday morning he met his first setback. The Mayor was not at home. Brett accordingly was left to stump the streets, jostling and being jostled by the sullen townspeople. 'Papists', 'traitors' and 'villains' were among the insults alleged to have been hurled at the official party. One of the inhabitants, Welch, was so offensive that Brett threatened to have him whipped. The Royalists retired in frustration to an inn where, over refreshment, Brett tactlessly rehearsed some of his new powers. He would lay the town constable by the heels. He had power to hang men. The reaction was not so openly hostile that Brett's party withdrew before the people got quite out of control. 'I shall hardly come thither againe', he wrote to the Mayor on returning to the castle, 'untill you have put the Towne into a more civell posture...I cannot compare your towne to anything but to a large Bedlam'.

It was no accident that Brett should have found that the bird had flown. Moses Read was fully informed about recent developments because the outgoing couriers had failed to get through the Parliamentary ships the evening before. In spite of their stout denials their boat had been thoroughly searched and all their letters found. The first public view of Brett's royal warrant was thus mere bathos. It was yesterday's news.

On Tuesday 16 August the Mayor and chief burgesses met to draft a reply to the rude letter that had now been received from Brett. The town's reply was lengthy and equally forthright. To a request from Brett for them to stand down the town militia they replied: 'As long as wee neither hurt nor disturbe any, give us leave within our selves to doe whatwee list (soe lawfull) for our owne guarde and Securyty the times must needes be confeste on all hands to be dangerous and we think it ther fore a preposterous kinde of care to bidd us be negligent'. The assembly then went on to pass a resolution to increase the town guard by sixteen men.

While this meeting was in progress things were going badly for the Royalists at Cowes. Captain Louis Dick, one of the commanders of the blockading ships, had come ashore with a warrant for the arrest of Captain Turney at Cowes Castle. When he arrived the first matter awaiting his attention was the disposal of two prisoners just taken by the watch at Gurnard, farther round the coast to the west of Cowes: a Mr. Southcot, and another of the Weston family, 'brother to my Lord of Portland'. The obvious course was to lock them up, but Cowes Castle was still in Royalist hands, so they were taken to 'a Mr. Monen's house'. Dick after a brief interrogation left them there while he sent off messages to consult the captains of the other Parliamentarian ships.

Southcot meanwhile was left with a problem. He was carrying letters to Island Royalists. So far these had evaded search, but they would certainly be found in due course. The house where he had been left was near the sea. It was now late evening, and getting dark. Southcot asked to be allowed to go to the privy, and two musketeers accordingly escorted him downstairs to 'an house of office'. Here was his opportunity. As he had suspected, there was a tidal outfall from the privy. Thankfully he threw his packet down it and watched the sea suck it away. His ingenuity deserved better success than it received. The tide washed the packet ashore again and it was found two days later 'within the Sea marke'.

Captain Dick however caught a bigger fish than the couriers. Over at Cowes Castle, Humphrey Turney had news of their arrest, and at once went to the house where they were being kept, to demand their release. Dick in turn had news of this development. He put a cordon of musketeers round the house and went in himself to arrest Turney. After a shouting match Turney succumbed to the inevitable. He and the two couriers were rowed out in a longboat and were made prisoner aboard various of the ships.

If the Royalists were to make an effort in the Island this was the time to try, for the vice was tightening. Parliament had already on 13 August agreed to supply the gunpowder needed by the town of Newport. On 15 August it had been confronted with a further appeal for the Isle of Wight to be sent some cavalry and weapons, and troops had accordingly been ordered to the area. As yet Portsmouth was the main target, but forces on and near the Isle of Wight were also being increased. By 18 August there were seven warships off the Island, and plans had been completed to take over the coastal forts one by one.

Cowes was the first to go. After Turney's arrest only two gunners – William Stanfield and John Galpin – were left there. On 17 August they sent an appeal to Sir John Oglander at Nunwell asking 'what Course we shall tak for the security of his maiestis Castell'. The letter evidently got through, for it is among Sir John Oglander's papers; but it was too late. Cowes Castle surrendered that Wednesday and a small Parliamentarian garrison was put in, with the master of Captain Swanley's ship in command.

Yarmouth was the next objective, and on Thursday morning Swanley sent Captain Wheeler to demand its surrender. Wheeler returned empty-handed. Barnaby Burley, commanding at Yarmouth, refused to hand over the castle without written authority from the King. Swanley, aboard Captain Jordan's ship the *Caesar*, now went to see for himself. Anchoring off Yarmouth Castle, he and Jordan rowed ashore and cautiously approached the moat 'thinking to have had a fair parley with the said Burley, but being before the castle we saw him on the wall like a mad man, having a barrel of powder at each corner of the Castle with a linstock in his hands, saying that before he would lose his honour he would die a thousand deaths'. Swanley waited a while for Burley to calm down and come out, on a safe-conduct, for a parley. Nothing was agreed, so Swanley left the castle surrounded by troops, and moved on.

The castle of Sandown was more easily taken. The captain there had a mutinous garrison who were effectively in control. When Swanley's ship appeared off-shore the gunner and some of the soldiers went aboard and asked merely for a warrant to take the castle for Parliament. So this new fort which had been completed by Charles I just six years before passed peacefully across to his enemies without a shot being fired. Meanwhile Captain Jordan, who had been sent to secure Hurst Castle, found the Royalist commander absent, and the garrison quite amenable to admitting a Parliamentary guard. By the end of that Thursday, then, all the coastal forts except Yarmouth were secured; and Yarmouth in fact surrendered the following Monday, 22 August, the same day that the King set up his standard at Nottingham.

In terms of closing the net round Portsmouth all this was very satisfactory, for the inland garrison at Carisbrooke was now effectively bottled up. The mere existence of the Carisbrooke garrison however was a threat to the town of Newport, and consultations had been in progress to arrange a joint operation between the Newport militia and troops from the Parliamentary fleet in the Solent, to capture Carisbrooke. It is not easy to estimate with any accuracy the size of the garrison at this time, but in spite of current rumours in Newport that 'Cavaleers resorted to Carisbrooke Castle in the night landed in by places of the Island' there are signs that it was quite small (the final terms of surrender name fourteen Royalists 'and all the servants belonging to any of them'); and it is probable that it had not enough food supplies to enable it to withstand a long siege. On the other hand Gianibelli's skill in the 1590s in designing the mile-long outer trace of artillery defences was such that this immense fortification could in theory be held by a moderately small garrison; and there was certainly no shortage of arms and ammunition, because this was the main arsenal for the island and the magazine at this time contained 60 barrels of powder and enough weapons for 1,500 men. As early at 15 August the wife of one of the castle garrison approached one of the Parliamentary sailors at Cowes and claimed 'that if speedy assistance could be provided, shee would shew a way to secure the said Castle'. It was already clear to Captain Swanley, however, that only a show of force would achieve the desired result.

The operation began on Tuesday 23 August with the landing at Cowes of some three or four hundred well-equipped musketeers and pikemen under the command of Swanley and five other naval captains. While the force was being quartered in Newport that evening, a delegation comprising Captain Jordan, Captain Martin, William Stephens (the Recorder of Newport; he later sat in the Long Parliament as one of the Newport members, after the death of Lord Falkland in 1643) and five trumpeters went on to the castle to offer terms. If Brett surrendered the castle, they said, he and the Cavaliers would be granted safe-conducts. Brett asked for time to consider this and was given until the next morning.

Brett had reasons for delaying: he was expecting more provisions, which might transform the situation. Also he saw no impressive show of strength in the token force that had accompanied the heralds. He prepared to guard the castle for his night vigil, and so did the thin cordon of pickets that Swanley now posted round the castle. As darkness fell Swanley's troops took their first prisoners of war: a flock of 25 sheep on their way in to augment the castle provisions.

It was a more imposing force that was seen from the castle the next morning, Wednesday 24 August. The full force of naval troops was now joined by the two town companies of Newport with their green and white flag, bringing the whole force up to 600 men. With dismay the watchers from the castle walls saw the moving forest of pikes as the enemy force took up its position on the neighbouring hill of Mount Joy overlooking the castle from the east. Richard Worsley (*History of the Isle of Wight* (1781) p. 116) adds the picturesque and familiar detail of William Harby the Newport minister whipping up the enthusiasm of the town guard to put out the Countess of Portland and her five children, who were still living in the castle. She was a papist, he said; and the troops should be valiant, for they were about to fight the battle of the Lord.

Swanley and Jordan now approached the castle and offered to parley. Edward Worsley came out to them (he was later to help Charles I in his attempted escape from the same castle) and was told that the castle would be attacked if Brett did not accept the terms offered the previous evening. Worsley now invited the two Parliamentary officers into the castle to meet Brett, and for the next three hours in the Captain's quarters the detailed terms of surrender were worked out, while the defenders on the castle walls enjoyed the mortifying spectacle of their captured sheep roasting over the camp fires on Mount Joy.

At last the terms were agreed. The castle was to be handed over on condition that the Countess of Portland was still allowed the use of her rooms there, at the discretion of Parliament, and that the principal Island Royalists were given safe-conducts to anywhere except Portsmouth. Richard Worsley (loc. cit.) records the defiant temper of the Countess of Portland: 'This Lady, with the magnanimity of a Roman matron, went to the platform with a match in her hand, vowing she would fire the first cannon herself, and defend the castle to the utmost extremity, unless honourable terms were granted'. (The Countess in fact left the castle within a month, to go to France).

Towards midday Swanley returned to his camp for a well-earned mutton dinner while Brett prepared to evacuate the castle. At last the signal came – a cannon fired from the castle – and the garrison marched out across the moat bridge.

Now the Parliamentary troops moved in, in an order previously agreed. Just inside the inner gates, at the entrance to the castle courtyard, they found a brass cannon loaded with a deadly charge of twelve flint stones and over a hundred pieces of musket shot, a sure sign that the storming of the castle would not have been a bloodless affair. While some of the incoming troops slewed the gun round and extracted the charge, others hastened to put a guard on the powder magazine and armoury. The castle was at last secured. It was left in the command of Captain Brown Bushell (the hero of a recent exploit of cutting out Goring's only ship *Henrietta Maria* from under the walls of Portsmouth) with fifty men (forty from the ships and ten from the Newport companies). The watchword at the gate that night was the *Marigold*, and at the powder magazine *Dick*.

The Island was now Parliamentary territory. On Monday 29 August Captain Dick left the Isle of Wight to report at Salisbury to the Earl of Pembroke, the new Captain and Governor, who finally arrived in the Island on 3 October, having been preceded during September by his deputy Colonel Carne. The Countess of Portland meanwhile had made preparations to leave for Rouen with Sir William Hopkins in attendance. The change of regime was complete, and the surrender of Portsmouth on 7 September removed the last element of immediate tension.

The revolution had been brought about in the Island with every sign of relative placidity from the population. Apart from Brett's turbulent and contentious visit to Newport on 15 August there was no sign of civil disturbance or of paying off old scores. The only case of looting was attributable to sixteen sailors from the fleet in the Solent, who apparently took advantage of the major operation against Carisbrooke Castle to plunder a house at St Helens belonging to Sir William Hopkins, a local Royalist who was in the Carisbrooke Castle garrison at the time (and in whose Newport house Charles I stayed during the Treaty of Newport in 1648). The Hopkins family later took some lugubrious satisfaction in the claim that 'their House was one of the first Plundered in England'.

Sir John Oglander, who was still at Nunwell, soon had news of this

Carisbrooke Castle from the south-east.

incident coupled with reports of the same sailors' threats 'that they will serve most of the gentlemen's houses in the Island as they have done Sir William Hopkins', and he was quick to send a protest to Swanley. The culprits were duly imprisoned in Cowes Castle, to the great consternation of the acting captain there, because the doors were without locks or bolts. Much of the plundered property was traced and returned. Certainly the Parliamentary officers were alive to the risk of pillaging resulting from failure to pay their sailors; but in this case the animus seems to have been of a political kind.

The epilogue on this Parliamentary take-over of the Island may best be left to the King himself. Sir John Oglander was informed ('and I believe by a good hand') that while in Oxford in March 1643 Charles I 'often sayde, That he had most Confidence of the Isle of Wyght, that they woold have stoode for him, than of any other partes of his kyngdome but now by his experience he fownd fewe honest menn there'.

So the Island was watching from the wings for most of the period of the Civil War. The inhabitants settled down to their new government under Pembroke's deputy, Colonel Carne – who, according to Sir John Oglander's gossipy and astringent report feathered his own nest in that office, to the extent of increasing his personal fortune from £2,000 to £10,000 in five years. For the local Royalists – now enjoying the name of Malignants – life was uncertain in this new political climate. In May 1643 some of the Island gentlemen who had joined the King at Oxford returned to the Island, and were promptly hustled over to Portsmouth for interrogation by a Parliamentary committee. They managed to talk their way out of this ordeal. Oglander himself was less discreet about his allegiance, and suffered for it. A Royalist news letter reported: 'Sir John Oglander, being in the Isle of Wight, one (who is a sufficient brother) said to him, that the Kings ships were goodly ships: yes, said Sir Iohn, but they would be better if they were restored to the true owner (meaning His Majesty) the Round-head replyed, why, what would you

61

gaine if the King had them all? No matter for gaine (said Sir Iohn), I would I had given 500 £ of my own purse, so as the ships were in the right owners possession. And verily (said the other) it shall cost you 500 £, and so presently informed against him, and caused him to be fetched to prison, where now the good Knight is kept close'. Carne meanwhile felt satisfied with the day's work, as he wrote to a friend in Parliament: 'I have sent up Sir J. Oglander, and sufficient matter to keep him awhile by the leg, if you will do him but justice; without it, peradventure the place will be the better for his absence, and some of the clergy (God willing) shall follow him'.

The recipient of that letter was Sir Thomas Barrington of Hatfield Broadoak in Essex who owned the manor of Swainston on the Island; and about that time his wife also heard from John Hall their steward at Swainston. Hall was explaining the general sense of insecurity on the Island: he wrote on 30 May 1643 'The Cavaliers coming so near these parts have put us in some fear here. Upon Saturday last they came into a town in this county called Ringwood, and there plundered the town, but chiefly such as they were informed of for Roundheads. At Salisbury and all thereabout they have done great spoil. I hear this day they are gone westward and intend to join with the Lord Hopton. But that which I cannot but acquaint your ladyship with (not doubting but my master hath notice of it already) is, that when the Cavaliers were come to Salisbury, Hurst Castle, the very key of the Island, was very much unprovided both of men and victuals, and most of the platform so much decayed for want of boards and other necessaries, as the ordnance can hardly be made use of there. I could not have believed it if I had not been there this day sevennight with Colonel Carne. If that castle should be taken, the Island would quickly be in a dangerous condition'.

As that summer wore on the feeling of general edginess continued, and morale on the Island cannot have been improved by the action of the citizens of Southampton in sending some of their goods across to the Isle of Wight before the expected arrival of a plundering Royalist army. On 11 August the Newport town assembly decided to increase the numbers of the night watch in the town. Meanwhile a formal request had now come from the town of Southampton for assurances of help from the Island in case of a Royalist attack. Colonel Carne summoned a meeting of the local gentlemen at Carisbrooke Castle to consider the appeal. Encouraged by murmurs of sympathy at the meeting, Carne suggested that the gentry should all sign a formal declaration of support against the Royalists. It was a nasty moment for poor Sir John Oglander, back in the Island once more after two months in prison in London. 'I confess I wished myself away, but that could not be. Then, considering the forwardness of the gentlemen, and how I was counted a great malignant, and that all their aim was at me, and that by setting my hand I might gain a better opinion, and be thereby better enabled to do his Majesty service when occasion served; and that if I did refuse it I was certain to be banished the Island, I did unwillingly set my hand'.

On the same day as Oglander's embarrassing meeting at the castle, 18 September, John Hall at Swainston was writing again to the Barringtons about 'the French fleet who are reported to have their intentions this way'; and, just as the Oxford colleges were even then melting down their silver plate for the King's use, Hall shows that Parliament too was seeking to finance the war in the same way: 'There will be some plate which is here gathered for the Parliament service shortly sent up to be exchanged'.

As the years passed, Island life tried to return to much of its normal pattern, but there were periodic reminders of the mayhem that continued across the water. There were special levies to pay for provisions or horses for the Parliamentary army; and the great effort, for this small community, of raising 500 infantry to serve in Waller's army. In May of 1645 the Newport town assembly called off the Whitsuntide fair 'in respect of the dangerousnes of the tyme'. It was observable however that the threat of invasion was increasingly remote, and that the Royalist cause was crumbling. Finally in 1646 the King surrendered and, it seemed, it was all over. Parliament had only to pay off the army, and everyone could go home. There was a problem here – no money; and there was the niggling question of Ireland, not to mention the continued embarrassing presence of the King.

From the perspective of the Island these issues seemed remote and unreal. Local concern was with the harvest and the price of corn; and, of course, the new Governor who in September 1647 set up his bachelor household at Carisbrooke Castle. He was something of a high flier. Still only twenty-six, Colonel Robert Hammond commanded an infantry regiment, had been governor of Exeter for the Parliament, and was beginning to wield some political influence in the army. His appointment now as Governor of the Isle of Wight – the Earl of Pembroke having been eased out of the job – was seen as the reward of a sinecure post after distinguished military service; and certainly there seemed every prospect of a spell of quiet away from the hurly-burly of army politics. He came to the Island not entirely as a stranger, for his aunt Jane Dingley lived in Shorwell, just four miles away from Carisbrooke Castle; and his acceptance into Island society was indicated by his admission as a burgess

Charles I and Colonel Robert Hammond,
his gaoler during his year on the Island.

63

of Newport on 18 September.

On the morning of Saturday 13 November Hammond set out from the castle on his way to Newport where he had called a meeting of some of the militia officers and the local gentry. A few yards down the hill he was hailed by two rather travel-stained gentlemen. They introduced themselves as John Ashburnham and Sir John Berkeley, and they had that morning made a choppy crossing from Lymington to Yarmouth before riding on to Carisbrooke in quest of Hammond. Berkeley cryptically asked Hammond whether he knew who was very near him: Hammond of course did not know.

'Even good King Charles,' added Berkeley, 'who is come from Hampton Court for fear of being murdered privately'.

If Berkeley had aimed to surprise the Governor he exceeded his expectations. Hammond was so perturbed that the messengers thought he was going to fall off his horse.

'O gentlemen, you have undone me by bringing the King into the Island, if at least you have brought him; and if you have not, pray let him not come: for what between my duty to his Majesty, and my gratitude for this fresh obligation of confidence, and my observing my trust to the Army, I shall be confounded'.

Berkeley assured Hammond that, if this was how he felt, the proposal of his receiving the King could be dropped, and no harm would be done. It was the thought of the harm all too possibly arising from his inaction that was now haunting Hammond's mind. If Charles should come to any harm, what would the Army and the kingdom say to him that had refused to receive him? Hammond could see his duty all too plainly, which was to scoop the King into custody as quickly as possible and discuss the small print later; but he could not give the needed assurance of outright support that the royal envoys wanted. Finally Ashburnham at least agreed to accept the Governor's assurance that he would do whatever could be expected from a person of honour and honesty. This was the kind of prevarication that the King would have admired, though he was not likely to welcome encountering it in this case. It was however agreed that Hammond should accompany the two envoys to meet the King, though Berkeley had misgivings. 'What do you mean', he muttered to Ashburnham, 'to carry this man to the King before you know whether he will approve of this Undertaking or no? Undoubtedly you will surprise him'.

And where was the King? He had two nights before escaped from house-arrest (or palace-arrest) at Hampton Court and was now in hiding at Titchfield House, the Earl of Southampton's home on Southampton Water, while the whole country and particularly the ports were being scoured for him. The occasion of his sudden departure by a back staircase from Hampton was apparently an anonymous warning that his life was in danger in London; but there is much evidence that Charles' choice of the Isle of Wight as a refuge was the result of long and serious thought. His attendant Ashburnham had first suggested it, and to Charles it was by no means unknown territory. He had in fact made four visits there, though the last had been nineteen years before. He had, as we have seen, been disappointed in his expectations of support from the Island at the outbreak of war in 1642, and this still rankled. On the other hand he knew that he still had loyal supporters among the inhabitants, not least poor Sir John Oglander now living a quiet life at Nunwell after serving two spells in prison for voicing pro-royalist sentiments. The King's mind at least was receptive, and Ashburnham developed his arguments in favour of the Island. The Army kept no units there, so at least the King would be safe from extremists; and, as the new Governor had access to the Army Council, Charles could keep his lines open through him to the effective power base of Parliament.

Robert Hammond had relations in interesting places. He was, to begin with, a cousin of Cromwell, and as well as his aunt at Shorwell, an uncle, Henry Hammond, was the King's chaplain. Moreover during that summer of 1647 the chaplain Hammond had taken his nephew Robert to meet the King; and the King's reading of Robert's temperament on this occasion was that he was eager to see a negotiated peace between the warring factions in the nation, rather than a bloodstained and imposed one. Robert Hammond was now on the royal list of hopefuls.

Some of the more subtle political wiseacres at that time saw the whole episode of the King's transfer to the Isle of Wight as a clever and convoluted plot by Cromwell, to get Charles out of the reach of the Army militants and into the hands of a trusted lieutenant. So, the proponents of this theory argued, Cromwell achieved his objective in three stages. He engineered the dismissal of the Earl of Pembroke and his replacement by Hammond as Governor of the Isle of Wight. He then enticed the King to escape from Hampton Court by contriving reports of threats to his life. Finally he steered the escape towards the Island – here the Cromwell connection is hard to demonstrate because it could practicably have been done only by inducing Ashburnham to argue the virtues of the scheme and thus convince the King. It would seem an unlikely story, yet many contemporaries accepted it. According to Clarendon Cromwell received the news of Charles's arrival in the Isle of Wight 'with so unusual a gaiety, that all Men concluded that the King was where He wishes he should be'; and there are the famous poetic lines of Andrew Marvell:

> '…twining subtile fears with hope,
> He wove a Net of such a scope,
> That Charles himself might chase
> To Caresbrooks narrow case'.

Nunwell House, the home of Sir John Oglander. It was here that Charles I made a visit soon after his arrival on the Island in November 1647.

There was too an unexplained visit by Cromwell to the Island in early September just after Hammond's appointment as Governor. We shall probably never know the truth. Here, as at most of the crucial moments Cromwell, like T.S. Eliot's Macavity, seems to have an alibi, but happily benefits from the result. Charles did indeed end up in the Isle of Wight, prised out of Titchfield by Hammond and another Parliamentary officer; and after spending the Saturday night at an inn called the 'Plume of Feathers' in Cowes (in a carved oak bed with a headboard adorned with the sobering text *Remember thy end* picked out in gilt lettering) he moved on to Carisbrooke Castle on the Sunday morning, cheered by some demonstrations of local support including – as he passed through Newport – the presentation of a freshly-picked rose by a lady called Frances Trattle. As news of the royal arrival buzzed round the Island it was received with dismay by Oglander, who wrote in his diary at Nunwell: 'I could do nothing but sigh and weep for two nights and a day. And the reason of my grief was that I verily believed he could not come into a worse place for himself, and where he could be more securely kept'.

Was he indeed secure? Hammond at first preserved the fiction that Charles was a state guest, and when Parliament reluctantly confirmed that he might stay in the Island, much of his furniture and library was brought over from Hampton Court, soon followed even by his coach which enabled him to enjoy some sightseeing and to catch up with views of parts of the Island that he had missed on his earlier visits. As the atmosphere became increasingly tense, though, it became clear to the King that any flitting down back staircases was to be infinitely harder at Carisbrooke than at Hampton Court. Hammond had no ambition to be the subject of a court-martial, and Charles was attentively followed in his daytime journeyings (more and more confined to the castle precincts) while at night his bedroom – in the centre of the walled courtyard – was guarded by sentries outside the door.

Within a few days of arriving at Carisbrooke the King, with Hammond's active encouragement, drafted a set of proposals for an agreement with Parliament. He was dealing from a rather weak position of course, after the outcome of the war and the success of the Parliamentary and Scottish armies; and his document was an assembly of all the concessions he had at any time offered, with a few new ones. It was in fact such a potentially conciliatory document that many Royalists in various parts of the country could not believe their eyes when the news presses published the substance of Charles's proposals. He agreed to accept Presbyterian government for three years, with the future of the Church left to be settled by the Westminster Assembly of divines along with twenty royal nomines. Amazingly he agreed to concede to Parliament the control of the militia for his lifetime, and to find out of the royal revenues the money necessary for the arrears of Army pay.

The King watched the castle gate in vain for sight of a courier returning with Parliament's reply. Their silence was deafening. Finally early in December he sent them a reminder worded with icy dignity: 'Had his Majesty thought it possible that his two Houses could be imployed in things of greater concernment than the peace of this miserable distracted Kingdom, he would have expected with more patience their leisure in acknowledging the receipt of His message of the 16 of November last'; and he repeated a proposal he had made for a personal treaty in London.

Parliament did react to this by agreeing to send commissioners down to the Island to deal with the King; but the remit of the delegation was only to present four draft bills which would in fact reduce the King to a mere figurehead, as a preliminary to any personal treaty in London, which after the bills would only be an empty formality.

The Parliamentary commissioners, led by the Earl of Denbigh, rode into Carisbrooke Castle on Christmas Eve, and early that afternoon, in the large presence chamber, they presented their document. The King asked for some days to consider it, and with his advisers withdrew to do some intensive reading. He found himself looking with horror, if not surprise, at what were clearly terms of total surrender.

Fortunately for him there were other bidders in this political auction. The next day some Scottish commissioners arrived, duly furnished with visas from London. They had to deliver a formal document dissenting from Parliament's proposals as being 'prejudicial to Religion, the Crown, and the Union and Interest of the Kingdom'. With the protocol thus out of the way the King's advisers withdrew, the doors were closed, and Charles and the commissioners began the real work of negotiation – Christmas Day at this time was in any case just another working day.

It was a remarkable diplomatic coup. That day, in the Great Chamber at Carisbrooke, detailed plans were made for the second Civil War. The Scots were to invade England, coinciding with English Royalist risings, to put Charles back on the throne – at a price. The King agreed that, as soon as he could, he would in Parliament recognise the Solemn League and Covenant by which Scotland had rejected bishops; and that Presbyterianism should be established in England for three years. Other articles laid the groundwork for a degree of political integration between England and Scotland. Importantly, the King kept control of the militia.

The detailed drafting was long and laborious and it took two days to complete the work. Two copies were written out and signed. One, the King's was temporarily hidden in a writing desk in his bedroom. The Scots were rather nervous about their copy. Understandably, they were quite prepared to be searched at their final departure, so they previously had the dangerous document encased in lead and secretly buried in an Island garden, to be recovered later by one of their agents. It was a prudent precaution but, as it turned out, unnecessary, and the Scottish commissioners got away without any impediment though with a frosty reception, on their way, from the town of Portsmouth.

The next problem was to decide what to do about the Commissioners from the English Parliament, who were still eating up their expense allowances and awaiting with stretched patience the royal reply to their paper, delivered on Christmas Eve. The King's policy here was to play for time. Now that he had achieved the treaty with the Scots, there were no considerations of policy to keep him in England, and indeed a boat was at hand to lift him from the Island and take him to France. First he had to send the Commissioners off to London reasonably contented.

The King had his own plans to achieve that. On Tuesday 28 December when the Commissioners filed in for their meeting to receive the royal reply, they found Charles sitting, flanked by his attendants and holding a sealed document. He asked the Earl of Denbigh whether he and the Commissioners were empowered to change any substantial part of the proposals they had brought. When Denbigh admitted that they lacked such powers, the King handed over his document, still sealed. This was not well received. After some heated argument they required the message to be unsealed and read out to them. The effect was dramatic, for the King had in quite forthright terms rejected all four draft bills and again requested a personal treaty in London. The Commissioners stumped out of the royal presence and peremptorily left the castle in high dudgeon.

While Hammond was seeing the angry Commissioners off, the King and his attendants moved quickly. Any escape, it was now clear, would have to happen without further delay. The King began putting on his riding boots, to leave the castle on the pretext of going hunting in the forest – such excursions had in fact been enjoyed during the past weeks – and then making a quick sprint for the boat.

Two things happened to prevent this. A last-minute glance through the window at the weather vane on the chapel roof showed that the

Captain John Burley who was tried and executed in 1648 for an attempt to rescue Charles I from Carisbrooke Castle.

wind – which until then had been favourable for the voyage to France – had now moved into the wrong quarter. Then a great bustle and shouting in the courtyard announced the return of the angry Hammond; and the subsequent activity was ominous. The castle gate was slammed shut, and then extra guards were seen to be set. Charles's imprisonment began in earnest in these final hours of 1647.

No more was seen, that day, of the Governor, who sulked in his quarters all evening. The next morning however brought sure signs of the new regime. Hammond announced that all the King's personal attendant must leave the castle and the Island at once – a step that must have been all the more embarrassing for him because those evicted included his own uncle, the royal chaplain Henry Hammond. It was the passage of these Royalists through Newport, and the feverish local rumours of affronts to the King, that sparked off one of the few cases of civil disturbance while Charles was on the Island. A local Royalist, Captain John Burley, seized the town drum and used it to assemble a crowd. Shouting 'For God, the King, and the People' he promised that he would lead them to the castle to rescue Charles from his imprisonment to prevent him from being murdered, and that he would be the first to enter the castle. Eventually the Mayor managed to get his drum back, and the demonstration fizzled out; but it gave a real alarm to the Army, and troop movements began at once. Early the next morning, 30 December, a hundred soldiers landed, and there were a further hundred following them from Portsmouth. These were men of Hammond's own regiment, veterans of the New Model Army, much more formidable than the four squadrons of Newport men with whom Hammond had hitherto been defending the Island. The same day three senior officers were sent to the Isle of Wight, from Army headquarters at Windsor, to help Hammond; and on 1 January the House of Commons ordered Vice-Admiral Rainsborough to go with some additional ships to the Isle of Wight, and granted Hammond powers of martial law. On 3 January it ordered that fifty barrels of powder 'with Match and Bullet proportionable' should be sent to the Island. It was a very large reaction to a very small riot, but one senses that a raw nerve had been touched in the realisation that the Army and Parliament had been tricked by the King and the Scots. 'The House of Commons is very sensible of the King's dealings, and of our brethrens, in this late transaction', Cromwell wrote to Hammond on 3 January. It was hardly surprising that John Burley's trial and execution at Winchester, on a charge of treason, should have followed very promptly after his abortive demonstration.

From the beginning of 1648, then, the King was closely watched and seemingly isolated at Carisbrooke; yet, strangely, he was hardly ever out of reach of a web of Royalist agents concerned in contriving his escape. As quickly as Hammond engaged new staff for the royal household, he unwittingly brought in covert Royalists among them, or else people of no special allegiance who proved susceptible to the royal charisma and were won over into helping the King.

Throughout 1648 Hammond was bombarded by supposedly helpful intelligence briefings, notably from the Derby House Committee in London – a kind of G.C.H.Q. which among other activities was fed with information by a network of spies. Almost every despatch from London seemed to include information about another projected escape, and if only half of these reports had any substance the King must have found himself fully occupied in escape plans. Potential routes out of the castle, as reported to Hammond, included getting Charles out disguised as the coalman; breaking a hole through the ceiling of the royal bedroom to allow an escape from the unguarded room above; another disguised escape, this time dressed as a country visitor to the castle; a daytime snatch by a 'Commando' party from outside the castle, using ladders against the outer wall; and a rather similar sudden rescue involving the starting of a major fire in the castle, and getting the King out in the resultant confusion. There was even a suggestion that Charles was planning to wriggle up a chimney flue, and according to one of the weekly news-sheets Hammond took this report seriously enough to order workmen to fit bars inside the flue.

To attempt even a few of these schemes the King would need fairly regular contact with his friends outside the castle; and rarely does he seem to have been cut off from such correspondence. Couriers came and went with bundles of letters from various people, but of course the dangerous part was to elude the scrutiny by the guards at the castle gate. This was where the household servants came in useful because it was unusual for them to be challenged or searched. During January and February 1648 there was an assistant laundress called Mary (her surname is not known) who, having access to Charles's room during the day, simply hid smuggled letters under the carpet, and collected the replies from the same place the next day. Eventually her identity was betrayed by a royalist courier – in the best laughing cavalier tradition – arriving drunk at the castle gate and asking for her by name. She was consequently ordered out of the castle; but there were usually others to replace her.

The main agent inside the castle during the early months of 1648 was Henry Firebrace, a young man of about Hammond's age, formerly a secretary to the Earl of Denbigh who had had that barney with the King the previous Christmas. Firebrace applied for a houshold post at Carisbrooke and, with such impeccable Roundhead credentials, he was appointed groom of the bedchamber. Hammond was not to know at the time (though he knew all too well later) that Firebrace was now already a Royalist. Once inside the castle he found various surreptitious ways of communicating privately with the King, and was soon busy with appraisals of escape possibilities.

He soon realised that a daytime escape was not practicable. The King was still allowed reasonably free movement at least within the defences; but as he walked the circuit of the medieval walls or, later in the summer, played bowls on the eastern barbican, he was always accompanied by one of the officers of the garrison, with other soldiers at an attentively short distance.

At night however Charles was locked in his room, and Firebrace saw this as the most promising opportunity to get him out of the castle without immediate discovery and pursuit. The King's bedroom was towards the southern end of the main wing containing the great hall, and the window at first floor level looked out on to the middle of the courtyard. Although guards were set outside the doors there was no sentry in the courtyard. The castle walls of course were patrolled, but at sufficient intervals to allow the King – with careful timing – to get on

to the south wall and to be lowered by a rope to the bank outside. From
there it would be a reasonably easy scramble on to the lower outer wall
of the Tudor defences, where friends could be waiting with horses to
meet him and take him on to the coast.

Firebrace put this scheme to the King, who approved the idea but
amended it in what turned out to be a significant detail. His bedroom
window was secured by a bar, and Firebrace's plan involved smuggling
a rope and a file into the room during the day, to be used during the
night escape. Rather than risk the noise of cutting the bar, Charles made
some measurements of the gap and pronounced that he would be able
to squeeze out without removing the bar. In spite of Firebrace's misgivings the file was abandoned from the escape plan.

Otherwise the arrangements went well. A ship was arranged to wait
off the coast at Wootton Park between East Cowes and Ryde, and two
Royalists – Edward Worsley and Richard Osborne – were to wait at the
arranged time outside the south wall with a spare horse. The night fixed
was 20 March. Firebrace reconnoitred the darkened courtyard to confirm
that it was indeed clear of guards, then threw a small stone up to the
King's window as a signal for him to come out. He heard the window
quietly opening, and a scuffling noise as the rope was lowered. Then
he could hear the King straining to get through the window and – as
he had half feared – not succeeding. Finally he saw the flare of a lighted
candle placed in the window and took this as a signal from the King
that the escape had failed. All Firebrace could do now was to warn the
two Royalists outside the castle wall, which he did by going up to the
battlements with some more stones and throwing them towards the
outer wall. Apparently the message was received, and Worsley and
Osborne vanished quietly into the night.

The conspirators outside the castle of course had no idea what had
gone wrong. Charles proceeded to tell them, in the course of his coded
and smuggled correspondence; and it was bad luck for Firebrace that
one of the Derby House Committee agents intercepted one of these
letters and managed to shake most of the sense out of the code. On 6
April Oliver Cromwell wrote to Hammond giving him an embarrassingly
full account of the failed escape on 20 March; and the result predictably
was yet another purge of castle servants, including Firebrace. He managed to hang on until the end of April, and before he left the castle he
had the arrangements for the next escape attempt near completion;

moreover there were other Royalists still in the castle, who had eluded Hammond's net.

As part of the new regime Charles had now been moved from his room inside the courtyard to one against the north wall, with a window looking out to the external bank and Tudor wall. The logic of this move was probably that it brought him nearer to Hammond's quarters where the Governor could keep more efficient surveillance; but the window, with only a short drop to the top of the outer bank, seemed an inviting way out in spite of its bars, and Hammond took the precaution of building a sentry platform immediately below it.

Charles's friends of course seemed equal to the problem. There was now no question that the window bar would have to be removed – after his previous experience Charles was quite ready to be convinced of this – and some acid was smuggled in to the King's room to allow him to do this quietly. The three sentries outside the window each night presented a greater problem, but the three who were to be on duty on 28 May were bribed to collude in the escape, and once again a ship was booked to await the King, while Worsley and Osborne again were to be stationed outside, this time below the north wall.

At the appointed time the King, having already removed the bar, opened the window, let the rope down for the short distance necessary, and started to climb out. He was soon back inside, for even in the murk of a moonless night he could see that the bank outside his window was bristling with troops. Two of the three bribed guards in a last-minute panic had informed an officer about the escape. The remaining sentry was arrested and replaced by a force of soldiers. The two Royalists outside, when they finally gave up waiting, rode away down the hill, straight into an ambush and a hail of musket balls. In the darkness they managed to escape the firing, and were then chased by cavalry over to Wootton where they found the escape boat just offshore. Turning their horses loose on the beach they ran up to the ship, but when its master found that they were without the King he refused to pick them up, and left them just time to dive into the adjoining woods.

As the pursuing soldiers reached the beach they found the two riderless horses and could just make out the shape of the departing ship, so they gave up the chase, leaving Worsley and Osborne eventually to find a boat and make their own escape from the Island.

During all these stirring happenings on the Island the rest of the country was having a summer of war, the product of that secret agreement in the King's room at Carisbrooke the previous Christmas. Already by May there had been Royalist risings in various parts of England and Wales; and early in July the Scots kept their part of the agreement by mounting an invasion across the border. Laboriously the various risings were put down, and when on 17 August Cromwell defeated the Scots at Preston it was clear that the time of reckoning had come for the King; and not only for the King – the Presbyterian majority in Parliament had its own misgivings about the future actions of its aggrieved and increasing radical Army.

A common interest in patching up an agreement before Cromwell and his friends were back, breathing vengeance, was the genesis of the final episode in Charles's year on the Island: the Treaty of Newport. Charles was released on parole and on 6 September took up lodgings in Newport.

The town began to fill with Parliamentary Commissioners, their camp followers, and a bevy of news-book correspondents eager to trawl for any gossip about the King.

Negotiations began on 18 September in the old Grammar School, which can still be seen, and ground on for more than two months with never more than a flickering hope of success. It was a busy time for the town inns – which saw the occasional fracas between supporters of the two sides – and for the posts between the Island and London as records of the negotiations were relayed to Parliament. Towards the end of November the treaty had reached a near-stalemate, when the whole issue was resolved by an Army coup. On 27 November Colonel Hammond was arrested and taken off to Army headquarters. Then on the night of 29 November, in blinding rain, more troops were brought into the Island, and in the early morning of 30 November the King was arrested and taken off, through Yarmouth, to Hurst Castle. It was the beginning of the journey to his trial and to his execution in London on 30 January 1649.

It was not the end of his family's connection with the Island. In August 1650 his two children remaining in England – Elizabeth, and Henry the Duke of Gloucester – were brought as prisoners to Carisbrooke Castle. Elizabeth was there for only a short time. Caught in the rain on the castle bowling green, she developed a chill which produced complications, and in the castle one can still see the room where on 8 September she died, aged just under fifteen. She was buried in St Thomas's church at Newport. Her brother Henry stayed on in lonely captivity at Carisbrooke for three years until in 1653 he was set free and allowed to join his family in France.

Sir John Oglander did not live to see the Restoration, as he died in 1655; but in 1665 Charles II visited the Isle of Wight and conferred a knighthood on Edward Worsley for his attempts to rescue Charles I from Carisbrooke. At last he had his reward for that hair-raising chase to the beach at Wootton.

Meanwhile Newport had adjusted to the change of regime. On 22 May 1660 the town assembly agreed 'that the towne maces be forthwith sent to Mr Richard Rudyard to London to have them altered out of the States Armes into the Kings armes about the same size they are now with as little charge as conveniently maybe'.

SIX

Plunder From The Sea

Wherever maritime traffic is moving, there is the temptation to steal it. Thus piracy was almost a natural condition in the Solent and surrounding waters during the medieval period and especially during the French Wars in the 14th century. In the reign of Elizabeth I however, the Isle of Wight acquired a particularly sinister reputation for interference with shipping. This period divides into an earlier phase from 1565 to 1585 dominated by plain piracy and the self-help methods of merchants in taking reprisals for losses; and the period from 1565 to 1603 marked by rather more organised privateering initiated with letters of marque and culminating in the appraisal of cargoes and the payment of government dues known as the Lord Admiral's tenths. In many cases however the dividing line between piracy and privateering is hard to find.

A fruitful ground for attacks on shipping was provided by wars of various kinds in this period – the French wars of religion, the revolt of the Spanish provinces in the Netherlands, and later the English privateering war against Spain. Much of the activity went on under foreign flags, but the mixed assembly of protestant corsairs that infested the Channel in the 1570s included many English sailors. When in the summer of 1577 a fleet of some fourteen ships of the King of Navarre (the French Huguenot leader and the future King Henry IV of France) put in to the Isle of Wight, Sir Amyas Paulet reported to the Queen that the only part of the fleet that was not English was in effect the flag.

The situation had its irony when English ships were the victims, as when in April 1588 the English pirate Gilbert Lee, sailing his ship the *Rat* under commission from the King of Navarre, captured an English ship with a cargo of wine which he later sold in the Isle of Wight. French Huguenot sailors, on the other hand, were accustomed to making themselves at home on the Island. When the Island Captain, Edward Horsey, was asked to make a count of shipping at Mead Hole (a bay between East Cowes and Wootton Creek) in July 1570 he reported that 'the frenche Captins have x sayle of shippes well trymed in warlicke order, and aborde them as I canne Lerne 300 of their Nation aswell Marriners as others'.

In December 1569 the Venetian ships *Giustiniana* and *Vergi* were only an hour out from the Isle of Wight when they were seized by four armed ships 'in the name of the Queen of Navarre and the Prince of Conde'. In 1575 the famous 200-ton *Castle of Comfort*, with its extended history of privateering ventures, was taken over by an Isle of Wight merchant Henry Jolliffe to operate under licence from the Prince of Conde, but the Queen got news of this and Edward Horsey was instructed to have the ship laid up in the Island.

With the Duke of Alva's arrival in the Netherlands in 1567 and the consequent intensification of the war there, the 'Sea Beggars' made their presence felt with some indiscriminate raiding of Channel shipping. In

1571 their victims included various Italian merchants,, and some ships of the 'Steelyard' company. The merchants were importunate and the Queen was in one of her anti-Flemish moods, so the Privy Council instructed Edward Horsey, along with all the other piracy commissioners, to look to their charges. Horsey did go as far as admitting, in a letter to Lord Bughley on 20 October, that the Prince of Orange's ships were getting out of hand.

There was a continuing background, then, of piracy and privateering under foreign flags; but there was also abundant native talent, from various parts of Island society, which deserves closer examination. There were first of all the gentleman promoters who financed and sailed their own ships as privateers. One such was Captain Edward Denny who, like many of his kind, seems to have worked on rather slender capital, leaving him vulnerable to any setback. When in September 1577 he brought in to the Isle of Wight two prizes, a French and a Spanish ship, these were impounded by Edward Horsey and Denny himself was required to discharge his crew, lay up his ship, and make his explanations to the Privy Council. Within two months he found it necessary to sell the ship in order to pay his debts. The following March the sale of some of his fish at Newport came under the scrutiny of the piracy commissioners. Apart from his trading activities he does not seem to have had any property links with the Island.

Another gentleman, John Vaughan, appears as an owner captain in June 1569, and his 60-ton boat the *Bowe* was one of those counted at Mead Hole by Horsey in 1570. Something of his volatile character may be judged from his appearance before the bailiffs of Newport in November 1568 for wounding his opponent with a dagger in the course of a fight with a sailor called Edward Clayse. Unlike Denny, Vaughan seems never to have been short of money. His house in Newport was apparently a large one, for a reorganisation of the town watches in 1574 specified that 'Mr. Vaughanes houseas longe as ther are 2 howseholdes to paie 2 watches as longe as they do dwell in hit'. He also had a house at Ryde, with storage for merchandise. He was involved with one of the ventures of the *Castle of Comfort* and, whether or not as a result of this, he spent four months in prison in 1574. Later that same summer he was making himself useful to Edward Horsey (and through him, to the Privy Council) by scouting for some sign of the Spanish fleet. In October 1581 when Bernardino de Mendoza (the Spanish envoy in London) reported to Philip II of Spain that 'the pirate Vaughan' was at the Isle of Wight he had four ships, as part of a larger squadron.

Apart from the gentleman promoters there were also the more prosperous Newport merchants whom mixed piracy with general trading. One of the chief of these was Henry Jolliffe, whom we have already encountered dabbling with the *Castle of Comfort*. As a merchant he engaged in the Normandy trade, and in the summer of 1576 a French pirate Captain Gilliam captured a ship of his loaded mainly with wine and canvas. Although he was on this occasion granted letters of reprisal, Gilliam evidently eluded him, for in 1579 he was still petitioning for the recovery of this loss. In 1578 he shared a warehouse in Newport with another local merchant Richard Markes, at which time he made sales of suspected stolen goods – bales of paper to a London merchant, and bell metal which he sold in Lewes – that he had acquired in Newport. In

1581 he acted for Edward Horsey as an entrepreneur to recover a pirated ship for its French owner. The years 1589-1590 brought several successful ventures. In 1589 he took a Catholic League ship with a cargo of fish and also captured a Spanish ship which he took into Cork. On 18 June 1590 he intercepted the *Renard* on a voyage from St Malo to the Isle of Wight and helped himself to the cargo of canvas, with some loose change and fifty gallons of sack as a bonus. Later that year, in the *Brave* of the Isle of Wight, he took another French ship.

Another prominent merchant-captain was Thomas Page. He was one of a group of young Island merchants who petitioned about piracy of their cargoes in May 1579. By 1590 he was captain of Sir George Carey's privateer *Commander*, and in 1592 he was sharing with Emmanuel Badd the large town warehouse at Newport quay. He prospered to the extent of becoming bailiff of Newport in 1595 but he obviously had a reputation for keeping dubious company, and in 1589 a Newport butcher, John Hallet, told him in public that he was 'a Raskall, Roage Knave Theif and that thou hast got thy goodes by theft'.

This then was some of the native talent, with money to back it. At another level there were the ordinary roughs who busied themselves with piracy. They were always described as 'of the Isle of Wight' but tended not to stay long in any one place: Baily and White in 1574; Austen and Daye in 1577; Yard and Gaskin in 1578; Nutshawe and Hooper in 1579; White and Foster in 1580; Corporall, Sawyer, Gisborne, Bord, and Pierce in 1581. The Isle of Wight served as their shop counter, and connections ashore are not easy to trace, though some turn up in surprising contexts. The well-known pirate John Callis for example does not seem to have had a residence on the Island, though he did operate from there – possibly his ship was his floating home; but his German colleague Kurt Hecklenburg, with whom he worked in the 1580s, did in fact occupy a house and garden in Lugley Street at Newport in 1583.

In the accommodating moral climate for the practice of piracy at this time, these people might on occasions be regarded either as criminals or as benefactors. In 1581 for example Horsey reported to Sir Francis Walsingham that John Story had captured a pirate named Fludd. In 1582 however it was the pirate Story and his crew who were now filling the Newport town prison; as for Fludd, in 1585 Sir George Carey was referring to him as a valiant and skilful pirate 'and now in mynde to be an honest man', able to do service against Spain.

Provisioning a privateer was a costly undertaking, and it may be wondered how the ordinary pirate, without merchant or joint-stock backing, was able to get to sea. An interesting story of the potential rewards of ingenuity and duplicity is seen in the methods of George Bord who in 1581 found himself at Cowes with a ship and with something of a crew, but without provisions. In May that year another pirate, Nicholas Gisborne, arrived at Cowes with a French prize containing a Flemish-owned cargo. He was closely followed by the indignant French owner of the captured ship, who duly applied to Edward Horsey for restitution. Horsey referred the matter to Henry Jolliffe, who had some experience of brokerage in such matters and had the additional qualification of being able to speak French. Jolliffe now passed the commission on to George Bord, who successfully arranged for his crew to seize Gisborne's captured ship while Gisborne was entertaining him to supper below hatches. Bord now transferred to his own ship all that was left of the Flemish cargo in the prize, delivered the ship itself to Newport for the French owner, and then went on to Poole to sell the cargo. He now needed provisions, so he returned to Newport to collect his fee from Jolliffe. Jolliffe in fact received £52 from the French owner, out of which he paid Bord £10 in cash along with '2 caste peeces of Ordenance called minniones and in vytalles an oxe & ½ of bread and 2 hogeshedes of beer'.

Jolliffe had made a quick and easy profit, but in fact Bord now had just what he needed. He now put to sea, and returned to the Island six days later with a captured French prize serving as his pinnace. Putting to sea yet again, within two days he had taken a Spanish ship. He now had a fleet of three. He next assimilated another Cowes ship as consort, and when last heard of he was planning an attack on two 100-ton French ships at St Helens.

Loot, once acquired, found a ready market in the Isle of Wight. Such shore-based support had long since been recognised and condemned by the Privy Council. A proclamation of 1565 complained that 'the said pyrattes…are at the handes of a nomber of disordred persons, dwellinge within or nere the havens, crekes and landinge places of this our realme, secretly refresshed with vitualles, furnyshed with munytion and other necessaries, and sundrye other wayes by byeng of the stollen wares ayded and relyved'. There were in fact several places in the Isle of Wight that mixed stolen merchandise with legitimate trade. The examinations by the piracy commissioners show that many of the cargoes coming in to Newport town quay were of dubious origin. Thomas Becket's house at Cowes was another disposal point for cargoes of all kinds, with few questions asked. Becket was apparently at one time an Admiralty officer. When, on the sale of the *Carricke Sidney* in 1570, the royal ordnance aboard was put into the custody of Edward Horsey on the Isle of Wight, it was Becket who received the guns from Thomas Finche (one of the former owners). A letter from Jasper Swift to the Earl of Lincoln in 1577 reported the drying, sorting and housing of 1,346 hides at Thomas Becket's house; and Swift himself was at one time an Admiralty officer. On 5 June 1581 he was working in consultation with an agent of Lord Burghley on the Isle of Wight, planning the arrest of some pirates. On the other hand, Becket's house was in 1588 the scene of some trading over stolen cargo brought in by a pirate.

It was common practice also for trading to take place actually on board the prize, and this was the method used by Gilbert Lee in 1588.

In fact the Island had a centre for both shipboard and shore-based trading in stolen cargoes, at Mead Hole. This was a not particularly sheltered anchorage and cluster of victualling and warehouse buildings ashore, between East Cowes and Wootton Creek. In a survey of the Island in 1559 it was described as being a mile west of Shofleet Creek and two miles west of Wootton Creek with 'fayre londinge at full see three quarters of a mile towardes the est at a faddom water and at lowe water dry and osy'. A survey of Island trade in 1569 referred to it, along with Yarmouth, Cowes, and St Helens, as an anchorage apparently already used for 'the stayeng of the shipes as well Englyshe as Straungers…be reason of contrarie wind'; and it was obviously the main anchorage when Edward Horsey made a census of local shipping in 1570.

By this time it had become a byword for felony. There was the South-

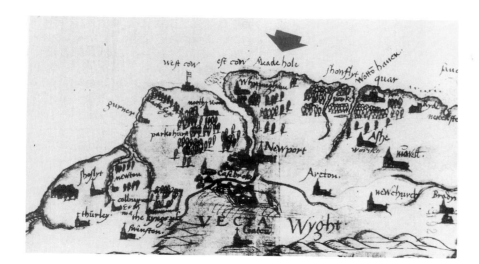

Detail from a map of about 1590 showing Mead Hole, the infamous pirate anchorage on the north coast of the Island between East Cowes and Wootton Creek.

ampton fishmonger who in 1577 protested that his barrel of eels was 'no Mead Holle goods nor thief-stolen'; and a deposition in the Admiralty Court in 1589 explained that 'meade holle…is a place not accustomed for marchanntes to make salle off goodes and merchandizes in…but rather suche as mak salle theare are suspected to have come evill by the goodes they there sell'. In 1570 the Spanish ambassador, having sent an agent to the Isle of Wight 'to see what was going on there', passed on his report to Philip II: 'In a town on the island called Medol there is a great fair of spices, wines, wool, saffron, oil, soap, woad, and a great number of other goods stolen from your Majesty's subjects and some from French and Portuguese'. Another witness of one of these Island markets, in 1581, wrote: 'Theyr weare above 30 bottes Abord the man of warre his pryes the pynes and the shipes so foull and soche a thronge as if it had bene at a feare byinge and sellinge and barteringe. The Seayllores browght hoes Reddy and doblyttes mantelles and gownes and towke lynen Clothe and wollen Clothe for the same in barter and some monny some wares. The goldsmythe with his wyselles in lyke maner so that he is no man in the shipe withowt he hathe a whisell and Acheyn Abowt his necke. The shewmaker with his shewes pompes and pantafelles. The brewer with his beere the backer with his bread and the boucher with his bifes Callefes and muttenes, and Eavery deayllor with his shares lyinge before him, on man bargeninge with this man one other with that mane and the bottes that gave attendance and browght men abord wolld not goe from on shipe unto Another, but he wolld have 12d. So that me thawght when I was amongeste them That I had bene in a goodly Feare'.

Foreign merchants must have felt a sense of despair at the apparent ease with which cargoes were plundered. In 1570 after the latest prize, a very rich cargo of wool, had been taken in to the Island, the Spanish ambassador lamented: 'If ships continue to come freely in this way trade will simply be to enrich the heretics'. At times the pirates seemed to have had the Solent to themselves. Henry of Navarre's ambassador M. de Segur, writing from Southampton in 1584, complained to Sir Francis Walsingham: 'The mouth of this haven is so well guarded by the pirates that yesterday a passage-boat from Jersey wishing to put to sea, was attacked and forced to return into this water. I could not pick a worse place for embarking than this, for the majority of the pirates of this country are between the Isle of Wight and Poole, past which I have to go. A few of the Queen's ships at Portsmouth would deliver the whole of this coast from these brigands, who are not content merely with robbing those at sea, but rather come into the harbours to pillage the merchants, and even come as far as in front of this town which is ten or eleven miles inland'.

He was not exaggerating. In 1581 a Spanish ship from Andalusia was taken by pirates from beneath the guns of Cowes Castle, causing the ambassador to complain forcefully to the Privy Council. This ship was probably the *Greyhound*, about which there is a grudging government minute that there appeared to be no alternative to making restitution. The Isle of Wight however was territory in which the government fiat would not necessarily prevail. There was for instance the case of Nicholas Vincent, a French merchant whose ship was taken by pirates and brought to the Island. Vincent, who had been set adrift in the ship's boat, survived the ordeal and later obtained an order from the Privy Council for restitution of the ship and cargo. Arriving hopefully at the Island with this document, he was forcibly carried aboard the pirate ship, had the Council's letter taken from him, and was thankful to escape with his life. About the same time, on 5 April 1587, a Danish ship carrying wheat and bacon to Rouen was captured by another pirate near the French coast and brought to the Isle of Wight. The owners in their complaint to the Admiralty Court did not conceal their view that the ultimate responsibility was with Sir George Carey the Island Captain. The pirate, Thomas Evans, detained the Danish ship at the Island for five weeks, in the course of which the crew had their money and clothing stolen, as well as all the grain and a large part of the bacon. Finally, with the ship and the meagre remains of the cargo, they were allowed to leave with Carey's permission. This voyage was not a long one. Still within sight of the Island they were captured and then taken into Falmouth by one of John Killegrew's ships – with every suspicion of Carey's collusion ('quae consulte, ut apparet, eos subsequebatur').

The inference may in this case have been unjustified, but Carey and his predecessor Edward Horsey were undoubtedly very involved with the flourishing piracy round their coasts. The reason was basically an administrative one. The legal redress open to an aggrieved shipowner was either an appeal to the Admiralty Court and thus down to the Vice-Admiral; or else to the Privy Council and thus down to the Lord Lieutenant or in this case the Captain of the Island. Edward Horsey (Captain 1565-1583) and Sir George Carey (1583-1603) combined the two offices and were thus will placed to block or at least interminably delay any litigation that might be launched in their direction. The office of Captain and Vice-Admiral did not automatically go together; but the commission making the exhaustive survey of the Island in 1559 had recommended that the Captain 'be vyceadmirall as the Capteynes heretofore hath bene'. Although this advice was not immediately adopted, the provision was written into the appointments of Horsey and Carey, and it so happened that both were resident mostly on the Island, and inclined to make use of the position. Repeatedly one finds that many of the lines of inquiry into local piracy lead to the Captain's study at Carisbrooke

Castle. Carey had the advantage of being related to the Queen and the Lord Admiral – as well as a business associate of the latter – whereas his predecessor Horsey had to live more on his wits. Much of the piracy and privateering encouraged or condoned by the Captain was of course within the ambit of Government policy, but when particularly important interests were offended there was pressure on the Privy Council and this was duly passed on to Carisbrooke Castle. Early in 1580 parts of pirated cargoes from ships returning from the East found their way into the Island, and the Council ordered Horsey to set about finding who was buying this stolen property. A cloud of suspicion was growing in London, and in June 1581 Walsingham passed on to Lord Burghley a report he had received from Julius Caesar (the Admiralty Court judge) 'by the which yt appeareth that the Yle of Wyght is a great favorer of Pyrates which groweth pryncypally thorrowghe the corruption of Sir Ed. Horseys Lieutennante...Sir Edward him selve promisethe to use all care in fynding owt sooche as are any waye to be charged and to offere them up to iustice that they may receyve punishment according to their demerytes'. Burghley would already have been well informed however, for earlier that month he had received a report from an informant, John Johnson, who had spent a short time on the Island sampling various shipboard markets and apparently looking out for particular cargoes that had gone astray. One night he had supper in Newport with several of Sir Edward Horsey's men and with the local merchant Henry Jolliffe. The conversation got on to the subject of piracy, with Jolliffe speaking 'crewell wordes agaynst pyrattes and them that had Anny maner of deayllinge with them...and Sir Edward Horseyes men in lyke order beinge at Soper with me ussing the lyke spyches sayinge That they wolld not for £20 anny of Sir Edwardes men showld be seene or known to goe Abord of A man of ware, neather showlld theyr any man of the ylland goe A bord, if theyre lyfftenant showlld knowe of Any it wear bettor for them, what eaver they be, to goe a honderethe mylles'.

The next day Johnson, posing as a prospective buyer, went aboard a pirate prize. Among the crowd of people on the ship he was startled to recognise Henry Jolliffe, eight of Horsey's men, and several Island gentlemen. 'They wear Abashed to see me', Johnson reported, 'and I wear muche more Abashed to see them, to Remember theyr wordes the night befor'. Jolliffe was seen to slip quickly down to the captain's cabin, and with equal speed Johnson climbed into one of the dinghies to be rowed ashore; but the boatman was recalled just as he was casting off. There followed a tense scene down in the captain's cabin, in which one of the pirate's chief advisers was Horsey's servant William Hopton, described by Johnson as 'A great dealler with pyrattes'. Finally, through Johnson's astuteness and through the intercession of another of Horsey's men, the prisoner was released under oath not to name names – though he seems to have done this with abandon in his letter to Lord Burghley.

'The Captaynes and theyre Companies', he continued, 'dowthe deally go on shore at the Wyght, and if Any man come on shore neer whear they are they by and by have warninge. If it pleayes Sir Edward Horsey, he may esely Cawse them to be stayed, for if the lifftenant at Any tym dowthe send for him Ashore he dowthe come strayght or if Any of his men dowthe send for eather bord or preese or Any of theayr companie they straight come withowt Any feare and if Any stranger Come then they haveword by and by. The comon Mareneres douthe come dely on shore they are esely to be come by, but not The principalles'.

Another of Horsey's associates was 'the pirate Vaughan' of the Spanish diplomatic despatches. Examined by the piracy commissioners in 1578, Vaughan pleaded that he had sailed in the *Castle of Comfort* with the knowledge of Edward Horsey. He had also accompanied Horsey on a diplomatic mission to the Netherlands in 1577, and used this alibi to plead ignorance of the alleged delivery of a load of stolen salt at his house in the Isle of Wight. Obviously Horsey was on personal terms with the local gentleman promoters, and prudently dealt through his deputies with the more ruffianly element at Mead Hole.

He was nevertheless reasonably diligent in his duties as Vice-Admiral. With a mixture of adroitness and guile he neatly took possesion of a Spanish treasure ship in Southampton water during the general seizures of Spanish bullion in December 1568; he used patience and persistence with obdurate characters like Captain Sconwall, reluctant to surrender their prizes; and in 1577 he achieved something of a coup with the arrest of John Callis and his crew. He did however provide the necessary easy climate for the dubious commercial practices that flourished under his rule.

His successor Carey had, in addition to higher social status, the pretext of the privateering war with Spain to invest with a sense of patriotism activities that were also personally profitable. He too could and did ensure that some piratical practices in the Island were not open to the full blast of legal sanctions; but the general pattern now changes from Channel ventures by small promoters, to give way to more heavily capitalised voyages by Carey and his Island associates into the Caribbean. Only when it came to arguing over the spoils brought back to the Island did he prove as unresponsive as Horsey had been to the claims of aggrieved merchants. Damaskette and the merchants of St Jean de Luz had a good legal case against Carey; but their captured ship, renamed *Commander*, remained in the Isle of Wight, flaunting Carey's colours and carrying one of the Newport town drums. Like Horsey before him, Carey was familiar enough with pirates.

With the end of Elizabeth's reign the age of piracy had passed as far as the Island was concerned. Peace with Spain tended to damp down such activity, and with the death in 1603 of George Carey (by then, 2nd Lord Hunsdon) the privateering voyages from the Island lost their main source of capital. The new Captain, the Earl of Southampton, after a brief experiment of residence at Carisbrooke Castle, soon lapsed into only occasional visits to the Island. Piracy round the Island continued, of course. Occasional prize cargoes came in to Cowes, such as a load of sugar and tobacco brought in by Captain Scras in 1629; and Sir John Oglander had a boat-load of butter and cheese taken by pirates in 1635; but the elaborate shore-based organisation had gone with the last of the buccaneering Governors, and there were also now more warships in home waters. Monsieur de Segur's wish, expressed in 1584, had been fulfilled. Some of the royal ships were at last clearing these brigands from the coast.

SEVEN

An Oligarchy of Gentlemen

Sir Richard Worsley, Governor of the Isle of Wight, 1780-1782 who wrote the important History of the Isle of Wight, *published in 1781.*

Wootton Bridge Tide Mill in about 1900. Large tide mills such as this were built at the end of the 18th century to cater for increased quantities of corn. The two built on the river Medina in 1793 and 1796 and the mill at St Helens built c1780 have disappeared, as has Wootton Mill – demolished in 1962. The causeway carrying the road at Wootton acted as the mill dam and two undershot wheels drove the machinery.

Any description of the Island in the eighteenth century must begin with Richard Worsley's *History of the Isle of Wight*, published in 1781. Worsley was able, through his paramount position in local society, to draw all the information he needed from men who were intimately involved in the local administration. When he states that the population was 18,024 he established this figure through returns made to him by the local clergy-men who, with their parish officers were best able to count the people in their parishes. When he described the imports and exports through Cowes harbour this information came directly from William Arnold, the Custom Collector, in reply to a request made in February 1781. It is not surprising that later writers of local history incorporated whole sections of his work into their publications. His was probably the last time a single writer could attempt such a survey of the past history and the contemporary social life of the Isle of Wight. The 'not over populous' countryside, the close knit society from which he could extract the raw information and his own leisure which he used so profitably made this valuable work possible.

For the Island generally there was little apart from agriculture to provide work. Most of the stands of timber had gone to Portsmouth and neighbouring shipyards, leaving only sufficient for local needs. The stone quarries at Quarr were still working and in the west there was alum at Alum Bay, fine white sand in the nearby cliffs and fullers earth near Freshwater. Great quantities of these fine sands were exported to London, Bristol and Worcester for glass and porcelain production, but as soon as the autumn gales set in the work ended and the labourers added to the problem of winter unemployment. Copperas stone was found in abundance on the coast and this was freighted to London. A modest production of salt provided work and a surplus for export and in the early part of the century there was work at Cowes cleaning the rice brought in from the Carolinas, but this ended when the Thirteen Colonies declared their independence.

The production of grain remained the major occupation. In the two years prior to 1781 this had increased amazingly, according to Arnold, to supply the armies in America and the West Indies. In 1780 32,499 quarters of flour were exported as well as wheat, barley and malt. Much of the flour processing took place in or near Newport. In 1796 there were eight or nine mills within a mile of the town including large tide mills each side of the Medina. One ancillary industry, starch making was also based at Newport.

Worsley described the farmers as a substantial class mostly living in stone houses. It was at this time that many seventeenth century manor houses began to be reduced in status to farm houses as gentry families moved into fashionable new 'seats' leaving their old homes to the farmers. It was only in the twentieth century that these old houses were re-gentrified into the manor houses of our own time.

Worsley lists the homes of the more important members of local society and occasionally adds his opinion. Of Osborne, a newly built classical house, the home of Robert Pope Blachford, he approved. North Court, Shorwell, was another house he admired, indeed this large seventeenth century manor house has remained an important Island house right up to the present. Of his own house, Appuldurcombe, he notes that it is surrounded by a deer park. Others would remark on the outstandingly handsome mansion which stood in the park. It was built from local stone, some taken from the old Elizabethan house which Sir Robert Worsley had demolished, leaving 'not one stone standing.' He then employed John James of Greenwich to design a baroque mansion equal to his standing and between 1701 and 1713 the new Appuldurcombe rose. It was Richard Worsley himself who employed James Wyatt in the 1770s to adapt the original building to the Palladian style. Here Worsley displayed the art treasures he had brought back to England from his extensive travels, including his collection of classical sculptures, some of the earliest to be seen in England, collected in Greece and Asia Minor. There might have been more but for an unlucky accident in 1801 when his 'valuable collection of antique sculptures, paintings etc.' were captured at sea by a Spanish frigate and taken in to Malaga where they were condemned and the best pieces bought for the National Museum in Paris.

Worsley's home was one of the grand eighteenth century houses which opened its doors to the discriminating traveller rather in the manner of the National Trust, even to allowing visitors in through the back door. After passing the servants' hall one came into Wyatt's new entrance hall with its eight scagliola pillars. The dining room was filled with fine paintings, the drawing room with elegant furniture. There was a large library and an interior library and finally the organ room. This completed the tour of the public rooms and the admiring visitor left to return through the landscaped park to Godshill.

At Nunwell in Brading the Oglanders refrained from pulling down the house Sir John Oglander and his wife had lived in but this was extensively modernized in the eighteenth century. In 1765 the garden front had an additional room added and a bowed centre made – although Sir John's little book room remained at the corner of the house. Other families were bringing their homes up to modern standards but some preferred a style which was quite opposite to the plain and classical.

North Court, Shorwell, in 1824 when the north front had been improved with Georgian sash windows and a classical doorway. This large manor house, built by Sir John Leigh, is dated 1615.

Appuldurcombe House, the home of Sir Richard Worsley as it looked in 1780, isolated in its landscape park from the village of Godshill.

The east front of Nunwell House, Brading, was re-built in 1765 to produce this attractive frontage. Behind it much of the old house built by Sir John Oglander still remains.

Westover, Calbourne, a Regency house which remains today much as this view drawn in 1822. It was the home of Sir L. T. Worsley Holmes, a magistrate and chairman of the Guardians of the Poor for many years.

Among the gentlemen listed by Worsley was William Tollemache who lived at Steephill Cottage, St. Lawrence, where the 'picturesque' triumphantly prevailed. A thatched roof and white walls were all it had in common with the villager's home. Internally it shared with Appuldurcombe a hall, dining room and a drawing room with a fashionable bow window. A contemporary writer commented, 'It is indeed covered with thatch, but that makes it … no cottage. Who would expect to find a fountain bubbling up under the windows … into an elegant carved shell to cool wine?' These cottage ornées were much admired and thought specially suitable to romantic coastal landscape.

The gentry families who occupied these country houses lived, with very few exceptions, throughout the year on their estates. The Worsley family in its various branches, with the Holmes family of Yarmouth were the main influence on Island life. They were related through a complex web of marriages and, which was more important, by further marriages they drew into their orbit many other local families; John Glynn a nephew of William Oglander of Nunwell, Alexander Campbell at Gatcombe Park, Thomas Dickenson a Newport merchant living at Bagwich, Godshill, John Delgarno of Woolverton Shorwell and Henry Roberts, the banker who lived at Standen near Newport. The ramifications of the Worsley Holmes families were important because they bound together the men who were J.P.s and active members of the Guardians of the Poor, those who administered the Island well into the nineteenth century.

The grand houses and sober farmsteads stood in an empty countryside. About fifteen thousand of the population were scattered in tiny villages isolated from each other and from Newport by roads that were in Worsley's time no more than dirt tracks through the fields. In the ten miles between Newport and Yarmouth there were fifty two gates, and carriages usually had a small boy seated at the back to open and close the gates as they travelled about the Island. In 1813 the local Highway Act brought some improvement but Loudon MacAdam thought little of the standard when he inspected the roads in 1822. The road work was undertaken by paupers who were paid by the day and had little supervision. MacAdam wanted them to be employed by piecework at reasonable rates but Highway Commissioners refused, anticipating an increase in the poor rate if this was done. And so the unemployed day labourers went on breaking stones and wheeling them in barrows to fill up the

A gateboy in about 1794. The Island roads were plagued by gates; there were 52 between Newport and Yarmouth.

The New Inn at Brighstone comfortably accommodated coaching visitors early in Queen Victoria's reign.

The entrance to Calbourne village from the Newport-Freshwater road showing the unsealed road surface in the early 20th century – dry and dusty in summer, muddy and treacherous in winter.

innumerable potholes. In 1834 a few improvements were made. The main road into Brading from the south was widened as was the steep hill at Shorwell and the routes over the downs to Niton and Bonchurch were improved, but in general the Island roads remained in a poor state throughout the nineteenth century.

Because of bad communications the southern part of the Island was so isolated that the inhabitants were regarded as a distinct race 'who seldom make their appearance at the capital'. The men of these coastal fishing villages were probably more familiar with the streets of St. Helier and St Peter Port than those of Newport as they made their regular smuggling trips to the Channel Islands. Freshwater Gate had one small cottage kept by a publican, 'a comfortable little inn, with decent accommodation, good port wine, and, uncommon in the Isle of Wight, a rational bill', a visitor wrote in 1794. In the east of the Island life was busier at St Helens where the haven was still important. Outward bound ships took on chickens and other stock, butter and especially spring water which had a reputation for remaining sweet throughout long voyages.

The cottagers in the villages made up the greater part of the population. It is difficult to re-create their lives, for their preoccupations, daily work and family budgets were almost never recorded by their own kind. The life of the rural labourer must be constructed from a variety of sources, all of which look at him from the outside. Worsley from his eminence saw that their cottages appeared neat and comfortable, each with its garden. And later visitors confirm this, comparing the Island cottages favourably with those on the mainland. There was usually about an acre of land attached, sufficient to grow potatoes and keep a pig. The cottages were well built in stone and brick although in the northern parishes cob and thatch hovels were common. The harvest month wage paid the rent, usually two to three guineas (£2.10-£3.15) a year. Wages were at all times very low. In 1774 seven shillings (35p) a week on average for family men. During the Napoleonic wars they did rise to ten shillings (50p) but nine shillings a week (45p) was to remain the average from 1815 and for most of the nineteenth century. Moreover, work was intermittent and in the dead winter months unemployment was unavoidable. This was when unemployed labourers went to work on the roads, their

St Lawrence in the early 19th century. Prawns and crabs were caught in the spring, lobsters in summer and crab in the autumn. A French visitor to the Island in 1879 spoke of the 'marvellous large prawns. They alone are worth a trip here.'

pay coming from the poor rates.

The Old Poor Law provided the poorest with a safety net from birth to death. Under parish administration the overseers could provide help using their own discretion; in 1748 Godshill parish lent Thomas Small £2.10s (£2.50) to buy a horse; Newchurch allowed a man £6 for repairing his boat, both important to the livelihood of the men concerned. Carisbrooke kept a parish cow, possibly to provide milk for the children in the poor house. There were sufficient of them for the parish to employ Widow Andrews at two guineas (£2.10) 'for schooling poor house children' and at Newchurch they spent money on 'writing books for the poor boys.' Every parish had some cottage poor house which could shelter the homeless and destitute but one or two went farther and built a workhouse with a master and mistress employed to manage it. Northwood was first to open its workhouse in 1727 on a five acre site near the church. Ten years later Godshill followed their example, spending £200 on buying land and building a brick house. But these, with the poor houses were swept away when the House of Industry opened in 1774 and all outdoor relief was determined from Newport.

From this time the Guardians of the Poor at their weekly and quarterly meetings settled all poor relief payments. The idiosyncratic relief of the overseers vanished but the assistance for basic relief remained. A birth

The interior of the Brighstone Inn in 1805.

allowance of 5s (25p) paid for the attendance of a midwife when necessary, child allowance was paid during exceptionally hard winters and some children from large families were taken into the House of Industry 'until the weather breaks.' Responsible women inmates were sent from the House as home nurses as were housekeepers such as Hannah Jenkins who went to look after a motherless family in 1782. Those who were incapacitated physically or mentally received a weekly pension of one or two shillings to help keep them at home, and the very aged, usually those over seventy years, were regular pensioners, guaranteed two shillings (10p) a week. And at the end a burial allowance of 12s (60p) allowed a modest funeral.

None of these very basic arrangements could withstand the general inflation at the end of the century. Wheaten bread which was now an integral part of the southern labourer's diet rose dramatically in price. In 1792 a gallon loaf, approximately 8½lb in weight cost 9d (4p) in Newport. In 1795 corn prices reached 56s (£2.80) a quarter in November and by January the following year one thousand families a week throughout the Island had to be relieved with a special child payment when bread prices reached 2s 6d (25p). In 1800 the situation was worse; a parish officer at Newchurch entered the horrifying facts in his account book; bread 3s 9d (19p), pork 16s (80p)lb, cheese 11d-1s 3d (4d-7d) lb – 'every Article in life was very dear'. Substitute foods had to be found and in December the J.P.s spent £300 buying herrings in Southampton to feed the outdoor poor.

Yet it was just this inflationary cycle which was transforming the farmers' way of life. With a new barracks opened at Parkhurst in 1798 and hundreds of troops camped about the Island any grain that could be got to market brought handsome returns and some of the money went to 'improve' the farmhouse. We can see the results today in the many farms that have late eighteenth century additions with neat sash windows and a symmetrical frontage. This gave the farmer's wife a pretty drawing room and dining room for special occasions, although the great old kitchen overlooking the farmyard remained the focus of daily life. From here the farmer, with his family, made the journey into Newport for the market.

Of the old medieval towns only Newport remained of any consequence. Newtown was a handful of cottages on the edge of mud flats, Yarmouth no more than a fishing village with unpaved streets, and Brading a long village street. Newport with its 2,778 inhabitants was the natural centre towards which trade was drawn with its markets on Wednesday and Saturday and the busy port at the head of the navigable Medina. Here corn was exported, and coal imported, a necessity for an Island that could no longer fell trees for fuel. The coal ships continued to make their journeys to Newport quay well into the twentieth century.

By the end of the century the town had a new look as sixteenth and seventeenth century shops and houses were faced with brick, given sash windows and dainty fan lights over the door. Walking in the streets was pleasanter, too. In 1786 the Newport Paving Act was passed and by the end of the century the main streets had raised pavements, although moonlight nights were still preferable if townspeople were to attend performances at the theatre in Holyrood Street. The first street lamp provided by the Improvement Commissioners was fixed to the wall of

A typical Isle of Wight cottage in the late eighteenth century. It was the home of The Dairyman's Daughter at Arreton. Elizabeth Wallbridge was immortalised by the Revd. Legh Richmond when his story of her Christian life and death was published in 1810 and became a worldwide best seller.

Brading Town Hall and main street in the early 19th century.

The 18th century Town Hall at Newtown where twelve burgesses elected two M.P.s by agreement before this 'rotten borough' was abolished by the 1832 Reform Act. One seat was filled by a member of the Worsley family throughout most of the 18th century.

Looking down High Street, Newport from St James's Square in 1821. Prominent in the square is the Literary Institute with its colonnade. This was built in 1817 in the style of the Town Hall, and is now the County Club.

St Thomas's Church, Newport in the 1840s before the present Victorian church was built. Opposite is the classical portico of the Corn Exchange where corn was sold by sample on market days.

the Vine Inn in 1801 and later six more were lit in the Castlehold area of the High Street.

On market days the town erupted with noise. Cattle and sheep were driven into the beast market in St Jame's Square where their cries, the smell and the flies in summer all contributed to a noxious atmosphere. Pedestrians had been partly protected from the hurly-burly since 1732 when the market had been railed off but no one could guarantee that a piglet would not scamper between feet and rush into a nearby shop. Down the centre of the square there was space for two teams of horses to pass and the noise they made as they passed through was considerable.

Up to two hundred waggons 'loaded with different grain' made their way to the corn market in the present St Thomas's Square in Worsley's day, but by the end of the century this was much reduced as farmers were selling by sample, a practical convenience to them but a loss to the poor who could no longer buy small amounts of unsold wheat cheaply. On the north side of St Thomas's church the tradition of the Shambles lingered on in a row of butchers' shops and at the north-east corner of the market, near the High Street was the cheese market where farmers' wives and daughters sold their dairy products. Several contemporary visitors commented on their style and good looks. They came in on horseback and when they arrived 'they have a room where they new dress' before they made their public appearance.

The pretty faces and clear complexions of these women may have resulted from their work in the dairy where attacks of cowpox protected farm workers from the dangerous and disfiguring disease of smallpox. Between 1778 and 1784 there was no year when smallpox was not present in the Island. Outbreaks began in the towns and villages nearest to the mainland and Newport was doubly vulnerable as a port and garrison town. As soon as it was obvious that an outbreak was spreading the surgeons employed by the Guardians of the Poor began inoculating. Twice within ten years nearly four hundred paupers were inoculated in Newport at a cost of £50 each time. Carisbrooke paupers were also inoculated at the rate of 2s 6d (12p) a person, a charge that remained

A carter outside Church Hill Cottages, Godshill, in about 1890.

constant throughout the century. 1787 was a particularly bad year when the disease spread from Newport to villages as distant as Chale and Niton, and in 1794 it spread again from Newport to Whitwell and Freshwater.

Inoculation itself was hazardous as it involved introducing a live disease into a healthy body; too weak and it was ineffective, too strong and it could intensify an outbreak. The Guardians of the Poor attempted to keep inoculation within the Island and refused relief to anyone treated by an inoculator from the mainland. It gave their own surgeons a monopoly but it also limited the dangers presented by 'quack' inoculators. Those who could left the neighbourhood when inoculation began. In the winter of 1790 when smallpox was present in Yarmouth William Devenish left his home in Thorley and took lodgings in Newport for three months until all danger to his health had passed.

In 1789 William Jenner's successful experiments with cowpox offered a safer protection against smallpox and three years later the Guardians offered it as an alternative to inoculation for children. But the poor were conservative in their habits and still preferred inoculation. It was only in the second half of the nineteenth century that vaccination became general. Vaccination stations were set up throughout the Island, sometimes in the village school as at Calbourne in 1880 or in the front room of a house. Mrs. Wheeler of Percy Cottage, Ventnor rented out a room for two pounds to the Medical Officer in the same year. It was a far cry from the fear that had sent Henry Devenish fleeing to Newport.

EIGHT

The Isle of Wight House of Industry
1771-1836

We must not pass unnoticed by,
The Spacious House of Industry:
...Here feeble poverty has found,
A Sanctuary to guard her round ...
Here the young race of casual birth,
Who would be outcasts on the earth,
Bred to no learning, taught to shun
No vice, but swift to ruin run,
Meet blessed Instructions' cheering ray
Their God to serve and Man obey ...
(A Rumble from Newport to Cowes)

The House of Industry stands today, a monument to the administrative drive of the late eighteenth century island gentlemen. Now it is one of many buildings in the complex that forms St Mary's Hospital at Parkhurst. When it was built it stood gaunt and alone on the extreme east of Parkhurst Forest, the largest public building in the island, a place that was eventually to influence the daily lives of most working families.

Sir William Oglander of Nunwell, Brading, and the ten gentlemen who published their intention to create an incorporation for the poor of the Isle of Wight in the *Salisbury Journal* on the 8 October 1770 were about to turn local government on its head. They proposed to end the traditional obligation of parishes to support their own poor by raising a parish poor rate and substitute instead a centralised poor law system radiating outwards from a single workhouse at Newport. In planning this major reform the gentlemen looked at East Anglia where consolidation of parishes and the establishment of centralised workhouses had been successful in reducing poor rates. They chose for their model the private Act of Parliament that established the Samford incorporation in East Suffolk, whose House of Industry was opened in 1766.

Very little time passed before a similar Isle of Wight private bill was presented to parliament. The second reading came in March 1771 but within a month opposition was expressed by over a third of the island parishes, who rallied to defend their local autonomy and demanded exclusion from the bill on the grounds that they employed 'great numbers of Poor Persons in the cultivation of ... the farms, and are well satisfied with the present mode of laying on and collecting the Poor Rate and maintaining and employing the Poor ...'. And so they might be, for a pool of low paid workers controlled by the individual parishes was a valuable asset.

The buildings that remain from the House of Industry. These now form part of the lower hospital at St Mary's, Newport.

The gentlemen, however, were determined to remove management of the poor from the parish vestries and on the 8 May 1771 the act which created the Isle of Wight Incorporation for the Poor came into being. The governing body of Guardians was assembled from twenty-four Directors and thirty-six acting-Guardians, that is, the gentry and the farmers with a very few tradesmen. The distinction was established by a high rating qualification for the Directors who served on a rotating principle while the acting-Guardians came as annual parish nominees from whom the Directors chose the required number. This gave the gentry and clergy firm long term control of this incorporation. It was a position they did not relinquish and one outstanding aspect of the Isle of Wight incorporation, unlike others of the eighteenth century, was the consistent and active participation of the local gentlemen in the management of the poor inside and outside the House of Industry.

Parish poor rates had now to be channelled to the Guardians. Each parish assessed the poor rates paid over the past seven years and from this the payment to the central fund was determined. This proved to have inbuilt defects which increased as time passed. Parish clerks were not skilled treasurers; some mistakenly assessed all the rates and made too high an initial return; other parishes, such as Newchurch, which included Ryde, grew so rapidly that their initial assessment had no relevance to their later rateable value. It was an imbalance that was not resolved until late in the nineteenth century when national legislation ended such inequalities.

The core of the 1771 incorporation was to be the central workhouse that took over parish responsibility for the indoor poor. It was to care for the aged and infirm, to give employment to the able-bodied, to correct the profligate and idle and to educate children in religion and industry. The site chosen, eighty acres of crown land, was leased for 999 years at a nominal rent of £8.17.9 (£8.89)p.a. This meant that expenditure could be directed entirely to building and furnishing the House. The Guardians could borrow up to £12,000 on the security of the poor rates, but this proved too little and in 1776 a further Act was passed giving the incorporation powers to borrow a further £8,000 to pay outstanding debts and complete the building. The final cost was between £18,000 and £20,000 the most expensive rural workhouse in the kingdom and also the largest as it was built to accommodate six hundred paupers.

The imposing main entrance to the House of Industry at Parkhurst. The classical frontage with its triangular pediment copied the style of gentlemen's houses being built at the time – old Osborne House has a very similar facade.

On the 9 August 1774 while the House was still incomplete the first inmates arrived, drawn from the old parish workhouses and poor houses throughout the island. The mental and physical shock to these first members of the 'family' must have been sharp. Used to small dark cottages, they were confronted by white-washed walls, large windows and immensely long public rooms and dormitories. Today virtually the whole of these original buildings remain, only the southern workshop wing and the farm buildings have disappeared. The principal block ran east-west for a length of 300ft. Extending northwards about mid-way was the chapel and southwards was the cross range, 170ft long. At the eastern end, also running southward were the dairies, wash house, brewhouse and wood house, all under one roof.

A huge 118ft long dining room was the main feature of the principal block, which also included the governor's and matron's rooms, the nurseries and sick wards. The ground floor of the cross range included the schoolrooms, the apothecary's shop, the kitchen, scullery and bakehouse. Upstairs were the lying-in wards and more sick wards. There were also twenty separate rooms for married couples and two sitting rooms for the old and infirm who could not get downstairs. In the manufacturing wing most space was occupied by two long spinning rooms, with weaving rooms above them, and here, too, were the shoemakers' and tailors' shops. All these were needed to supply material for the house and clothes for the inmates, but the manufactory also produced sacks for grain and flour. These had never before been made in the island and they were a commercial successful enterprise bringing in about £200 a year.

At the head of the household was the governor. He was paid £50 p.a. in 1789, a not untypical salary, and this remained unaltered until 1834 when it was raised to £75, but this reflected increased work as the effects of the New Poor Law were felt. The governor of the Island workhouse had considerably more security than men in many other incorporations. His salary was guaranteed, irrespective of the profits of pauper labour and, in the eighteenth century, there was little pressure on any of the men who held this office. They were correctly described in 1834 as being drawn from 'broken down tradesman and farmers'.

The matron received only £30p.a. from 1778 to 1836 although she carried the heavy burden of the day to day management of the House. She supervised the washing and cleaning, saw to the inmates' clothing and was in charge of the sick wards and lying-in wards. Mrs. Jane Adams, who was appointed in 1779, was both capable and intelligent. In 1783 the Guardians took her advice and brought into the House a new water pipe from a near-by reservoir. This meant that clothes washing no longer depended on hard spring water and expenditure on soap was reduced. She was also a competent nurse and when she resigned in 1794 all her accounts were in good order. In general the matrons were more satisfactory than the governors and they served for longer periods. Hannah Burge who bridged the change from the Old Poor Law to the New remained in office from 1826-1848 and retired with £10 superannuation and the thanks of the Guardians' committee.

Because of the large number of children in the workhouse a schoolmaster and schoolmistress were employed from the outset to teach reading. At first their status was lowly but it rose in the early nineteenth century

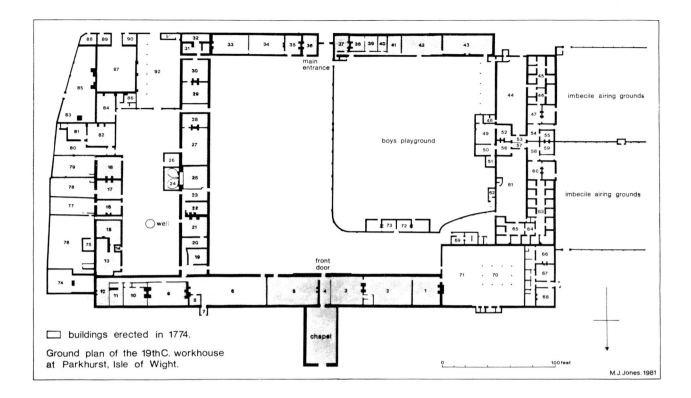

buildings erected in 1774.

Ground plan of the 19thC. workhouse
at Parkhurst, Isle of Wight.

M.J.Jones. 1981

when a major advance in teaching methods was adopted. In 1810 the Guardians began a correspondence with Joseph Lancaster and were so encouraged that they adapted the boys' and girls' schools in the House of Industry to suit his Lancasterian system. This began in January 1810, the first use of monitorial teaching in the island. It was at this time that Elizabeth St John of Brighstone became school-mistress. She was twenty-seven-years-old and she remained in charge of the girls' school for the following fifty three years, dying in office, although now with assistants, in January 1864.

The schoolmaster had assistance from the time the Lancasterian system was established. One interesting appointment was James Tucker from Godshill who entered the House as a pauper child in 1804 to receive special education as a withered hand made him unfit for general work. He was sent to school in Newport to learn writing and arithmetic and this led to Tucker being employed as an assistant teacher in 1824 with a gratuity of £1.00. Two years later this was raised to £6.00p.a. and in 1828 he was recognized as a schoolmaster. In 1832 when more professional standards were required Tucker became the governor's secretary.

The Guardians attempted to keep up standards in the schools. Before Tucker was appointed in 1824 he was sent to the National School in Newport for training. Two years later he and George Riall, the schoolmaster, went to Portsmouth Central School to learn improved methods and Miss St John went to Winchester Central School for a week. From 1835 only schoolmasters trained in Central Schools were appointed. This could not guarantee good results, however, and the boys' school was not

1 Able-bodies Men's Day Room. 2 Cripple Ward Dormitory. 3 Cripple Ward. 4 Hall. 5 Old Men's Day Room. 6 Dining Hall. 7 Porch. 8 Porter. 9 Board Room. 10 Master's Office. 11 Clerk's Office. 12 Bread Room. 13 Laundry. 14 Pump. 15 Wash house. 16 East Ward 2. 17 East Ward 3. 18 East Ward 1, A.B. 19 Store. 20 Master's Pantry. 21 Master's Sitting Room. 22 Master's Kitchen. 23 Serve-out Passage. 24 Ovens. 25 Bakehouse. 26 Store. 27 Nursery Bedroom. 28 Nursery. 29 Old Women's Day Room. 30 Old Women's Dormitory 31 Wash-house and bath. 32 Girls Laundry and Scullery. 33 Girls Day Room. 34 Girls School Room. 35 Class Room. 36 Cottage. 37 Clerk's Sitting Room. 38 Sitting Room. 39 Band Room. 40 Kitchen. 41 Lavatories & Bath Room. 42 Boys Dining Room. 43 Boys School Room. 44 Males Back Yard. 45 Males Receiving Ward. 46 Males Imbecile Ward. 47 Day Rooms. 48 Disinfecting Room. 49 Open Ward. 50 Wash House. 51 Drying Room. 52 Males Kitchen. 53 Males Lobby. 54 Staircase. 55 Male Attendant's Room. 56 Females Kitchen. 57 Females Lobby. 58 Staircase. 59 Female Attendant's Room. 60 Day Rooms. 61 Females Back Yard. 62 W.C.s. 63 Female Imbecile Wards. 64 Bath Room. 65 Female Receiving Ward. 66 Kitchen. 67 Dining Room. 69 Urinal & W.C. 70 Open Shed. 71 A.B. Men's Yard. 72 Shoemaker's Shop. 73 Tailor's Shop. 74 General Store. 75 Store. 76, 77, 78, 79, 80 Open Yards. 81 Boiler House & Scullery. 82 Kitchen. 83, 84 Open Yards. 85 Coke Yard. 86 Infants Wash House & Store. 87 Coal Yard. 88 Smith's Shop. 89 Weighing Shed. 90 Bricklayers Room. 91 W.C.s. 92 Girls Playground.

93

satisfactory. Miss St John did manage the girls' school well but she probably had less problems of discipline than did the schoolmasters who often had disruptive pupils to manage.

In 1813 as part of an extensive reform of the House the Guardians introduced 'proper hours of play and recreation' for the children, 'which at present does not seem to be the case'. It was at this time that part-time schooling began; half the day was spent in school and half in the manufactory. But the Guardians emphasized that work was not to impair 'the other and not less important part of their education'. The large manufactory had space for one hundred and fifty workers and could well occupy the children on a shift system. The boys were set to weaving while the girls earned a small profit from spinning worsted thread. In the early nineteenth century the manufactory was mainly employed making material for the inmates clothes, but as cheap cloth rolled onto the market this became uneconomic. The manufactory closed in 1832 and the south wing was converted into a new boys' school. In this way the long association of children with that part of the House was continued.

Living in the House of Industry was rather like being in a boarding school where the day was punctuated by the clanging of bells. Each new arrival had a thorough wash and new clothing if this was necessary, although under the Old Poor Law they could keep their own clothes if these were decent. There was no official uniform although there must have been a standard type of clothing. Certain of the 'family' were distinguished by their clothes; the nurses who looked after the infants wore different gowns from the other women and in the 1830s the school monitors wore superior clothing. In the eighteenth century the most distinctive dress was the bright yellow gowns worn by the women who were in the House for persistent bastardy, an unruly and unsavoury element. The prostitutes were given hard scrubbing and washing to do and in the eighteenth century some received severe punishments. In 1791 two were publicly whipped and in 1795 another was sentenced to two weeks solitary confinement and had 'her curls cut off'. Young prostitutes remained a problem and the Guardians were only too pleased to send some to Australia in the 1830s. Of these, a few proved a match for the emigration agents. Of seven destined for Van Diemen's Land in 1834, one disappeared in London wearing her new clothes and four were returned to the workhouse because of their bad behaviour!

In 1834 the *Hampshire Chronicle* reported the death of Nancy Orchard, a pauper in the House of Industry. It was a newsworthy item because Mrs Orchard had lived 101 years and had been one of the first paupers to enter the House in 1774. She had remained there for the rest of her life. But Ann Orchard's life was not restricted to the House of Industry. She was in her forties when she arrived and she proved to be capable of general nursing and attendance at births. She soon became one of the regular home nurses, and, what we would know today as 'home helps', who were sent to poor families when illness, births or deaths put extra strain on the family. The Guardians undertook this out-relief from at least 1779 and it was still part of their work in 1835, the year before the New Poor Law was introduced into the island. Ann was mentioned by name several times in the 1780s; in 1784 and 1785 she attended women lying-in, whilst four years later she was allowed 2s 6d

(25p) maintenance for nursing a pensioner.

Over the sixty years she made the House her home Ann Orchard would have experienced a long period of continuity. The rising bell rang at 6am in summer when the House doors were unlocked, and at 7am in winter. After prayers came breakfast at 8 o'clock, dinner at noon and supper to fit in with the end of work. A roll call of all inmates was made before the doors were locked at 8pm in summer and 6pm in winter. Before everyone retired there was another call-over of women, at 9 o'clock in summer and an hour earlier in winter.

During the day the work of the House went on. The girls were taught cookery, washing and scouring by the matron and the older women. There were instructions for opening the sash windows each day for a good through draught; rooms were to be swept regularly and washed when convenient. Clean linen was distributed each Saturday evening and clean sheets each month. This was a counsel of perfection and experience must have been rather different, particularly at the times when up to eight hundred paupers were living in the workhouse. In one respect, however, the inmates were better off than most workhouse paupers. From 1813 the Guardians began buying in iron bedsteads so that the Poor Law Commissioner was able to report in 1832 that each pauper had a single, unshared bed.

A large part of the daily work was spent in preparing meals. Baking and brewing were done with the help of the inmates as was all the cooking, and there was an amazing constancy about the food. Ann Orchard would have eaten bread with cheese or butter, or potatoes, for

The weekly diet of the workhouse inmates in 1837.

Mens diet Scale.

Breakfast	Dinner	Supper
Onion Soup 1 pint ½ lb. Bread	**Monday** Pease Soup 1 pint.	½lb Bread. 2oz Chee.
D°. — —	**Tuesday.** Salt Pork 4oz. 1lb Potatoes.	1lb Potatoes with Salt.
D° — —	**Wednesday.** Pease Soup 1 pint.	½lb Bread. 2oz Cheese
D°. — —	**Thursday.** Salt Pork 4oz. 1lb Potatoes.	1lb Potatoes with Salt
D° — —	**Friday.** Pease Soup 1 pint.	½lb Bread. 2oz Cheese
D° — —	**Saturday.** Rice 4oz 1oz Treacle.	1lb Potatoes with Salt
D° — —	**Sunday.** Salt Pork 4 oz. 1lb Potatoes.	Onion Soup 4oz Bread.
Note—	Women, Bread less 2oz Nurseries at discretion Beer 1 pint.	School Children as heretofore

95

supper every day. Baked potatoes were a very cheap meal, 10 bushels could be cooked for 3s (15p). From 1796 to the day she died there was always onion soup for breakfast. One day each week the main meal was rice pudding with treacle added, always on a Saturday from 1804. Meat appeared only at dinner. In 1813 9oz of meat was allowed for each person on Sundays, 4oz pork on Tuesday, Thursday and Friday. On Monday came broth with baked potatoes and on Wednesday bread and butter pudding or suet pudding. This was much more food than poor labourers were eating in their cottages but the effect of inefficient communal cooking had to be taken into account.

This was shown at its worst just before 1813 when conditions in the House reached a scandalous state, when food was prepared in filthy conditions, when many inmates had no eating utensils and others little food because it was unfairly distributed. The governor, John Pierce, who had allowed a state of near anarchy to develop was dismissed and the Guardians set about reforming the House. This they did by dividing the inmates into seven categories each headed by a responsible inmate. Ann Orchard would have been in the over fifty class and her sub-governor received all the meat for his group's dinner. This was tied in nets and clearly labelled before it was boiled. Every inmate was responsible for a knife, wooden plate and wooden spoon and had two towels woven in the House. In this way Order was brought out of chaos and the standard set for the following twenty years.

When Ann Orchard died in 1834 she was probably buried in the House of Industry cemetery. The service would officially have been taken by the chaplain but, in fact, his deputy, a completely unofficial person, acted for him. The chaplain, George Richards, was first appointed in 1798 when he was already master at Newport Grammar School. He was still holding both posts in 1834 but his chaplaincy was by then a comfortable sinecure of £100 p.a. from which he paid his self appointed assistant. It was a situation that ended sharply in 1837 at the insistence of the Poor Law Commissioner who refused to accept such a lax and improper arrangement.

Ann Orchard's funeral coincided with the end of the Old Poor Law which had provided for her during most of her long life. During that time the island incorporation had established itself as the main organ of local government, collecting rates, distributing out-relief and acting as an embryonic welfare body. The Directors, who were the driving force, never let management pass from their hands and extended the work of the incorporation to meet changing circumstances. The coming of the New Poor Law to the island in 1836 was, therefore, no dramatic change but an evolution. The island already had its central workhouse and administration and the constitution of the incorporation continued unaltered, but the Guardians welcomed wholeheartedly the support and intervention of the Poor Law Commissioners in London. In the House of Industry there was indeed a change, the 'family' however badly it was managed at times, was gone – an institution took its place.

NINE

Smuggling – the Secret Economy

The great days of smuggling came during the eighteenth century and the early years of the nineteenth, when high duties on imported goods made the clandestine trips across the Channel worth while, while the danger of capture was relatively light for the Revenue service boats were no match for the smuggling gangs. The forerunners of this flourishing trade in the Isle of Wight, however, can be found in the sixteenth century when privateering, or pirate, ships preyed on Spanish, Portugese and French merchant ships as they returned to home ports laden with valuable cargoes. By 1570 Mead Hole, between East Cowes and Wootton Bridge, had established itself as a secure haven for stolen goods. These could be bought by the knowledgeable in surroundings that were more like a fair than a secret hiding hole. It gradually evolved into a receiving depot for smuggled goods and remained, well into the nineteenth century, a notorious hide-out for smugglers.

Smuggling that was undertaken from the Island itself did not compare with the large scale ventures promoted by mainland entrepreneurs, but this modest trading was suddenly expanded in the early eighteenth century when a bold adventurer set up in Ryde. David Boyes of Alverstoke had family connections in the Island but his considerable fortune, estimated to be about £40,000 had been made from large scale smuggling before he came to Ryde. With this he bought an estate at Appley and Appley House at the eastern end of Ryde shore. Today the old house is incorporated into the Benedictine Convent of St Cecilia, but beneath the ground floor there still remain the fine vaulted cellars in which Boyes stored his wines. He and his partner John Hatch dealt chiefly in French and other foreign wines, keeping twenty boatmen and labourers on call to help when cargoes were run. Not all the boats escaped capture but Boyes himself never doubted that any jury would find him other than not guilty. His own men were trained to be word perfect in giving false evidence when they testified in the London courts. Jurymen were also corrupted and the flagrant misuse of justice in repeated cases brought against these two smugglers contributed to the Ballotting Act of 1730 under which twelve jurymen were picked indiscriminately from a large number of names concealed in a ballot box. With the aid of this Act Boyes was convicted and imprisoned in the Fleet prison where he is said to have died about 1740.

It was not often that gentlemen were found among active smugglers but in 1744 the excise officer at Brading faced just such a situation. Thomas Fisher, with John Cross and eight soldiers were on duty at Shanklin on the 9 August. About midnight they saw a boat come ashore and watched while the boat party landed a five gallon cask of brandy. This was immediately seized by the excise men but Thomas Fisher was himself seized by one of the smugglers who abused him as a rascal and a rogue and threatened him with dismissal from the service. This high-handed attitude taken by Mr J. Popham of Shanklin was based on his standing as Justice of the Peace! But both Fisher and John Cross stood firm. They returned to the boat but, 'as soon as we got there a great number of Persons came upon the Cliff and assaulted us with great Stone's.' It was only when the soldiers opened fire that the gang withdrew and the excise men were able to remove the boat and its contraband goods.

When Boyes was enjoying his new house at Ryde and Popham was smuggling at Shanklin, a few miles away at East Cowes the officers at the Custom House were doing their best with inadequate resources to contain smuggling around the Island waters. This headquarters of the Custom service had been established in 1575, before the little town of West Cowes evolved. By the mid-eighteenth century, however, the shore on that side of the harbour was already well built on and it was here on the sea front that the Custom's Watch House stood, well sited to observe shipping in Cowes roads.

The separation of these two buildings made for inconvenience and in 1766 raised the nice point as to why two ensigns, with their significant portcullis were needed for the Cowes station. The Collector of Custom had to explain to the Commissioners in London that they were used not only for festivities, but that each House needed to raise an ensign when the Tide Surveyor and boatmen were called out on either side of the harbour. It was only in 1839 when the Custom House was finally moved to West Cowes that this historical anomaly was finally resolved.

The harbour at Cowes had changed little in the first half of the eighteenth century but by 1757 a new quay had been built, together with two large warehouses, whose total value was £1,151. Trade increased in the 1760s with many transient ships passing through. The additional traffic put considerable pressure on the Custom Station and in June 1765 a report was made on the shortage of men at Cowes. There were then eight rice ships in from South Carolina and Georgia and only nine established boatmen and tidesmen with five extra men, that is, boatmen and tidesmen who were called on when needed, to cover all the work. It was not surprising that the Collector of Custom complained that he frequently had no officers to guard shipping.

The Collector was the chief officer and the second senior officer, in a separate capacity, was the Deputy Controller, responsible for accounts. Below these principals there were in 1758 twenty five other officers including searchers and waiters, land waiters, a tide surveyor, tidesmen and boatmen and four riding officers. Of these the riding officers and boatmen had much the hardest and most dangerous work. James Blake, the riding officer at Yarmouth, surveyed all the coast from Newtown to the Needles, a solitary and isolated figure who received £10 a year in 1769.

The established boatmen were paid £30 a year but their work was exceedingly hard and dangerous. Those least paid were the extra boatmen and tidesmen who got two shillings (20p) each day they were on duty. All men in the service could count on rewards, however, when smuggling boats were taken and their goods impounded. But there were often difficulties for the boatmen even when they had caught their prize. In August 1767 a new six-oar boat was bought for Cowes and a new 'Sitter', Francis Arthur, arrived from Dover with his six boatmen to take charge of it. Arthur was an experienced officer and he lost no time in telling the local Custom House that his men were 'very uneasy because they have no Commissions'. The 'Sitter' himself had authority to make seizures but in his absence the crew were without legal authority. What was worse, they were vulnerable to crews of the cutters working for the Board of Excise, who all had commissions, and had warned Arthur's men that they would take from them any goods they had seized, if Arthur himself was not in the boat. This was a very serious threat because the Custom boatmen would then have lost their share of the rewards that came with confiscated goods. Once two of the boatmen had received commissions the boat's authority was secured.

Coming from Kent Arthur was acquainted with the problems of smuggling gangs on land and at sea. In September he asked for and was given arms for his men; two muskets, '12 pistols 8" long in the barrel' and six cutlasses. With the advance of autumn he also pointed out the weakness of having only oared boats in service. It was 'impossible in bad weather to be at sea, which being the only time the smugglers carry on their illegal practices —'. He pleaded for a 'small deck cutter' which would put him on equal terms with the smugglers who were laying up their open boats for the winter and preparing their cutters for trading. In November he reported that he had heard that three of the smugglers' cutters had landed ten tons of tea every dark night during the winter for the past three years and he could do nothing to stop this trade. But no cutter was supplied and the service continued to work only with oared boats to guard the coasts.

Many of these worked until they were completely worn out. The four-oared boat at Yarmouth was declared useless in 1765 and was replaced with a clinker-built boat, 16 feet wide at midships, with a depth of 2 feet, at a cost of eleven guineas (£11.55). A similar boat at St Helens was ten years old in 1767 when it was finally replaced at a cost of £26.5.0 (£26.25). At South Yarmouth the seventeen year old punt, so useful for gliding up the river Yar, finally gave out in 1768 and was replaced with a new one, 9 foot 6 inches long, built by Isaac Mitchell for £3.3.6 (£3.17)

The men who rowed these boats often had long distances to cover. In March 1768 the Custom House received information that a small sloop, the *Nimble Ninepence*, had sailed to Alderney and was expected on her return to run her cargo between Culver Cliff and Sandown Bay. At three o'clock on the afternoon when the sloop was expected to return, William Mouncher and four boatmen set out from Cowes in the six-oared boat to pull round to Sandown, where they arrived at about six in the evening. As dusk was closing in they rowed on to Shanklin where they intended to remain until dark before returning to Sandown Bay. By now, however, the sea had risen dangerously and they made for the safety of St. Helens' harbour where they patrolled on land for some time. While on this duty Mouncher observed a boat come ashore and he at once challenged its crew. It turned out to be the St Helen's boat, whose Sitter, Andrews, in turn demanded to know who the strangers were! Both parties were on Customs duty but such was the isolation of each station that the officers were unknown to each other. Good relations were established over a drink and then they separated, Mouncher and his men guarding Mead Hole and Kings Quay, notorious smuggling haunts, all night, while Andrews, the senior officer, took his crew overland to Sandown where they seized sixty nine casks of brandy at exactly the place the informer had indicated. While the operation had been completely successful it was complicated by the fact that the Cowes crew, because of bad weather and the re-arrangement of duties lost their chance to make a seizure, and with it their claim to a bonus on the goods seized. The reason for the lengthy report made by Mouncher was summed up in his last sentence – 'As I gave Mr Andrews the above information of this vessel I hope you'll think us entitled to some part of the seizure'.

Captured goods were taken to the Custom House at East Cowes where they were sold off for the best price possible. Rum, gin, brandy, wine, many pounds of tea, cigars, silk handkerchiefs, silk stockings and fine lace were all offered in the eighteenth century and the proceeds were allotted to the Customs men. The hulls of the captured ships were burned; later they were broken into three parts, but whatever the means used, for small owners this would mean the end of their livelihood. In June 1763 a 15-ton sloop the *William and Mary* was burned and in August another sloop, the *Wheel of Fortune* went the same way. In 1766 the cutter *Miller's Maggot*, 15 tons, and a 34-ton sloop, the *Launceston* were destroyed. Even a good small cutter the *Tartar's Defiance*, 'a prime sailor … not 9 years old … in every respect fit to be used for the service …' was not spared but went up in flames the same year.

With inferior boats and insufficient men the Customs relied on information such as that given on the *Nimble Ninepence* and informers were valued for the inside information they brought. They were often disaffected smugglers wanting to score off their old companions. But they took considerable risks when they turned traitor. In February 1767 the Custom Office at East Cowes was very much concerned over Isaac Peru who had been imprisoned in the House of Correction at Winchester for two years. In that time the Cowes officers had supplied him with clothes, paid 3s 6d (17p) a week for his subsistence and had already written three letters to London asking for Peru's release. With his information they had seized and burned two vessels and now they wrote again, concerned for the man himself – 'he is a real object of pity' – as well as with the long term result of such treatment which would not encourage other informers.

In the same year a remarkably bold smuggler-turned-informer, Thomas Mead, completed his rehabilitation by joining the service. He was a very useful recruit who had been involved in smuggling 'along the coast from North Foreland to Landsend, there not being a creek or harbour but what I am acquainted with …'. Unfortunately for Mead his old companions were all too well acquainted with him and when he rashly went ashore at Yarmouth he was set upon and badly beated by members of the local smuggling gang. They escaped to Hurst, but not before threatening Mead that others would murder him. He was indeed intimidated and asked to be moved to a station in far off Wales, but as his evidence was needed in several cases Mead was obliged to remain in the Island. His work was, however, restricted to Cowes harbour but even here he was persecuted. Most of the smugglers against whom he informed were Cowes pilots and they lost no opportunity in letting captains and crews of incoming ships know of Mead's infamy. 'The few ships I have been boarded on the captains told me that everybody at West Cowes says I was an informer and ought to be hanged.' This accompanied his final plea to leave, made in April 1769, just over a week since two sailors had come up to his house and threatened 'by God, I will have a limb of him.' At last, at the end of the month, the Commissioners of Custom agreed that all his evidence was completed, and Mead, with his long suffering family were free to leave.

Eight years later in 1777 a new Collector of Custom was appointed to the Island. He was to remain for twenty three years and make a notable impression on the work of the Customs at Cowes. William Arnold was thirty-two when he exchanged work in the General Post Office in London and settled at Cowes. Although he was a bachelor he had elderly parents to provide for and a long standing attachment to Martha Delafield whom he later married. With this in mind he leased a substantial house in West Cowes, Birmingham Hall, overlooking the harbour with its own landing steps at the bottom of the garden. Here he brought Martha in 1779 and here they remained for sixteen years, the family gradually growing in numbers. In 1795 their last son Thomas was born, the seventh of their children, and the one who was to achieve national distinction as the headmaster who reformed Rugby School, making it a model for later nineteenth century public schools.

William Arnold, Collector of Custom at Cowes, 1778-1818.

By this time the house at Cowes was already cramped and it was a great joy to Arnold when he was able to buy his own land at East Cowes, a farm above Old Castle point. The farmhouse was demolished and in its place Slatwoods was built, looking out to the harbour and Cowes roads. The family moved across the river in 1796 to enjoy life on their little estate, but Arnold had only six years in this pleasant home. He died in March 1801 at the untimely age of fifty five.

The Collector's long period of service began and ended when the nation was at war. In 1777 the American War of Independence was already two years old and when he died Britain had been at war with France for eight years. Both these national trials gave opportunities for smuggling to flourish and Arnold was not slow to inform the Commissioners of the problems that faced him. Fast, twenty-oared boats which also carried sail were used by smugglers; no Revenue cutters could catch them, while at that time there were no cruisers at all at Cowes.

During the war smuggling ships became increasingly bold and without well-armed ships the Customs could not match them. The Commissioners had few cutters of their own but they contracted for suitable ships with private persons who were willing to risk them, hoping for good returns from seizures. In 1783 Arnold himself found a suitable cutter and, with his brother-in-law, fitted her out. She was the *Swan*, the first of many Revenue ships to carry that name. Her life was short, within a month she was wrecked off the Needles and Arnold lost all his investment. But within six months a new *Swan*, a 90-ton cutter arrived. She was armed with ten guns salvaged from the old *Swan* and, in company with another contract cutter she covered the sixty miles from Lyme Regis to Beachy Head. She also cruised from Bembridge to the Needles and occasionally around the island. The Preventive officers around the coast were in touch with her commanding officer so that there was much more unity in operation than there had been in earlier years. Arnold could also call on the naval cutter *Expedition* which patrolled Hurst roads and a formidable sloop-of-war, the 300-ton *Orestes*, with its eighteen guns.

This considerable fighting strength might seem excessive to combat

Smuggling equipment. These were the essential tools for retrieving tubs that had been put overboard to escape the coastguard. The wooden 'peep' tub with a glass base allowed the smugglers to see where the tubs lay, whilst the grapnel was dragged along the sea bed to catch the ropes linking the tubs. The scissors-like 'tonges' were attached to a long handle and were used to raise the tubs.

The Ariel *of Bembridge, showing the false bottom by smugglers for concealing tubs.*

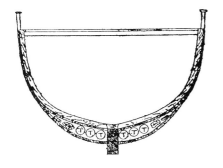

smugglers but their ships were by now heavily armed. One of the first triumphs of *Orestes* was the seizure of a 200-ton cutter armed with twenty 6-pounder guns laden with 2000 gallons of spirit and nine tons of tea. In June 1784 the *Orestes* had a serious engagement with a twenty gun smuggling cutter that was guarding a smuggling boat the *Orestes'* men had boarded. The cutter's guns killed one officer and seriously injured two others.

By 1786 the presence of armed Revenue and Naval vessels made the smugglers much more cautious but expediency produced new methods to outwit the coastguard. The smuggling ships took to carrying large stones as 'ballast' and long hawsers were coiled up on deck. Small casks were sunk in slings attached to ropes and weighted by the stones, to be raised at a time safe to the smugglers. This was the introduction of a method that was to be refined and improved until it became general in the period following the Napoleonic wars.

In 1793 France declared war on England and Holland, and Cowes became increasingly busy as a port of call for vessels going up and down the Channel. All these, together with their cargoes and passengers had to be checked, adding to the work of the Customs, who were still keeping watch on the armed smuggling craft. Their vigilance was rewarded and in 1795 Arnold could report that smuggling had not increased since the outbreak of war. Other factors also helped; many smugglers were serving at sea and some ships were in government service as tenders, while others were laid up because of difficulties in finding crews.

There were also problems peculiar to smugglers in the Isle of Wight. In contrast to mainland smugglers the Islanders were men with little property and they found it difficult to get credit. The main trade from the Island was with Guernsey and Alderney, while south coast smugglers dealt directly with France and the east coast men with Holland. When the French army occupied Holland both these traditional sources were lost and these experienced traders moved into the Channel Islands. Increased demand meant increased prices for spirits and men from the Isle of Wight did not have the financial resources to compete. They were forced to buy inferior spirits or to water down and adulterate good spirit they could afford. The most telling evidence for the limitation on Island smuggling was that given by the riding officer on the back of the Wight. In 1795, within five months, only one hundred casks of spirit had been landed between Bembridge and the Needles.

This coast was reasonably well guarded by a little cutter carrying ten men, armed with a swivel gun. At this time the Commissioners were ordering many fast-cutters and Thomas Gely's Yard at East Cowes always had one on the stocks. In 1797 he received the contract to build *Swan V*, a large cutter of 140-150 tons, costing £1,230. This *Swan* was capable of covering long distances, frequently crossing to the French coast, exposing herself to considerable danger. Both *Swan III* and *Swan IV* had themselves been captured by French frigates and the large, well-armed *Swan V* went the same way, taken by French privateers in March 1807, when her mate and three of the crew were lost.

Nearer the Island the Revenue cutters tried to intercept the smuggling boats as they approached the coast and from these captures came the largest hauls. A brig at anchor between Yarmouth and the Needles in 1803 had 780 tubs aboard; in 1804 a tub-boat with 270 four-gallon casks was seized between Yarmouth and Cowes; in 1805 another tub-boat had 800 four-gallon casks aboard. Many of these boats were sailing directly for the mainland but at this time smugglers were also using Island waters as staging points en route for the mainland. The tubs were attached to long lines and sunk off shore, from where they were later 'creeped up' by crews coming out of Hampshire. The owners of the smuggling boats bought the undiluted spirit in lots, paying ten, twenty or thirty pounds according to the number of casks supplied. Some large hauls made by the Revenue men were these sunk casks dragged up before the smugglers got to them. In October 1804 200 casks were taken up near the Needles; in June 1805 228 casks were picked up off St Catherines. In 1818, within six months, 1200 casks were seized from points all round the Island coast.

Contraband taken on the shore was never so great, usually between fifty and a hundred tubs. During 1816 there were several hauls beginning in February when 51 casks of brandy and gin were seized at Luccombe; in March 62 casks were hidden in cliffs at Shanklin; in May 49 were seized at Compton; in June 32 were hidden near Bembridge; and in December 80 casks were seized in Orchard Bay, St Lawrence. The men who ran these goods could not be compared with the armed gangs who worked along the Sussex coast but danger was always present for the handful of officers who had to confront the smugglers.

All Saints Church, Freshwater, showing the tower which was a convenient store for smugglers in the opening years of the 19th century.

Some of the crew from the Preventive boat at Yarmouth were patrolling Totland Bay in October 1817 when they surprised a party of smugglers carrying tubs up from the beach. At first the shock of meeting the officers demoralised the smugglers and they fled, leaving the Customs men to seize some of the tubs. But the gang soon regrouped and attacked the officers, who could not have been more than five in number. They injured two of them and made off with much of the contraband. This was quickly carried off to Freshwater parish church where the tubs were hidden in the Gun Room of the belfry and the next night the smugglers set out to 'clandestinely run them in that parish'.

Churchyards proved useful hiding places. Table top tombs were particuarly well designed for hiding goods but in Niton one proved to be a more than welcome refuge. In the early 1830s three or four of the local men were surprised on the shore carrying off spirits and bags of tea. The Customs men followed them up into the village and managed to pen them into an area surrounding the church. There seemed no way of escape but quick thinking by one of the party found the answer, 'they prised up the stooan on one o' they gurt high brick tombs … and got inside, tubs and all, and bid quiet'. The officers could make nothing of the mystery and finally went away but the smugglers sat tight. Early next morning a young labourer was passing on his way to work. Suddenly he saw the top of a tomb begin to rise, a man's face appeared and out came the words, '… can ye tell me what time tes?'. The young man's hair shot up in his fright, he shrieked and fled to a neighbouring house, shouting out to the astonished family, 'the dead vokes in the churchyard be gitten out o' their graaves.' Later the whole village enjoyed the joke and probably the spirits that had been so astutely saved.

St John's Church, Niton, showing the table top tombs which were a convenient hiding place for smugglers.

Even finding unattended tubs could be hazardous. John Clark, the Ryde boatman, found 59 when he was patrolling the beach near St Helens in February 1838. He fired off a pistol to call up his colleagues and sent for a cart to transport the seizure. By 1.30am five officers were

The 19th century lighthouse at St Catherine's, first lit in 1840. Elegant as the 120ft tower was, it was still affected by sea fogs and in 1875 it was reduced to 86ft.

loading up the tubs when they noticed a gang of about thirty men creeping from the salterns, forming a half circle to surround them. They were armed with strong staves and in the fight that broke out one of the officers was hurt, but this time two of the smugglers were taken and ended up in Winchester gaol.

In the 1820s and early 1830s the Island smugglers went about their trade with little hindrance. The Poor Law Commissioner reported in 1832 that the population was 'nearly all more or less concerned with smuggling'. Charles Deane, the coastguard commander in 1836, concluded that '8 out of 10 of the whole population are consumers of contraband Spirits, tobacco and tea, and … they consider … there is no harm in it.' Deane complained that with only fifty men to deploy around the entire coast at night he could not prevent widespread smuggling. He estimated that 33,000 tubs were landed 'for home consumption' alone and the Island was full of 'pop shops' selling cheap liquor.

The 'pop shops' were usually small houses where a glass of brandy or gin could be bought and no questions asked. The owners were particularly vulnerable and came before the local magistrates regularly, charged with harbouring and concealing contraband. In March 1838 Robert Ridett of St Helens was unlucky when he served a plain clothed Excise man with a glass of brandy costing a shilling (5p). The following day his house was searched revealing a tub of foreign brandy under the stairs and more jars of brandy in small cupboards each side of the fireplace. He was fined fifty pounds and was apparently able to pay. Very different was William Newbury of West Cowes who was caught in the same month selling an Excise man two glasses of brandy for sixpence (3p). He was fined only £12.10.0 (£12.50) but was too poor to pay and went to prison for seven days.

In the countryside harbouring and concealing was on a grander scale. Tubs had to be stored while the spirit was diluted before being sent on in smaller containers. Cornelius Jones of St Helens was a well established smuggler who could afford to employ an attorney when he was brought to court in December 1829. Both his house and garden had given up casks containing brandy and gin and in the house was all the apparatus

St Catherine's Lighthouse today.

needed for preparing the spirit for distribution. The searchers found eight recently emptied casks, two measures and several bottles with colouring made from burnt sugar, as well as bladders and skins for carrying the liquor. Jones was fined a hundred pounds. At Whitwell a much smaller haul was made in William Stone's house. He had three jars of brandy and a quantity of tea concealed in the ceiling. He too, was fined a hundred pounds.

Where spirits were found in outside buildings, gardens or hedges it was more difficult to convict. Joseph Jupe of East Cowes was able to argue successfully in 1832 that a tub found in his shed was not his responsibility as his garden was open and there was a field adjoining. Other pleas, while charmingly naive, hardly held up when evidence was heard. In July 1837 James Hillier of Freshwater claimed that the brandy in his house had been brought for his mother who was very ill. Her health cannot have been improved during the ten minutes it took the search party to break through a barred door, time which Hillier used to get rid of the spirits in the house. There were six tubs in the wash-house, together with empty broken bottles still with traces of spirit about them. The magistrates, not surprisingly, fined Hillier fifty pounds and he went to gaol until it was paid.

From the kitchen or wash-house the foreign spirit was carried on the final stage of its journey to the customer. Although tubs were carried about the island – one man at Bembridge regularly walked over to Newport with two half anker kegs on his back – most contraband was reduced to small amounts that could easily be hidden and carried by men, women and children. These, too, were the cases that came most often before the magistrates. Sarah Neason went to Winchester gaol for carrying two bladders of brandy in her basket; Ann Dyer had one pint of brandy and eight skins of Geneva on her when she was arrested and her companion Elizabeth Trubbeck also had eight skins 'under her skirts.' Fish wives were particularly useful distributors as they sold their goods from house to house. The Bembridge fish woman was long suspected and was finally stopped and told that she must go to Portsmouth where a female searcher was employed. While she waited with the Excise officer on Ryde Pier

The first attempt to protect the seas around the Needles came in 1785 when a lighthouse was built on High Down but the perennial problem of mist made this ineffective. In 1859 a new lighthouse was built at the seaward end of the Needles and has continued to be manned to the present day.

the woman retired behind some sheds to relieve herself, but the person who re-appeared astonished the officer as a previously buxom figure was transformed into a gaunt woman with little shape. And the illicit brandy had disappeared into the sea! Even young children were used as carriers. John Benzie was stopped by the Ryde boatman on the pier in December 1836 and found to be carrying six skins of brandy in his basket and four of gin tied around his body, altogether about ten pints. He was eleven years old but his age did not prevent him from being sent to Winchester gaol for six months.

At this time steamers crossing to the mainland were used regularly to carry spirits off the Island. Not only by couriers wearing the goods but also in packages sent to fictitious addresses. Edmund Barnacle was arrested at Cowes in December 1832 when he was about to put a hamper addressed to the Rev Romney, London, on board the Steam Packet. His defence that he was doing this for an unknown man he had met at Osborne and was quite unaware that it contained foreign brandy carried no weight with the magistrates and he, too, ended up in gaol.

By 1836 the high days of smuggling were drawing to an end. In the previous autumn the *Hampshire Advertiser* described the Island smugglers as being in despair at the alertness of the Preventive men, and worse was to come. At the end of 1836 the guard between Bembridge and the Needles was doubled, nine additional stations were established and two wherries came on duty at sea. Smuggling did not, of course, end but it ceased to involve large numbers of the population and by the 1880s was restricted to summer months and particular areas, particularly the back of the Wight. The parish of Chale was a smuggling centre in the opening years of the nineteenth century and benefited from the hidden income that came in. Here even farm labourers owned their own houses, an unknown situation in most rural parishes. The average labourer's wage was nine shillings (45p) a week in the 1830s but 3.6d (18p) could be made in one night when tubs were safely removed from the shore and the profit from the sale of a tub was twelve shillings (60p). What this represented in hard physical effort, however, was considerable. After a day's work labourers would walk, sometimes many miles, to the shore and then back with the tubs on their backs. Unemployed labourers fared rather better until 1836 and the introduction of the New Poor Law. Most were employed on the roads, in theory repairing the surface, in practice, as the Poor Law Commissioner acidly commented, they 'sleep away their day' so that 'they will be fresh and ready for the night exertions smuggling requires'.

106

There was also the ever present anxiety that smuggling tales gloss over. Conviction meant prison, transportation or years of service in the navy while families were left to survive on out-door relief or in the workhouse. One of the young smugglers who found himself sentenced to serve in the navy was James Buckett of Brighstone. He had been a regular smuggler but when he married his wife persuaded him to give up the trade. It was his generous nature that led him to stand in for one of the crew on an arranged trip, and his misfortune that the smugglers were caught. He served for just under five years before he was given an early discharge for good conduct in May 1837 when he was thirty-two-years old.

For smugglers who crossed the Channel there was always the hidden threat of the sea itself. In November 1816 three noted smugglers were drowned at Fecamp as their boat crossed the bar. The *Hampshire Telegraph* recorded their deaths, adding that within the past four years twelve young men had been lost while smuggling. The tubs and skins that arrived at the back of gentlemen's houses and farmers' porches had a real price far higher than the money that changed hands.

*   *   *

James Buckett's 1837 discharge certificate from the Navy, 'in consideration of his good conduct.'

Blackgang Chine in the 1840s, with visitors admiring the waterfall while wreckage is hauled ashore.

Mr James Buckett of Brighstone wearing the silver medal of the Royal Lifeboat Institution which he was awarded for his part in the rescue of the Woodham in 1873. He remained coxswain of Brighstone Grange lifeboat until he was 72 years old.

On the 24 December 1859 the first formal moves were made to have lifeboats stationed in the Island. In a petition signed by the rectors of Brighstone and Brooke the immediate reason was given – 'fourteen lives were lost by Shipwreck at the back of the Island, about three weeks ago. It was stated by the officers of the Coast Guard and by others at the Inquest, that if a Lifeboat had been at hand, the whole of these might have been saved.'

The Reverend Edward McAll, rector of Brighstone, initiated the movement with a meeting in the rectory, following which a survey of the coast was made by an Inspector of the Royal National Lifeboat Institution. His report recommended that two lifeboats were needed, one at Brooke and one at Brighstone Grange. Each was expected to cost about £350 and the annual expenses would be £20-£25, later raised to £40-£50. The initial outlay would amount to £700, of which the R.N.L.I. would pay half. By February 1860 local subscriptions had raised sufficient to fund one boat and, independently the Royal Victoria Yacht Club had undertaken to fund a boat themselves. This meant that no help was needed financially from the R.N.L.I. and the first two lifeboats in the Island were provided entirely from local initiative.

The Seely family at Brook House contributed generously to the subscription fund and they remained closely associated with the service; none more so that Jack Seely, 1st Lord Mottistone, who was a crew member, coxswain and supporter for forty years. A member of the Brighstone crew illustrates the contribution ex-smugglers made to the service. Only men used to handling oars in rough weather could attempt to save lives in stormy seas and smugglers with their experience of crossing the Channel were eminently suitable for this work. James Buckett of Brighstone was coxswain of the first Brighstone boat, *Rescue*, and he remained in the crew for eighteen years until he reached the age of seventy four, receiving in 1783 the R.N.L.I. Silver Medal for bravery.

The lifeboat stations in Brooke and Brighstone were opened on the 13th August 1860. In 1867, at the most easterly point in the Island Bembridge lifeboat was launched following a brave rescue by the local fishermen in their own boats. Ryde followed two years later and in 1885 and

1890 Totland Bay and Atherfield boats came on station. At Shanklin *The Dove* was paid for by subscriptions raised from Island Sunday School children.

Launching these boats was heavy, laborious work and required many hands. When a carriage was used this first had to be pulled from the boathouse with the boat on it. Strong cart horses from the local farms were enlisted, eight to ten in number, and they had to be led into the rough sea as far as it was possible in order to turn the boat to face bow first into the waves. Then the sixty or so helpers took over, listening for the coxswain's crucial cry to launch at exactly the right moment. Finally the ten oarsmen had to pull together immediately and in unison when the boat was waterborn. The whole experience was a united effort drawn from a close knit community.

Danger was ever present. The efforts made to rescue the *Sirenia* off Atherfield Ledge in March 1888 is only one dramatic occasion when exceptional bravery was shown. The *Worcester Cadet* was launched in the afternoon and took off the captain's family, a maid and an apprentice. At midnight when the weather had worsened she returned to the ship pulling through huge seas and took off thirteen members of the crew. As the lifeboat was returning a rolling wave capsized her and both the coxswains were drowned, together with one of the *Sirenia's* crew. And yet the lifeboat went back again to complete her work. The three members of the Brighstone crew who went out for the third time Frank Salter, Rufus and David Cotton were all awarded the R.N.L.I. Silver Medal for bravery.

Today fast boats at Yarmouth and Bembridge are the descendants of these manually operated lifeboats which began the modern service of saving life on the seas that surround the Island.

The lifeboat Worcester Cadet *with her crew in 1881. At the extreme left of the crew in the boat are Tom Cotton and Moses Munt who were to be drowned seven years later during the rescue of the* Sirenia.

TEN

Expansion and Crisis

The head of Shanklin Chine in 1821. This highly dramatised view shows visitors being conducted down the nearly 200ft deep chasm by William Colenutt, in the white hat. He lived in a cottage on the shore and maintained the path in exchange for the sole right to act as guide.

The high living which farming sustained at the turn of the 19th century could not be sustained when the Napoleonic Wars ended. While the 1820s were not consistently bad for agriculture they did not offer the high returns which farmers had enjoyed. The results of this were seen in the ports along the south coast thronged with ships ready to take disenchanted farmers to the United States. Many Island farmers were among them. In 1821 about sixty Islanders sailed for Philadelphia in the *Nepos* and in the following year yet more boarded her, including many 'respectable farmers'. They were following the example of John Pittis, an enterprising brewer and hop merchant who was sufficiently well off to charter the brig *Resolution* and set off with his large family, fourteen indentured youths and fifty five paying passengers. Eleven years later he returned from their new home at Brownsville, Ohio, on the edge of the unsettled wilderness, and took back with him a party of unemployed young labourers whose passage was paid by the Guardians of the Poor. This was the first step in a policy which helped young people to emigrate to the United States, Canada and Australia.

From 1836 assisted emigration became for about six years an important part of poor relief. Most emigrants went to the neighbourhood of Toronto in Upper Canada, travelling in the care of the Petworth Emigration Committee, a well-organized body who saw all the emigrants safely settled on their land or in employment. The Guardians adopted this standard and between 1837-1842 at least 325 of the poor, all young and all actual or potential paupers, had gone to Canada, while others travelled individually to America and Australia. It was an expensive way of reducing the pauper population but removed some of those most likely to produce large pauper families. And the poor wanted to go; places were always over subscribed and for those selected the prospects, despite much hardship, were more rewarding than they could hope for at home.

While agriculture was entering a period of stagnation the attractions of the Island as a holiday area were growing. Before Worsley wrote his history it had acquired a reputation as the 'Garden of England' and visitors were already arriving to please themselves with 'a sight of Carisbrooke Castle, and perhaps the Needles' before the end of the century. Shut out of Europe by the French wars the English traveller had to satisfy his love of the romantic in his native land. The Isle of Wight offered the adventure of a sea voyage, the charm of wooded slopes, and sandy bays. There was, too, the healthful prospect of yachting, sea-bathing and 'water pick-nicks' during the summer season.

Taking in summer visitors was established in the very early nineteenth century. At Shanklin the dramatic chine drew admirers of the picturesque and 'nearly every cottage … being in the habit of letting cottages in the Summer Season is surrounded by a garden of flowering shrubs and is

itself adorned … with whitewash and green paint.' The real development of Shanklin came later but for the intrepid traveller the tiresome journey from Ryde was worthwhile. Before the 1830s and the regular steam passenger services 'sailing packets were formidable conveyances', to which had to be added 'a post chaise from Ryde' with numerous gates to pass before the beauties of the southern shores could be enjoyed.

This isolation held back the development of the southern villages but at Ventnor aristocractic influence was also important. Lord Yarborough who owned the land between St Lawrence annd Steephill in the 1820s absolutely refused to allow his tenants to take in lodgers. At Steephill John Hambrough refused to allow road improvements which would intrude on his views. He had bought the estate, demolished Hans Stanley's Gothic cottage and was now watching his own Gothic Steephill Castle rise in its place. From the later 1830s, however, the back of the Island became more accessible as steam packets took some of the anxiety out of sea travel. It had a distinct advantage over other parts of the Island for the exceptionally mild climate attracted visitors throughout the year. Ventor suddenly became popular and houses were built to accommodate invalids escaping the rigours of winter on the mainland. 'The land has been let in small portions to needy people, who have run up cheap small houses for the sake of immediate gain,' wrote a lady in 1841. Two guineas (£2.10) a week for a small house was then the usual rent although this rose by a further guinea in high summer. Bonchurch was much more attractive, being more sheltered, and here some very superior houses were found, including East Dene, where Swinburne spent his childhood. Later in the nineteenth century this soft climate was fully appreciated when the Royal National Hospital for Diseases of the Chest was opened at St Lawrence in 1861.

A few miles away the fashion for improving health by drinking mineral waters encouraged a small development at Niton, the most westerly point of the Undercliff. Here Thomas Waterworth, a Newport surgeon, exploited a chalebeate spring at Sandrock where he opened his dispensary in 1810. The strength of the mineral content made this spring unique and it was admired for its success in treating 'debility, prostration of the nervous energy … and many disorders of the female constitution'. But fashions in health cures pass and by 1860 this little spa had closed.

The coast nearest to the mainland prospered most. Before the end of the Napoleonic wars 'families of distinction' were passing through Southampton and boarding ships to carry them to East and West Cowes. Here the aristocracy had been attracted by the sailing since the late eighteenth century. Cowes grew slowly during that time and brought itself up-to-date in the 1790s by hiding the seventeenth century buildings behind

All the picturesque character of Shanklin village is captured in this view; deep thatched roofs and elaborate bargeboards. The Crab and Lobster Inn with its flag pole stands in a central position in the village.

Steephill Castle, Ventnor, the Gothic fancy of John Hambrough, begun in 1833. It was designed by James Sanderson, of Ryde, and cost nearly £250,000.

The Sandrock Hotel, Niton. This was originally a small inn but the wings were added in 1812 and it became a cottage ornée, with wide verandahs and a thatched roof, designed to fit the picturesque scenery of the undercliff. The hotel was associated with the nearby chalybeate spring which attracted visitors hoping to improve their health by drinking the water.

Ventnor began to develop as a resort in the 1840s when rented houses for visitors were being built up the hillside: the population more than doubled between 1841 and 1851.

At the end of the 19th century Ventnor still retained its earlier charm. The inevitable bathing machines line the shore and houses have now spread to the skyline.

This 1848 view of Bonchurch Pond, illustrates its attraction to visitors as both a summer and winter resort.

Georgian frontages. But there were too few houses for the growing numbers of visitors and new building supplied marine cottages and villas. Queen's Road began to be developed in 1829 and the elegant houses that remain near Holy Trinity church are a reminder of the fashionable society Cowes attracted. This whole area was the property of a Mrs Sarah Goodwin and it was she who paid £6687 for building the church as a place of worship 'for sailors and seafarers' – and to provide a living for her son-in-law Maximilian Geneste. The sailors proved to be a very superior class as, since its consecration in 1832, Holy Trinity has always been associated with the Royal Yacht Squadron and it is here on the first Sunday in Cowes Week that the Regatta Service is held each year.

On an elevated site above the town a splendid house was being built in the 1820s, replacing the earlier Belle Vue which perfectly described the outloook onto the Solent. Now there was a new name for a new family, Northwood House, the home of George Ward, the first of a family which was to take an active part in local affairs well into the twentieth century.

The grandest houses, however, were across the river at East Cowes. Here in the 1790s two fashionable architects were each building Gothic

112

castles. Much the finer was Norris Castle, built by James Wyatt for Lord Henry Seymour between 1795-1805. The house is wonderfully sited commanding the Solent and Wyatt's building, a pseudo-Norman castle was designed to fit this landscape, a strong building in a strategic position. There is nothing false about Norris Castle. Wyatt was a serious architect who links the eighteenth Gothick with the earnest medievalism of Victorian times.

Nearby John Nash was building himself a castle very like those he had been designing in other parts of the country. He had bought the land in 1798 and by 1802 he and Mrs Nash had moved into their new home although many additions were to be made before the castle was completed. The roof line was particularly dramatic with a circular staircase tower, a massive octagon and a square tower at the north-east. Below the house were fine terraces and the beautiful formal gardens were laid out by the distinguished landscape gardener Humphrey Repton.

Here Nash enjoyed entertaining in lavish style. During Regattas there were breakfasts and receptions. In August 1815 there was a great fête to celebrate the final defeat of Napoleon and two years later his patron and friend the Prince Regent dined at the castle. Nash also involved himself in Island life, designing Gothic villas and classical houses as well as public buildings. He even found time to attend meetings of the Guardians of the Poor when he was elected a Director. In 1830 Nash suffered a stroke but he continued to work, enjoyed having visitors to stay and the soirées continued. But on his death in May 1835 he was found to be deeply in debt, the castle and its contents were sold and Mrs Nash retired to their shooting lodge at Ningwood.

East Cowes was at this time so attractive that a major development

East Cowes Castle in 1824. John Nash began it in 1798 and lived here until his death.

James Wyatt's spectacular Norris Castle, East Cowes.

Newport Villa, East Cowes. This villa with its Tudor-style chimneys and elaborate barge-boards is an example of the superior houses being built in East Cowes in the 1840s. It can still be seen in York Avenue.

This 1847 view of Ryde shows the first pier head built by James Langdon of Ryde and opened in 1842. On the shoreline the newly built Royal Victoria Yacht Club stands out with its colonnade of columns. To the right behind the white flag is Henry Players manor house built c1706. It was this family who began the development of Ryde. Brigstocke Terrace with behind it the spire of St. Thomas's Church is a prominent central feature. At the top of the hill on the right is Westmont, the home of John Lind, and now the central part of Ryde School.

was conceived in the 1840s to create a garden village for the middle classes. East Cowes Park with its 'detached villas surrounded by gardens and embosomed in shrubberies' was advertised as a British Madeira where each plot had a 100ft frontage and a depth of 300ft. A variety of house designs was offered from classical temples, Swiss chalets to miniature castles. By 1843 a central Botanical Garden was laid out encircled by Victoria Drive and the prospectus issued that year projected a picturesque park with fountains, bowers, exotic trees and shrubs. On paper it was an attractive venture and, with the completion of the railway to Southampton London was no more than four hours away. But by 1859 only twenty villas had been built and the future of the Garden Village faded. Two factors probably contributed to this. The long sea crossing to Southampton was a deterrent to permanent development of this kind, but more significant was the imcompatibility of planning a superior middle class estate in a district whose natural growth was concentrated among a population 'chiefly composed of mechanics and others dependent on the shipping and shipbuilding establishments' crowded together near the river. While Cowes and East Cowes were growing, a few miles along the coast two hamlets were beginning their transformation into the first new town of the nineteenth century. Upper Ryde, in the present High Street area and Lower Ryde, straggling along the foreshore saw the first stage of their later unity in 1780 when William Player the landlord, laid out Union Street, a wide direct road between the two communities. Before this new thoroughfare was fully developed Ryde was already attracting superior visitors as newspaper accounts of the opening years of the century show. It was full of 'genteel company', the 'Beau Monde', all 'literally crammed' into the available accommodation. In 1810 Jane Player, William's widow, was able to exploit this demand when she obtained a private act of parliament which allowed her to grant building leases on the estate. In 1814 the pier opened and at last travellers could step from the ferries without facing the hazards of Ryde's muddy foreshore. From this time the town expanded and many of the elegant villas that were built may still be admired today. Between 1827-1832 the Town Hall, St Thomas's Church and Brigstock Terrace were built, all designed by John Sanderson who set a standard of elegance that local builders adopted in their domestic buildings. In 1829 the local Lighting and Paving act recognized Ryde as a town and it continued to be the most rapidly growing area in the Isle of Wight.

But in the opening years of the century Newport was the only town of any size and its civic pride determined that the old Town Hall should be replaced with a modern building. John Nash was engaged and in 1813 when his plan was accepted the grateful burgesses elected him a free burgess. They had every reason to be pleased with the classically plain building which is today the most important feature of the High Street. Building operations were supervised by a local man, William Mortimer, and two years later he profited by his experience when he built the new Isle of Wight Institution, a meeting place for gentlemen in St James's Square.

Newport remained the centre for trade and business. It was here the banks were concentrated. One eighteenth century bank had already disappeared – Roberts and Gregory were bankrupted in 1791 due to the fraudulent dealings of Mark Gregory – but Kirkpatricks and Bassets remained with a branch of the former at Ryde and Bassets at Cowes. By 1841 they faced competition from the mainland when the Hampshire Banking Company had branches in each town. It was probably to face this intrusion that the Isle of Wight Joint Stock Bank was formed in 1842. It bought Basset's Bank in St James's Square but kept the two remaining partners as managing directors. But within a year they were dismissed for fraud and in 1844 the National Provincial Bank, with a branch already in Ryde, swallowed up the last remnant of local banking.

Commercial banking could not help the poor to save although it was well known that the poorest did save when they were offered the opportunity. Even Friendly Societies were beyond their reach, indeed some specifically excluded the lowest paid workers. The Isle of Wight Brotherly Society excluded anyone earning less than 18s (90p) a week and in 1843 ordered that 'no … labourer whatever' should be admitted. These societies catered for artisans and small businessmen and in the 1830s they were flourishing with good memberships and sound finances.

The servant and labouring classes had to wait until 1817 when the Savings Bank Act was passed before they could invest their savings safely. In October that year a meeting in Newport, largely supported by active members of the Guardians of the Poor, inaugurated the Isle of Wight Trustee Savings Bank. William Yelf was appointed secretary and in 1836 his house in Holyrood Street was bought by the bank, his front room serving as an office. One shilling would open an account and once £1.5.0 (£1.25) was credited for one month interest of 4% began to accumulate.

This bank was an outstanding success from the moment its doors opened. In 1828 finances were so satisfactory that every depositor recieved a bonus of ten shillings (50p). It was unusual in having the largest number of depositers and most money invested drawn from labourers and journeymen and not from the servant class as was most common.

Lind Street, Ryde. This important street in the growing resort was built after cottages had been demolished by the Town Commissioners. St James's Church in the distance was built in 1827 preceding the Town Hall by three years. The original Town Hall, with its classical frontage was extended in 1868. The clock tower was built to carry a clock presented to the town by the Brigstocke family and an assembly room with rounded windows was added at the same time. The colonnaded building was built c1835 by James Sanderson. Apart from intermittent alterations to the windows the facade has remained unchanged.

Every market town needed a large clock and the position of the Newport Town Hall facing up the High Street made it a convenient building on which to fix a bracket clock. It is a reminder that Nash's classical building did not remain unsullied in the earlier years of its life.

	1821	1822	1823
Labourers and Journeymen	3515	3745	6547
Apprentices and children	1858	2375	2824
Servants	2229	3195	2817
Others	1749	2566	3844
Benefit Clubs	820	845	1098
Other Charities	143	443	740

In 1825 a branch opened at East Cowes where shipyard workers might

This view of Cowes in the early 19th century illustrates the importance of shipbuilding; even the houses are surrounded by the keels of vessels in the course of construction.

A design of lace taken from the pattern book used at the Lace Factory. The designs were so successful that in 1833 an imitation of French white silk lace sold undetected for a whole season, bring a profit of £40,000.

be expected to have money to save, but the second branch, opened the same year, was at Shorwell, a totally rural parish. In November 1834 another branch was opened at Calbourne where the agricultural labourer was the typical worker. The Cowes branch opened in 1829 and Ryde's in 1832, but Ventnor and Yarmouth had to wait until 1841 for their savings banks.

Unfortunately the bank was not well supervised and in 1853 the secretary admitted 'a considerable defalcation' in the accounts going back many years. Business was immediately suspended, an inspector from the Controller of the National Debt arrived from London to investigate and by the 9 May all was resolved. The depositors were to receive 17.6d (87p) in the pound and the administration of the bank was severely overhauled. Compared with gross frauds suffered by some Savings Banks in other parts of the country the Island came off lightly but the loss on each pound fell hard on poor people. A committee was immediately formed to raise money and make good the losses and the long term success of the bank was not harmed by this unhappy experience.

Investors in this bank would certainly have included the skilled employees at Broadlands Lace factory. This extension of the Nottingham lace trade was brought by John Nunn after he lost a complicated legal battle over his right to the exclusive use of improved lace making machinery. At the end of an expensive trial in 1816 Nunn was determined that some of the machines should be brought to the Island. Thomas Sewell, the Newport lawyer and land agent, reported in 1817 that land had been bought near Newport 'for carrying on a lace thread manufactory'. This was at Staplers on the eastern outskirts of the town, now the offices of the Department of Health and Social Security. The factory appears to have opened in 1826 and was a typical manufactory employing mainly women and children with a few skilled men as overseers. It made a real impact on Newport where 'a large portion of the children of the labouring poor – nearly eight hundred' were employed. In 1832 eighty machines were at work but it was a vulnerable industry,, so closely linked with the volatile fashion trade. In 1832 during a slump half the employees were dismissed. Following the practice of northern factories Broadlands had outworkers and in some country cottages girls of eight used their soft supple fingers to embroider elaborate patterns onto fine net. From this basically industrial process the traditional Isle of Wight Lace was born. The factory continued until 1868 when Mr Nunn retired and could find no one willing to take on the business.

Around Newport houses were springing up. Rows of cottages at the lower end of Castle Road became New Village and near the Lace Factory Barton's Village was being built. Within the town open spaces were filling up and in the poorest areas such as South Street alleys and courts were crammed with families. The dismal conditions in which the poor lived was revealed in 1850 as part of the report on the sanitary conditions in East Cowes, Cowes and Barton's Village. All shared the same problems of lack of water and bad sanitation. Even the new cottages at Barton had bad sewerage, and although wells had been sunk the water was undrinkable. Drinking water had to be carried from the nearest well in South Street or had to be bought at a cost of up to 5d (2p) a week.

At Cowes and East Cowes the situation was worse. At the Point in Cowes about one thousand people were living in courts and alleys which they shared with piggeries, dung heaps, offal pits and cesspools. There were two free taps in the town and three public pumps which had to serve everyone who had no private well or, after 1848, was not served from the newly opened waterworks. East Cowes was no better. There one well with no pump or windlass supplied 150 families. Drawing water was so slow that the first persons arrived at 3am, and even this supply was contaminated by sea water at high tides. Sanitation was just as bad, 'every house or court has its cesspools, which are emptied every two years', while streets near the slaughter house and stables suffered from their waste flung into open gutters. None of this was peculiar to these places; they illustrate the normal conditions of life in any town at this period and it is not surprising that in Whippingham the average age at death was 27 years 5 months when one child in eight died before its first birthday.

In the countryside many labourers had, at least, space around the cottage to grow potatoes and keep a pig but not even this could be assured as the century advanced. New cottages with rents as high as 2s to 5s (25p) a week often had no land attached and there were few allotments. Most farm workers were now day labourers as farmers found this more economic than contracting with all their workers for annual terms. Since the introduction of the local Highway Act in 1813 an arrangement between the Highway Commissioners and the Guardians of the Poor had established a system where road work was offered to unemployed men, the Guardians paying them a graduated rate according to the number of children in the family up to the 9s (45p) weekly wage. This suited the Commissioners who were mainly farmers. It gave them

The blacksmith was essential to communities where iron was used in every part of rural life from shoeing horses, making and maintaining machinery, repairing shovels and picks used by paupers on road work, to clandestinely making smugglers' tools.

a guaranteed supply of low paid workers who could be laid off whenever the weather was bad in the secure knowledge that the poor rates would make up their wages to the usual day rate. Road work was not hard, there was little supervision and gradually men who had no connection with agriculture were taken on; in the 1820s mechanics, journeymen, sailors and pilots could all be found on the roads. At the same time the guardians continued to subsidise shoemakers, buying in the shoes they could not sell, building up a mountain of 1,000 pairs which somehow had to be sold.

This was expedient but it was not a recipe for contentment. Men working on the roads had long hours and ample time to brood on their condition and among the gentry and farmers in their isolated houses there was always latent fear. This was grounded on their vulnerability to fire, the one weapon always to hand for the poor. An ill-written but clear notice pinned to the church door at Newport in early October 1804 sets out the threat:

'A Cousen for the farmers and those that was the incegation of the unecesary rise upon flower and Bread we do hearby declare and give public notice that if you dont lore the price as before we will put fire to every Wheat Rick within our Reach For we think it necessary that the rich should starve as well as the poor and so you may depend on this as truth'.

The writer kept his word. A few days later Widow Cole of Rew Farm, Gurnard had her barn, stables and five ricks of hay and corn destroyed by fire. In May 1816 a poster at Ryde encouraged 'the lower orders of society to acts of violence against Millers, Farmers and Landowners' because of a rise in corn prices. Arson continued intermittently and with no soldiers in the Island and no police any change which seemed to threaten the security of the poor had to be considered carefully. In 1829 the Guardians determined to refuse road work to all men who were not agricultural labourers, offering them and their families instead relief in the workhouse. Immediately rumours spread claiming that all out-relief was to end and in this unsettled atmosphere the autumn of 1830 arrived and with it the 'Labourers' Revolt' that swept through southern England.

The Isle of Wight was not as seriously affected as the neighbouring mainland counties but it experienced a traumatic week-end at the end of November. Earlier in the month farmers who owned threshing machines received threats that they would be damaged and these now stood idly on the farms. On 25 November two hundred and fifty paupers employed by the Guardians on Forest Farm near Carisbrooke left their work and went in a body to neighbouring farms, complaining of low wages. This uprecedented 'strike' spread alarm throughout the Island. Local magistrates were urged to action and in Brighstone Samuel Wilberforce, the rector, could not escape an anxious neighbour, 'coming up to me twice a day ... requesting me to swear in special constables, appoint patrols ...'. Constables were sworn in and a public meeting was called at Newport on the Saturday to discuss the situation. By this time the justices were so fearful that they ordered the Preventive men to stand guard with their arms while the meeting was held. Their fears were justified for that night a Newport farmer had his ricks burned, an attempt was made to fire a rick at Gate House Farm near Ryde and a threshing machine was destroyed at Rookley. At Freshwater the absentee rector was the target for local anger. A doggerel verse delivered to his house shows that the arsonists were united against tithe collection. 'For the last 20 years we have been in a starving condition to maintain your Dam pride' and later that day his hay rick was burned down.

This frightening week-end and a second strike by the Forest Farm paupers in January 1831 convinced the Guardians that they should not proceed with their intended plans to reduce relief to the able-bodied. Instead the overall total of out-relief payments for the following year doubled as the Guardians and the justices bought security, at least for the time being.

Arson was not given up, however. In the following years it continued intermittently during the dark nights and in January 1837 the magistrates appointed an inspector and ten police officers. Ryde Town Commissioners had already agreed to appoint an inspector and in late 1837 Newport did the same. The reasons for these innovations were related to the introduction of the New Poor Law in the Island.

In April 1836 the Poor Law Commissioner, Colonel Ashe a'Court, arrived to make arrangements 'for carrying the Poor Law Bill into operation.' The Directors of the incorporation welcomed the new law but they were faced with a potentially dangerous situation when Colonel a'Court insisted that pauper road work must end. In future farmers would no longer be allowed 'to send their paupers (very often their own independent labourers in wet weather) on the public roads.' The Highway Commissioners were furious and retaliated by dismissing all their workers, about four hundred, on the 5 July. It was a tense new committee of Guardians who met to hear the claims of these men on the 16 July. They sat for nearly nine hours considering each claimant and were thankful that 'although there was ... a good deal of bluster ... no acts of open violence.' The transition from old to new passed off quietly enough on the surface but the strengthening of the police reflected the apprehension of the upper classes.

One year later in Ryde this concern was fully justified. On the 8 August polling in the 1837 election took place. The voters in 1832 had elected Sir Richard Simeon, a Liberal, as M.P. for the Isle of Wight by a majority of 600 but in 1835 this fell to 146 and when he retired the new candidate, Captain Pelham, faced a strong conservative challenge in William a'Court Holmes. When the votes were counted the Conservatives had won the seat and this signalled serious disturbances in Ryde where the Liberal was strongly supported. But this was an extra-parliamentary protest by the dis-enfranchised who combined it with economic grievances. In the afternoon a large crowd threatened Mark Allen, a local butcher, accusing him of extortionate prices and burning his effigy before his shop. In the evening trouble began outside Yelf's Hotel, the Conservative headquarters, but soon spread. At about 7 pm a crowd of men marched through the town and at 9 am a second more serious march began. The leader was dressed entirely in white and carried a bludgeon and nail-studded stave. The smart villas in Wood Street and George Street were attacked with heavy stones and in Castle Street the command 'Fire!' was heard, followed by the report of a pistol or gun. This riot was more serious than the usual election disturbance of a few broken windows. It had been planned, the leader in white was in the mould of radical agitators elsewhere and those who met the rioters concluded that they were country people, those who had been refused out-door relief during the previously exceptionally hard winter and spring.

The following day a misjudged attempt to provide military protection allowed a party of troops from Portsmouth to enter the town, re-kindling the agitation, which was only quelled when the magistrates agreed that the soldiers should be withdrawn.

This riot was exceptional but it came out of a radical tradition that had shown itself during the passage of the Reform Act. At the end of March 1832 when the second reading was going through Parliament the paupers in the House of Industry contributed what little they had to buy candles and light every window in the vast building to show their support, and the following May the workers at Nunn's factory carried a lace banner through Newport inscribed 'We must we will be free'. The Mechanic's Institute in Pyle Street was regarded as a school of radicalism by the Conservatives. In the 1840s Newport was the centre of the Chartist movement in the Island, with a second branch at Cowes and a small group at Ventnor. The Island Chartists were unusual in the south of England which was virtually free of these radicals and they were equally unusual in being mainly small traders rather than operatives. Barnabus Urry, millwright and founder, was the chairman and Phillip Brannon, son of the engraver, was an active missionary. He started a Ragged School in Newport and taught there himself. Mr Self, a baker in Crocker Street, was the vigorous secretary in 1842 when the Island members sent £6.18.0 (£6.90) to the Chartist Political Victims and Defence Fund, following the riots in the north earlier that year. The fear of a Chartist uprising in 1848 was so great that rumours spread that a large party had landed in the Island to capture the Queen. They were, in fact, an innocent group of Oddfellows on a day trip from the mainland!

The years 1830-1836 were a significant period in Island history. They were a watershed which separated the old independent life of the Island and the modern period. In 1832 political influence changed. The pleasant charade of the burgesses at Newtown electing their M.P.s over an oyster lunch ended; the six Island M.P.s were replaced with two, elected on a wider suffrage. In 1836 the Guardians of the Poor adopted and administered all the regulations of the New Poor Law, ending their personal administration of much of local government. This marked the beginning of the modern period when government policy increasingly determined the management of local affairs.

*   *   *

When Queen Victoria and Prince Albert decided to make Osborne their sea-side home they were not deterred by the working population living near the river. The estate was isolated from the community and remained completely private. The Queen took little part in Island affairs that were not included within the estate, but she remembered the school children at Whippingham each Christmas and all the estate children enjoyed a tea party and presents at Osborne on Boxing Day. Her determination to live a secluded family life may have been formed when she reflected on the public duties she had undertaken as a girl under the direction of her formidable mother. In 1831 and 1833 her holidays at Norris Castle had been punctuated with official engagements and public parties, including both laying the foundation stone of Nash's St James's church at East Cowes and attending its consecration in 1833. But those holidays had shaped an affection for the Island. In addition her doctors' thought the air good for her health and that of the family.

Life at Osborne was totally different to her own childhood. It was above all family life that was enjoyed, first in the eighteenth century house they rented for 1844 while the complicated process of buying the land went forward. Two parties were involved, Lady Isobelle Blachford who owned Osborne House and two hundred acres and Winchester College who held Barton Manor, Dashwoods and Little Shambles Farm, all needed to guarantee seclusion in a large estate. Together the estates cost £44,000 but there was no difficulty in finding the money. Prince Albert's ruthless pruning of the existing overstaffed households in the three royal residences allowed them to buy their own home entirely from their resources. In the spring of 1845 the Royal Family spent their first holiday at Osborne; 'our new and really delightful home … we can walk about anywhere without being followed'. Old Osborne was charming with its bowed windows, chintz covers and beautiful views down to Osborne Bay but it was much too small for all the state business that inevitably followed the Queen.

The newly built Pavilion, the first part of the present Osborne House, with the old house in which Queen Victoria and Prince Albert first lived beside it. The two houses were linked by a corridor before old Osborne was demolished.

It was Thomas Cubitt, the fashionable builder-contractor who advised the Queen and Prince Albert to build anew rather than extend the old house and he with Prince Albert designed its replacement. Osborne was planned to fit a landscape; in summer weather with blue skies and sparkling sea Albert compared the Solent with the Bay of Naples and so an Italianate design was chosen, Palladian with loggias and a campanile. The foundation stone was laid by the family in June 1845 and work on the Pavilion began.

The choice of Cubitt to design and build the house shocked Victorian society. He was not an architect but he was exactly the type of man Prince Albert most liked, a competent business man, with the most modern and well organized firm in England. He built well, offered fixed price contracts and a stated completion date and his works on the Isle of Dogs was a model of concentrated efficiency.

His chief concern in the new house was to ensure that it was fireproof. 'A fireproof building [puts] a most heavy responsibility upon the Builder and I endeavoured to provide against the slightest danger'. To achieve this he created a structure based on brick arches with cast iron girders, insulated between the floors with finely crushed shells and he used cement for all the skirtings. Cubitt and Prince Albert were also economical; most of the interior woodwork was deal, only in the reception rooms was oak used for floors and mahogany for window sashes. Here, however, newly invented 'plate' glass was put in the windows, and in those of the Queen's sitting room on the first floor, so that large spans of glass gave wide views down to the Solent.

The Pavilion was really two houses, with formal state rooms on the ground floor, where gilt and gold brocade furnished the drawing room and solid mahogany was used in the dining room. The monumental side board by Whitaker was not solely for display. At Christmas a baron of beef weighing up to 250lb was sent down from Windsor, garnished and decorated with the Queen's monogram in horseradish in the Os-

Queen Victoria and Princess Beatrice in the private sitting room at Osborne House. The empty chair beside the Queen was use by Prince Albert who shared the desk with his wife.

Her Royal Highness Princess Beatrice dressed for her wedding on the 23 July 1885. The white satin dress had a lace overskirt and was trimmed with lace on the sleeves and neckline. The Princess was an expert on lace and in a particular gesture of affection Queen Victoria allowed her to wear the Honiton lace veil she had worn on her own wedding day.

borne kitchens, which had no ovens large enough to cook it, and finally became the centrepiece on the sideboard for dinner on Christmas Eve. Upstairs was the family home with its cosy cluttered appearance, over-blown roses woven into the carpet, balloon backed chairs and chintz curtains, a picture of a well-to-do English family living room rather than that of an aristocratic household. On the 15 September 1846 the Pavilion was ready for occupation and the Queen found it 'like a dream to be here now in our house of which we laid the stone 15 months ago'. Old Osborne was still standing and before it was demolished during further building the careful Cubitt removed everything that could be used.

For Prince Albert much of the joy of Osborne lay in the gardens and the estate. From the top of the Flag Tower he supervised the grading and planting of terraces, using signal flags to direct the workmen. The rough ground was seeded to grass lawns and he planted trees, thinned woodland and took a keen and intelligent interest in his new model farm. He was as he described himself, 'partly forester, partly builder, partly farmer, and partly gardener.' The children ran about the grounds and joined their mother in bathing which she greatly enjoyed, stepping from her high-wheeled machine into the secluded bathing area. When the pre-fabricated Swiss Cottage arrived in 1854 the children's education widened as Prince Albert was able to introduce his own ideas in which practical education was important. Each child had a garden and an individual set of tools made by Cubitt's workmen. They cultivated their own plots and when the under-gardener was satisfied with the quality of the vegetables their father bought them at current market prices. They washed potatoes, shelled peas and cooked them in their own kitchen, in their own house and altogether enjoyed an idyllic life. Only the Prince of Wales was excluded, his unenviable position as heir-apparent forced him into a straight jacket of academic learning unsuited to his character or abilities.

By 1850 the servants' quarters were finished and in 1851 the main wing for the Household was ready, freeing them from their lodgings all over the estate and in East Cowes. This was celebrated with a great open-air dinner for the workmen who had been employed on the house, on re-building Barton Manor and other works about the estate. Two hundred and seventy sat down to dinner and there was dancing and games until sunset, a splendid conclusion to Thomas Cubitt's direct association with the building of Osborne.

This happy era ended abruptly on the 14 December 1861 with the unexpected and tragic death of Prince Albert and it was to Osborne that the Queen returned to mourn. For the remainder of her life summer holidays and Christmas visits were spent there, always with her youngest daughter Beatrice at her side. On the 23 July 1885 the Queen and the Islanders were able to share in the happy celebrations of the marriage of Princess Beatrice to Prince Henry of Battenburg. The wedding took place at St Mildred's, Whippingham parish church, in the building designed by her father, and later in the day Prince Henry and his wife left for a two day honeymoon at Quarr Abbey, then a private villa, before returning to live with the Queen.

There had always been problems about accommodating large numbers for special occasions at Osborne; receptions were held in a marquee on the lawn beside the Pavilion but in 1890 an additional wing was com-

pleted, including a large reception room. The elaborate Indian style decoration of the Durbar Room was a complement to Victoria as Empress of India, which she had been since 1876. Above this a new suite of rooms was provided for Princess Beatrice, Prince Henry and their family. Six years later he was no longer there to share it with them. Prince Henry had joined the Ashanti Expedition and in Africa was attacked by malaria which, within ten days had killed him. His wife had at first received encouraging reports of his progress and was preparing to meet him in Madeira when the news of Prince Henry's death was brought to her. 'The life has gone out of me', she said. On a cold February morning in 1896 she joined the funeral procession at Trinity Wharf and went back to Whippingham Church to see her husband buried.

Both Princess Beatrice and her mother were widowed when they were only forty two years old but Princess Beatrice with her four young children did not retire into seclusion. She was appointed Governor of the Isle of Wight in succession to her husband and she remained so until her death in 1944. For the remaining years of her mother's life she was her constant companion becoming increasingly important as the Queen grew older.

In the autumn of 1900 Queen Victoria's indomitable constitution began to show signs of weakening. Yet she determined to spend Christmas at Osborne as she had done for so many past years. But by mid-January the end was drawing near. The Prince of Wales arrived on the 20th and her grandson, the German Emperor on the following day. Now it was only a question of waiting as her life slipped away. Outside Osborne House reporters waited as the hours passed and at last, on the evening of the 22 January the official announcement came: 'Her Majesty the Queen breathed her last at 6.45pm surrounded by her children and grandchildren.'

It was Princess Beatrice who administered the precise instructions the Queen had left for her funeral arrangements. The catafalque was set up

Osborne Naval College was opened in 1903 to provide initial training for boys entering the Navy. The separate houses and buildings were pulled down after the College closed in 1921 and the site is now used as the main car park for Osborne House.

in the dining room and over the tiny figure was placed her wedding veil. There was no black on the coffin that was carried away from the Island on the *Alberta*, only white and gold, with the royal arms embroidered on the pall.

In an astonishingly short time after the death of the old Queen the family home was granted to the nation under the Osborne Estate Act of 1902. On the day of his coronation King Edward VII wrote to the Prime Minister expressing his wish that 'his people should have acccess to the house' although the private apartments were secured against intruders by strong ironwork gates which were only opened during our present Queen's reign. The Household Wing was to become a convalescent home for naval and military officers, certainly the most attractive in the country. In the dining room all the table furnishings were white, the Irish linen tablecloths having the King's cypher with a Tudor crown woven into the material; white china was decorated in gold with the same design and it was engraved on the table glasses. Each of the individual bedrooms was decorated in pale green or pink with white painted furniture. As the patients gained strength they could walk in the grounds, play golf and tennis as they returned to health.

In 1903 a further phase of Osborne's life begann when Edward VII opened Osborne Naval College. Here the cadets received their first two years training in the Royal Navy before passing on to Dartmouth. Nearly four thousand boys entered the College before it was closed in 1921, among them Edward VIII and George VI, as well as the late Governor of the Isle of Wight, Lord Louis Mountbatten.

After her mother's death Princess Beatrice lived in Osborne Cottage, but in 1912 she moved to Carisbrooke Castle which was to remain her summer home until the outbreak of the Second World War. She celebrated her eightieth year with a special gift from the people of the Isle of Wight, a tribute to her long years of service as their governor. In the courtyard at Carisbrooke she received an ornate and charming chamber organ, then believed to have been used by Princess Elizabeth, the daughter of Charles I who had died in the Castle. It was a pleasing gesture to a much loved Governor and the organ remains in the building that was her home.

ELEVEN

Railways and Tourism

The elegant, coach-borne visitors of the 18th century had come in relatively modest numbers to sample the arcadian scenery of the Island; but there were changes to come, and they came with the hiss of steam.

By the early 1840s the completion of a railway to Southampton, and a branch line to Gosport, signalled the gradual advance of a transport revolution.

Steam locomotives hauled visitors in increasing numbers to the south coast, to be greeted there by steam navigation across the Solent to the Isle of Wight where Ryde pier, opened in 1814 and grown by 1833 to half a mile, reached out to welcome them and ensure a landing without the muddy hazards of the 18th century.

So the railways promoters looked across with hungry, appraising gaze at the Island, and sized up the bucolic landscape for gradients and cuttings and viaducts. They made a brave try in 1847 when Newport enjoyed a rowdy public meeting to thrash out the pros and cons of a railway from Cowes to Newport, and all the vested interests had their say. In favour were the railway promoters, who wanted the dividends; Mr Pring and the town radicals, who wanted cheap transport; and many of the local shopkeepers, who saw the chance of commercial expansion for the town as an important transport centre. Against were the backers of a project to improve the river navigation up to Newport harbour; and – conclusively in this case – the landowners who did not want their estates noisily invaded and besmutted by trains. A good time was had by all, and the evening ended with the railway promoters being escorted by a silver band back to their hotel; but, for the time, victory remained with the opponents of the railway.

It was the twilight of the coaching age, and the Island was one of its last outposts. One observer commented in 1860: 'The treat of a ride on the top of a well-appointed four-horse coach, on a fine day, through beautiful country, is one peculiar to the Isle of Wight'.

That particular idyll was soon to finish. On 16 June 1862 the first trains began running over 4½ miles of track between Newport and Cowes; and on 23 August 1864 the Isle of Wight Railway opened a service between Ryde, St John's Road, and Shanklin. The ambition of the company was in fact to link Ryde and Ventnor, but they were having landowner trouble, and their chosen scenic coastal route from Shanklin to Ventnor through Luccombe and Bonchurch was firmly blocked. The railway builders however were determined to reach Ventnor by hook or crook, because it abounded in lush scenery and because of its sheltering cliffs behind the village which gave it a mild climate. So, as they could not go along the coast, the company went inland through Wroxall, and drove an approach tunnel through St Boniface Down to Ventnor. This extension opened on 10 September 1866.

'The treat of a ride on the top of well-appointed four-horse coach, on a fine day, through beautiful country, is one almost peculiar to the Isle of Wight ...' wrote Edmund Venables in 1860. Day visitors could buy a return ticket on the ferry which included a horse drawn coach tour such as this party is about to take.

The locomotive Bonchurch *coming into Ventnor station in the mid-1920s. A tunnel was driven under the downs in 1864-5 to connect Wroxall with Ventnor.*

The well-house at Carisbrooke Castle has long been an attraction to visitors. This Victorian view takes liberties with perspective but all the features present day visitors see are here. The axle shaft dates to the late 16th century when the present well house was built. The well is the only one in the country that continues to use donkey power.

The first harvest of this Ryde to Ventnor railway was an encouraging crop of dividends for the investors. The second was a cluster of three new towns for the Island, along the railway holiday coast. The medieval towns – Yarmouth, Newport, and Brading – had grown where they were for commercial reasons, at the limits of sea navigation for merchant ships (though, with the haven now drained, Brading is an inland town). the only newcomer since the medieval period had been Cowes which, starting in the 1550s as a scatter of houses adjoining the new fort, grew to be a bustling town by the 1630s because of the maritime traffic that the safe anchorage around the fort attracted. Now the railway had created the three Victorian towns – Ventnor and Shanklin from tiny fishing villages, and Sandown from almost nothing but a fort. This process began a little ahead of the Ryde to Ventnor line itself, benefiting indirectly from the holiday-makers who were being decanted in growing numbers by the railway service to the Hampshire coast, and who came on to the Island on a self-help basis; but when the Ventnor line opened, the pace of growth was most noticeable.

So far, the Island had two disconnected lengths of track. Enter now the Isle of Wight (Newport Junction) Railway which in 1868 received authority for a nine-mile line between Sandown and Newport. They must have been sunny optimists because the engineering problems were all too clear, notably the fact that the existing Newport station was on the west side of the harbour with most of the built-up town between it and Sandown. The only obvious approach from Sandown was from the south-east, which involved a costly viaduct over the harbour. The company beavered away, and on 1 February 1875 a service opened from Sandown to Shide on the south-eastern skirts of Newport; by 6 October the same year the line had been extended to Pan Lane; and on 1 June 1879 it finally reached Newport.

Meanwhile the Ryde and Newport Railway Company had on 20 December 1875 opened a line between Ryde St John's Road and Newport, so something like a network was beginning to appear. Until July 1887 the lines from Cowes to Newport and Ryde to Newport were administered by a joint committee; then in 1887 they merged with the Isle of Wight (Newport Junction) Railway to form the Isle of Wight Central Railway.

Still the system grew. Stirring things were happening in Brading harbour with its long history of attempted reclamation. An attempt to build a sea embankment in the 1500s having already failed, Hugh Middleton in the 1630s seemed to have had better success with the same project, but his embankment sprang a small leak, and by the time a messenger had toiled up to London to give Middleton the ominous news the sea

The level crossing at Shide, on the line between Sandown and Newport.

had broken through the dyke. Now in the 1870s there was a proposal to try again, and in 1874 the Brading Harbour Improvement and Railway Company was granted powers to build 2½ miles of railway line across the reclaimed marsh, linking Brading with Bembridge. Work proceeded, though with some setbacks. By 1880 the embankment was complete, but only wide enough for a footpath at the top, and not reinforced. During bad weather the sea broke over the top of the bank and went on to carve out a breach in it. This was repaired, and a new embankment was built inside the dyke; and, on 27 May 1882 the new railway opened, linking Brading with Bembridge through St Helens.

The great empty waste on the railway map was now West Wight, where of course the population was smallest and the financial pickings were not likely to be encouraging. Even here, though, the railway companies tried their luck, and on 10 September 1888 the Freshwater, Yarmouth, and Newport Railway began working its new line from Newport to Freshwater. It was, not surprisingly, rather undercapitalised, and the shortcomings of the track were such that the line began with freight traffic only. Finally, by using borrowed rolling stock from the Isle of Wight Central Railway, the line was able to open to passenger traffic on 20 July 1889. Those who were lucky enough to travel on it before its closure in 1953 will recall with pleasure the scenic quality of this delightful line. (British Rail used to run a crack 'express' called *The Tourist* from Ventnor to Freshwater, stopping only at Newport and Yarmouth). Relations between the F.Y. and N. Railway and the I.W. Central Railway were usually acrimonious, a particular flashpoint being the size of Central's proportion of the takings in consideration of their provision of the rolling stock.

Things came to the boil in 1913 when the F.Y. and N. Railway bought in some worn-out secondhand locomotives and coaches and cancelled its agreement with the Central Railway for the use of borrowed trains. Central's reply was to close Newport station to Freshwater trains. F.Y. & N. replied to this by building their own ramshackle station a few yards down the line, and the wretched passengers for Newport or for through connections had to disembark there and tramp in all weathers from one company's platform to the other's until the general outcry induced both companies to patch up the dispute. It was just at this time that a scheme was put up to the Government on strategic grounds, for a national subsidy towards the construction of a railway tunnel to the Isle of Wight. The most practicable route, according to the engineers involved in the project, was from Lymington to Yarmouth. If the Government had taken

Steam train and pier tram at Ryde Esplanade station, 1955: oil painting by John Fitzmaurice Mills.

The Victoria Pier, Cowes, was built in 1901 but its life ended when it was demolished after the end of the Second World War.

The chain pier at Seaview was built between 1879-1881 and the pierhead was added in 1889. Its life ended in December 1951 when two days of severe storm broke it up.

the bait, all the other railway companies in the Island would have been at the mercy of the Freshwater, Yarmouth, and Newport Railways for access to their vital line. It was a good try, but nothing came of it.

Meanwhile one more branch line had appeared in this remarkable microcosm of a network. The Newport, Godshill, and St Lawrence Railway Company built a branch line from Merstone – a truly rural station on the Newport to Sandown line – to St Lawrence just west of Ventnor, opening its service on 20 July 1897, though it was worked and eventually absorbed by the Isle of Wight Central Railway. On 1 June 1900 this line extended its service to Ventnor. By a quaint misnomer this terminus was called Ventnor Town, though in fact it was right away from the town centre, where the other station was.

In 1923 all the companies were absorbed by the Southern Railway – though, characteristically, in the case of the Freshwater, Yarmouth, and Newport Railway there was a seven-month delay while the company unsuccessfully took the Southern Railway to arbitration about the amount of the compensation – and in 1948 Southern became the Southern Region of British Railways. It was in 1952, way ahead of the Beeching era, that the closures began; and, sadly, the only part of the British Rail network still functioning in the Island is the line from Ryde Pier Head to Shanklin, now electrified and worked with former London Underground stock. Fortunately though, the flavour of the old tank engines with their noisy Westinghouse pump, and the aroma of the carriages, can still be sampled thanks to the enthusiasts of the Isle of Wight Steam Railway Centre at Havenstreet, where a length of the old Ryde to Newport line is still worked by steam trains.

The holiday trade thus generated by the trains has left another piece of tourist archaeology – the seaside piers. Ryde pier, opening in 1814 at first had the field (or, rather, the sea) to itself, and it went through various improvements and enlargements to accommodate such aids to transport as horse-drawn trams (later electrified) and finally steam trains making the link all the way from the pier-head to Ryde St John's Road. Then, as tourism grew spectacularly later in Victoria's reign (helped of course by her choice of residence at Osborne House) there was a succession of other piers: Ventnor in 1872, Yarmouth in 1876, Sandown in

1878, Seaview in 1880-81, and Shanklin in 1891. These piers had two functions. They made the various resorts directly accessible to visitors arriving by boat, thus providing healthy competition for the railways; and secondly they were strolling grounds for visitors once arrived, where the holiday maker could enjoy something of the sensation of being aboard ship without the discomfort of any movement. Ryde pier was described in 1860 as 'a most delightful promenade, crowded during the season with the usual tribe of walkers and loungers'.

The success of tourism is reflected in the extent of successive investment in amenities for the visitor. Ryde with its early pier had got off to a flying start. Apart from the various pier improvements such as the pier pavilion of 1842, the Esplanade was completed in 1856, and the canoe lake in 1880. Even in 1926 – at the time of the General Strike and on the eve of the Depression – a bandstand was built on the Western Esplanade at a cost of £4,000, and the following year the Eastern Esplanade Pavilion, built at a cost of £15,000, was opened.

Perhaps there was less evidence of conspicuous amenity spending on the new south-east holiday coast, but here the tradition was still to be established: these resorts were newcomers compared with Ryde. Nevertheless Shanklin sought to make the delights of the Old Village on its clifftop, and the scenic beach below, equally available with the opening in 1892 of the cliff-face lift. The tariffs for its use are perhaps revealing about the Shanklin clientele in the 1890s: passenger, 1d; bath chair with attendant, 3d. Even so, the recovery of the capital outlay of £4,000 must have been spread over many years, even if the bath chairs rolled in convoys along Shanklin esplanade. The opening of Shanklin pier the year before certainly provided a focus for seaside entertainment in the season. Applications immediately poured in from 'troupes and pierrots' to provide entertainment on the shore and the esplanade, and German bands were also among the performers.

There was some gathering of skirts about the impact of holiday entertainment on the local life-style, and one observer of the Sandown scene in 1902 complained that 'the Esplanade and Pier provide an undesirable accommodation for nigger troupes and hungry trippers'. Sandown moved up-market in 1934 with the building of a large Pier Pavilion, costing £26,000, but before that its holiday regime seems to have been simple and homely, relying mainly on the attractions of its gently sloping, sandy bay which justifies the place-name – and 'no shingle', added the Warde Locke guide's account of Sandown in 1925. This went on to describe bathing as 'the pride and glory of the place'. Bathing was allowed from the pier-head all day, Sundays included. Even at this date there was every effort to extend the season. The Carlton Private Hotel on the Esplanade ('terms 3 to 4 guineas according to Season and Rooms Chosen') was open all the year, with the added and necessary assurance that there were gas fires in the bedrooms. The Sandringham Hotel was a place for those interested in eating. They kept a Continental chef, and assured their guests of separate tables.

The Sandringham's inclusion of mention of a 'large garage' suggests that its guests might include several car owners – this well before the days of vehicle ferries with their convenient ramps. For those without cars however the 1925 season included coach tours in charabancs 'with resilient tyres equal to pneumatic tyres'. For 6s 6d (32½p) you could

This lively scene at Ryde captures the excitement and bustle as the paddle steamer Lorna Doone arrives at Ryde Pier in the 1890s.

The lift at Shanklin was opened in 1892 at a cost of £4000. For the first time visitors had easy access to the beach for a charge of 1d.

Beneath Seaview Chain Pier a pierrot troupe entertains visitors on a chilly summer day.

An afternoon tour from Sandown to Blackgang Chine and Carisbrooke Castle cost about 6s (35p) in the late 1920s and 1930s.

A fully-laden bus grinds slowly up Brading High Street towards the Bull Ring. The conductor is poised to leap out and place a wooden chock behind the rear wheel when the bus stops.

Some of the local place-names provided material for a popular holiday postcard in the 1930s.

Doubledecker buses were introduced by the Isle of Wight Motor Express Syndicate in 1905 and are here standing before the entrance to Ryde Pier.

St James's Square, Newport when it was the hub of Island life.

have a 55-mile afternoon outing to Freshwater, Alum Bay, and the Needles. The public bus services in the Island were for long run by a variety of family firms. Among these a private company, Dodson and Campbell, began operating in the Isle of Wight with three solid-tyre Daimler buses in 1921. When in 1923 they became Dodson Bros. Ltd., their little fleet had grown to 18 29-seater buses. When in 1929 they were taken over by the specially formed Southern Vectis Omnibus Company (in which the Southern Railway Company had a 50% share) this fleet had doubled to 36 vehicles. The expansion of the country bus routes certainly helped to hasten the decline of the railways; and this in turn is now helping the buses to fend off their modern competition from the private car.

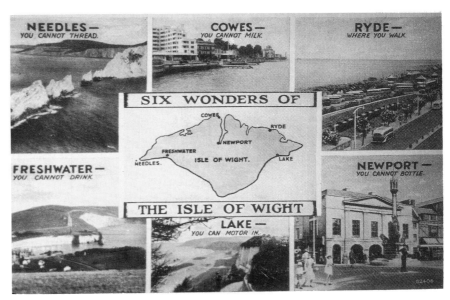

The two buses standing on the esplanade at Ryde were part of the Motor Express Syndicate's fleet. The company provided the only complete coverage of the Island in the early 20th century, travelling as far as Totland. A well-to-do party is approaching the motorised taxis, which outshine the horse cabs.

This tranquil scene at Bembridge explains the charm of this most easterly village, summed up in a 1925 guide, 'the average tourist passes unheedingly by ... but if you care for a place where the only daylight occupations are yachting, golfing, bathing and fishing ... then Bembridge is not likely to disappoint.'

A summer day at Cowes in the 1930s with visitors enjoying the view from the Green.

Tourism was not entirely an industry of private hotels and boarding houses. Bembridge at the eastern tip of the Island had been from its earliest days in the 1820s a particularly superior seaside village, but it also developed in the early 20th century as a holiday area for tented camps. In 1905 the 76th London Company of the Boys' Brigade established their first camp on Peacock Hill above Whitecliff Bay, then so empty that to meet someone on the beach was remarkable. From this the white tents blossomed each summer, followed by caravans and holiday chalets. Holiday camps were already opened in the Island before the second World War, but it has been the post-war period with its profusion of transport – ferries, catamarans, hydrofoils, hovercraft, and light aircraft – that has brought so many thousands of annual visitors eager to enjoy the pleasures of a seaside holiday.

During the present century tented camps have been a feature of the holiday scene at Bembridge. This one was photographed in 1987.

TWELVE

When the Sirens Sounded

About the middle of the afternoon on Wednesday 23 August 1939, with Hitler's forces massing in preparation for an attack on Poland, a telegram was received in County Hall at Newport from the Government in London: LOWIN TAKE ACTION PARAGRAPH SEVEN ACKNOWLEDGE.

'Lowin' was the code word governing the elaborate emergency procedures that had been prepared for a wartime situation, and this message was to lead to a ferment of activity by the County Authority on the Isle of Wight as elsewhere in England and Wales.

On 25 August the County Council Chairman decided to recall all officials who were on leave. Meanwhile further instructions kept coming from London and from the Regional Commissioner at Reading: about the supply of sandbags, evacuation of schoolchildren from city areas, painting of white lines on roads because of the blackout, and air raid precautions generally.

On Friday 1 September, the day on which Germany finally invaded Poland, the first evacuee schoolchildren from Portsmouth were received for billeting in the Island; fewer, though, than had been planned: 4,040 on the first day (8,000 expected) and 1,070 on the second day (5,700 expected). The Portsmouth parents were reluctant to trust the evacuation scheme and many held their children back. The official report to the Regional controller at Reading went: 'Temper and condition of children very good'.

The first impact of the war on many people was of course the blackout. The Isle of Wight Emergency Committee working from County Hall logged on Friday 1 September a message from the police : ALL LIGHTING RESTRICTIONS IN FORCE TONIGHT. So, two days before the outbreak of war, the Great Blackout had begun. The shop stocks of torch batteries disappeared within days, and enterprising electrical shops produced a reserve supply by breaking up high-tension radio batteries for the individual cells. Cars and buses had their headlights shrouded in blackout masks, and drivers had to adjust to the lower visibility.

Air Raid Wardens began to utter the familiar cry of 'Put that light out' on sight of any transgressing chink of light. On Monday 4 September a complaint was received at County Hall, from Portsmouth Dockyard A.R.P. station, that an Air Raid Warden at Bursledon near Southampton had reported seeing lights showing prominently at Cowes. There was an immediate hunt for the offender, and the answer was forthcoming within twenty minutes: the lights were caused by the reflection of moonlight on the roofs of buildings.

One inhabitant of Newport recalls experiences of the blackout in the town: 'Air raid shelters partly blocked the pavements in many streets, their ends marked by tiny lights from oil lamps at night. One man had a nasty accident when he walked into one after its light had gone out

A team of Red Cross volunteers practising rescue work while wearing gas masks. The nurses' training was used to the full when parts of the Island were bombed.

Territorials running to take up position in one of the coastal batteries in the early days of the war.

in the blackout. The streets were of course pitch dark at night and one had to find one's way about with a torch, the glass of which was covered with blue paper. It was so dark that I once walked into the next door neighbour's house by mistake one night'.

In other ways adjustment to wartime life in those quiet early months was gradual. The Territorials, the 189 Coastal Battery (Princess Beatrice I.O.W. Rifles) Heavy Regiment, R.A., manned the coastal batteries from as early as 22 August. The Island shipyards and aircraft factories, already working on contracts for the Services, intensified their work and took on extra labour. The Civil Defence Corps and the Observer Corps became fully operational, and the Women's Voluntary Service, the St John's Ambulance service and the Red Cross prepared for more intensive duties.

When in May 1940 the Germans broke through the Allied defences and occupied northern France there was a surge of signals traffic being received at County Hall in Newport from Whitehall. Arrangements were made for the receipt of foreign refugees in the Island, a check was made on the nationality of all aliens involved in Civil Defence, passes were issued to control admission to report centres, and the Island sprouted a crop of concrete pillboxes and tank traps, and the seaside had a changed vista of barbed wire entanglements on the beaches, and piers with their middle sections lopped away.

On 14 May 1940, even before the fall of France, the War Minister Anthony Eden made a broadcast appeal for recruits to a force of Local Defence Volunteers. They would have L.D.V. armlets as uniform and – although Mr Eden did not say so in the broadcast – nothing in particular for weapons. 'Dad's Army' had been born.

The response in the Isle of Wight was good, and the police soon had the job of checking about 4,500 enrolment forms. At first Hampshire and the Isle of Wight were divided into five sub-areas of which the Island was No. 4, under the command of Major T.C. Cunningham. It comprised five company areas: 'A' Company, commanded by Major-General W.R. Paul, for north-west Wight; 'B' Company, under Lieut.-Col. S. Davenport, for north-east Wight; 'C' Company, under Brigadier-General A.C. Aspinall-Oglander, for south-east Wight; 'D' Company, under Captain F. Nevill Jennings, for south-west Wight) and 'X' Company, under Major Musgrave, for East and West Cowes.

The L.D.V. were initially without uniforms and mostly without weapons, but in June the U.S.A. made available to Britain half a million

Waiting for Operation Sealion, 1940: a concrete pillbox guarding the causeway at Freshwater.

.30 calibre rifles, and the first L.D.V. issue of 250 rifles and 2,000 rounds of ammunition was delivered to the Isle of Wight – fifty guns to each of the five companies, with about eight rounds per rifle. As these guns had been made in 1917 and stored for more than twenty years, the grease in which they were packed had gone hard inside the barrels. 'C' Company in Shanklin hit on a drastic but effective solution to the problem: they took their rifles to the local bakery and left them in the ovens at a temperature high enough to allow the barrels to be cleared subsequently with ramrods and 'pull-throughs'. History relates that no complaints were recorded from customers about the flavour of the bread.

With the progression of the Local Defence Volunteers to Home Guard, the Island on 12 July 1940 became an independent zone under the command of Major T.C. Cunningham, with two battalions: the 19th (West Wight) Battalion Hampshire Home Guard, commanded by Captain F. Nevill Jennings, with headquarters at Fairlee House in Newport; and the 20th (Nunwell) Battalion Hampshire Home Guard, commanded by Brigadier-General A.C. Aspinall-Oglander (later succeeded by Lieut.-Colonel C.W. Brannon) with headquarters at Nunwell near Brading.

Thus the Island reverted to a centuries-old command structure for defence, with forces based on East and West Wight. The zone headquarters was at Fairlee House.

Other preparations had been made, too, in case the Island should be invaded and occupied. In conditions of extreme secrecy an underground resistance cell had been formed with the object of carrying out enough sabotage to tie down a substantial occupying force. 'Our training, of course, was very, very amateurish', the leader of the group recalled many years later, 'I called it completely Heath Robinson; but however we were very proud of the work which we were asked to do'. Some lengths of railway line were obtained, as well as explosives, and at a remote Island farm the group successfully practised demolition. The unit was later brought under the aegis of the Home Guard, and its members were provided with carefully disguised radio equipment. Secret dug-outs were made out in the country, and members of the unit had to practise living literally underground for extended periods.

German photograph of 'Fort Freshwater', part of a detailed briefing about the south coast of England prepared for Hitler's invasion forces in 1940.

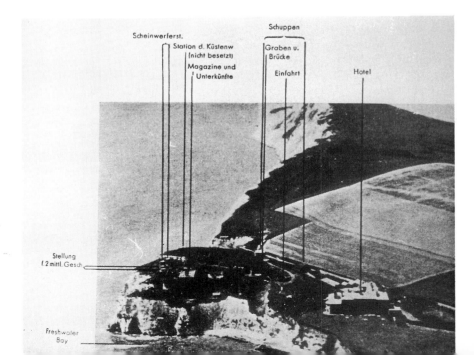

The Island was certainly, for a time, at risk of invasion. On 16 July, two days after Anthony Eden's broadcast setting up the L.D.V., Hitler issued his directive no. 16 ordering the planning of an operation against England.

> 'The landing will be in the form of a surprise crossing on a wide front from about Ramsgate to the area west of the Isle of Wight ... The possible advantages of limited operations before the general crossing (e.g. the occupation of the Isle of Wight or the County of Cornwall) are to be considered from the point of view of each branch of the Armed Forces and the results reported to me. I reserve the decision to myself. Preparations for the entire operation must be completed by the middle of August'.

In fact Hitler's staff quickly dissuaded him from attempting a Channel crossing on such a broad front as he had asked, and the Isle of Wight was taken out of the invasion area, at least for the initial landings. The atmosphere on the Island of course was tense. On 9 June the 12th Brigade of the 4th Division came over from the New Forest to form an Island garrison under the command of Brigadier Beak V.C. They made their Brigade headquarters at Billingham Manor, and Battalion headquarters for the 2nd Battalion the Royal Fusiliers was at North Court in Shorwell. In the east of the Island a battalion of the Black Watch was based at Havenstreet.

One quiet summer night a sentry of the Royal Fusiliers, on duty at Shorwell, heard the distant sound of a church bell, signal of an invasion. He called the guard commander, the guard commander called the duty officer, and then the lines started to buzz. Brigade headquarters was alerted, and it was only when someone telephoned the local vicar that the truth emerged: the sound was coming from a bell buoy off Brighstone. the sentry was said to have kept a low profile for a few days after this excitement.

With nerves so tense, though, there was always a risk from sentries mistaking natives for invaders. In Brighstone a sentry fired at an Air Raid Warden but fortunately missed. There was one tragic accident when a deaf farm worker at Fishbourne not hearing a sentry's challenge, was shot and killed.

If Hitler's operation 'Sea Lion' failed to materialise, the Luftwaffe certainly made its presence felt after the occupation of France. On 12 August Goering began his offensive against Britain's air defences with raids on five of the radio-location stations on the south coast, including the one at Ventnor which suffered serious damage, putting it out of action for eleven days. Next the aerial attack shifted to East Wight between Sandown and Ryde; and then to Cowes, though other parts of the Island had their air raid incidents. Someone in Newport recalls: 'Vivid memories ... rather like strips of film; hot summer days, with the wail of sirens and thudding of anti-aircraft guns. White puffs of shell bursts in the sky and twisting sheaves of contrails, accompanied by the wail of aircraft in combat and the sound of far-off machine guns firing. I particularly remember one raider, pursued by one of our fighters, clipped leaves off a fifty-foot high tree in the orchard behind our house in Caesar's Road, near to what is now the dairy boiler house in Westminster Lane'.

The build-up of troops and defences continued until by 1942 there were 17,000 men and two Home Guard Battalions in the Island. The defensive force was organised as an Independent Brigade, the 214th, with three beach defence battalions: the 7th Somerset Light Infantry, the 5th Duke of Cornwall's Light Infantry, and the 12th Devons who later fought their way with great distinction from Normandy to the Baltic as part of the 43rd Wessex Division.

Local industry meanwhile had stepped up its war production. At Cowes, J.S. White's shipyard was turning out a destroyer or other major naval craft every three months; and they and smaller firms at Bembridge, St Helens, East Cowes, and Wootton were also building motor torpedo boats, gunboats, launches, and landing craft. The Saunders-Roe factory at East Cowes was also busy,and apart from repair work it was also producing a stream of new aircraft, mainly Walrus and Sea Otter flying boats. Many of the war workers commuted each day from the Island holiday resorts, where the wartime collapse of the hotel and tourist industry had produced ample spare accommodation.

Even after the Battle of Britain the bombs kept falling, and the Civil Defence log shows a steady stream of incidents throughout the war. There was one raid of exceptional severity, on Cowes on the night of 4/5 May 1942. It was a fine evening with very little cloud, and a waning moon. The first attack came just before eleven in the evening. Mr Ransome, the bomb reconnaissance officer for Cowes, recalled the experience: 'I was on duty at the car park post in Northwood grounds when the alert went; and going outside of the post I saw the first bomb fall. I passed the remark to my co-warden. "That is not far from Beckford Road". In fact we found that it was in the next road. And then the raid started. The people began to come up to know where they could get shelter; we had a concrete shelter which we filled up; and half a dozen soldiers came along, and they said they had to get back to camp, and they didn't feel like it, so they stayed. So we were outside most of the time, and we could see these bombs coming down all around; and we saw the incendiary bombs, and just above us – less than a hundred yards – the road was lit up with the incendiary bombs. I've never seen anything like it. And away on the river bank the big fires – the yacht

Members of the Women's Voluntary Service assembled behind County Hall Newport before setting out with a street organ to raise funds during the 1939-45 war.

136

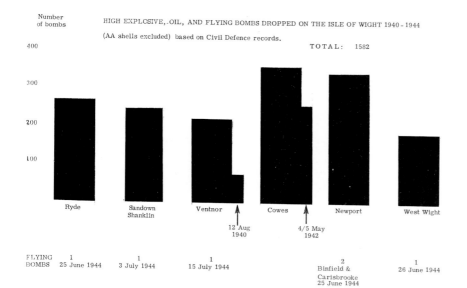

Number of bombs

HIGH EXPLOSIVE, OIL, AND FLYING BOMBS DROPPED ON THE ISLE OF WIGHT 1940-1944

(AA shells excluded) based on Civil Defence records.

400

TOTAL: 1582

300

200

100

Ryde	Sandown Shanklin	Ventnor	Cowes	Newport	West Wight

12 Aug 1940   4/5 May 1942

FLYING BOMBS	1 25 June 1944	1 3 July 1944	1 15 July 1944	2 Binfield & Carisbrooke 25 June 1944	1 26 June 1944

stores were on fire, and we also saw a small fire in the town near to my own place; and later I found that it was my own roof that was on fire'.

The bombers had gone soon after midnight, and the rest of the Island prepared to move to the help of the crippled community. Most of the public services in Cowes were out of action, including the telephone lines, so communication was mostly by despatch rider. The W.V.S. opened rest centres at Newport and Ryde, and the Southern Vectis bus company was put on standby to evacuate people from Cowes. Meanwhile the St John's Ambulance and other rescue services were busy on the dangerous job of extracting seriously injured people from houses that were in some cases on the point of collapse. As further reports from both sides of the river indicated the extent of the devastation, some mobile kitchens and supplies for a thousand people were sent to East Cowes. Over about two hours of the emergency rescue incidents thinned out; but as the medical services took breath and began to sort their equipment further reports came in of seriously injured people being found under the debris.

It was while this rescue work was going on, just before four in the morning, that the air raid sirens could be heard on the neigbouring mainland – the Cowes siren was not working because they had lost the electrical supply along with the other main services. Before the wardens could get everyone back into the shelters the next wave of bombers was overhead and the ordeal had resumed. The carnage was all the greater because the area was now full of the rescue services who had come in from other parts of the Island. This second wave of bombing lasted for an hour, and when daylight came a large part of the town was seen to be in ruins. The Saunders-Roe repair plant, situated where the hoverport now is, had been completely destroyed. Other large buildings including the main aircraft works in East Cowes, the Somerton works in West Cowes, and the Free French base off Arctic Road, were seriously damaged. The military canteen was damaged, and the British Restaurant contained an unexploded bomb. Church halls were full of homeless people, and the W.V.S. set up emergency feeding centres on both sides

This scene sums up the work of the WVS in the last war and during the period of severe food restrictions that followed it. With more modern equipment the members still continue to serve the community today.

137

of the river – at Trinity Hall in West Cowes, and at the Osborne Road Centre in East Cowes. 162 tons of bombs had been aimed at the shipyard and aircraft factories, of which 69 tons were on target. Four of the bombers were brought down by the intense anti-aircraft fire – much of it from the Polish destroyer *Blyskawica* which was refitting in Cowes at that time – but none of them came down on the Island. 68 civilians were killed, 48 seriously injured, and 70 slightly injured.

In the three days after the raid the W.V.S. cooking depots served between 15,000 and 20,000 light meals (tea, soup, and sandwiches) while the billeting officers struggled to place the homeless people elsewhere in the Island. It had been a raid not lightly forgotten, and Cowes had a much needed morale-booster when the Duke of Kent made a visit there on 19 August.

During the next year German 'tip and run' raids on the Island introduced a new tactic in the air war. Single planes would come in at low level to escape radar detection, drop their one bomb on a selected target and then return to the attack with their guns. These raids were unsettling because they came during the working day, and were quite without warning because of the ineffectiveness of the radar defences against this kind of attack. The first such raid on the Island was at Ventnor on 1 September 1942, and the last at Niton on 1 June 1943. There were nine of these raids altogether, and other targets included Ryde, Shanklin, Sandown, Cowes, and Newport – virtually all the towns. 33 people were killed, 61 were seriously injured, and 95 slightly injured.

Meanwhile the Island was taking on a role rooted deeply in its history: as a potential base for offensive military operations. In 1626 it had accommodated the Scottish troops involved in the expedition to La Rochelle, and in 1708 it was the base for General Erle's force of 6,000 men intended by Marlborough for a descent on the French coast and a march on Paris. Now in 1942 it held allied troops doing cliff assault training, and – during that summer – the Canadian forces in the later stages of their preparation for the raid on Dieppe. The Canadians had their headquarters at Osborne Court, Cowes.

Already from 1942 the Island was a controlled area. There were regulations limiting the entry of unauthorised persons, and those who were not normally resident in the Isle of Wight were banned from making their home there. Then security became even tighter. On 1 April 1944 the control was extended to a band of coast twenty miles deep, from

Preparations for the invasion of Europe: the 1st Independent Guards' Brigade Group on a landing exercise in Thorness Bay.

Newquay in Cornwall to the Wash. Even members of families were prohibited from moving into this area, and this ban included movement from the Island to the mainland, as well as vice versa. Day trips from the Island to Portsmouth and Southampton were, temporarily, a thing of the past. There were exceptions to these movement controls, for close family, and for school or college pupils, but permits were not easily given; and the security people had their ears to the ground, to say nothing of the phone line. A. L. Hutchinson in his history of the Island in wartime tells of a Land Army girl in Surrey phoning her sister in Carisbrooke at this time, suggesting that she should visit the Island in a borrowed W.A.A.F. uniform. The sequel to that conversation was a detective on the sister's doorstep in Carisbrooke the next day.

Well might security be strict, for the fleet of invasion vessels now filling the Solent was of prodigious size. More than 600 vessels were moored in 22 anchorages reaching from Spithead in the east, past Cowes and Calshot opposite Southampton Water, to beyond Hurst spit in the west. That was the main ship park. Then there were three more anchorages, one off Yarmouth and two off Seaview and St Helens. From the Observer Corps look-out on the summit of Mount Joy hill at Carisbrooke the Solent seemed to be so choked with shipping that one might walk across to the mainland from deck to deck. Yet this armada was only one of several massing at different points around the English coast.

With the exception of capital ships the Solent fleet comprised vessels of every kind: drifters, trawlers, motor minesweepers, colliers, tankers, fresh-water vessels, ammunition ships, transports, sloops, and all kinds of special landing craft. Then, overnight on 5/6 June 1944, in the best Thomas Woodroffe tradition, the whole fleet disappeared.

Preparation for D-Day: Churchill tanks being loaded onto tank landing craft in Thorness Bay.

The eve of D-Day: landing craft with warships anchored in the Solent.

A.L. Hutchinson in *The Island at War* tells how at 7.30 am on 6 June an officer at the War Office telephoned his wife at Seaview to tell her that the invasion of Europe had begun. Putting the phone down, she went to an upstairs window to survey the now empty Solent, and came back to say: 'Yes, the fleet has sailed'. Many of those aboard it, moreover, had been quartered on the Island. One Islander, Mr. Sam Watson, in his recollections of this event, described the very gradual build-up of the huge fleet, and went on: 'Then the Island was invaded by thousands of troops, billeted in empty houses near Ryde and Seaview, and places around there. And on the Saturday night the whole Island was full of troops. Sunday night, not one to be seen! They had gone aboard; and I have yet to find anyone who remembers seeing those troops leaving the shore in boats and going on to the landing craft'.

The fleet, having sailed, assembled with others some 20 miles south of the Island and then proceeded along a swept channel towards the designated landing beaches in Normandy. Not far behind it – also emerging from creeks and harbour in the Island – went sections of the Mulberry harbours that were to serve as do-it-yourself ports on the French coast; and tugs towing the huge bobbins of Pluto (Pipe Line Under the Ocean) oil pipe, which entered the sea at Shanklin, and with Brown's ice cream factory at Sandown converted into a pumping station for it; the Island's final umbilical link with the invasion to which it had given birth. The assembly of the Solent armada had been mainly the responsibility of 'Force J' at Cowes which had been established two years before for the planning of the Dieppe raid, and had now grown into the organising of the Normandy invasion. The Island moreover was the vital link between General Eisenhower and the landing beaches, because messages passed from the headquarters at Southwick by cable across the Solent and the Island, to the marine radio station at Niton (appropriately on the site of some of Marconi's earliest radio experiments) near the southern tip of the Island. When however contact was lost with Niton just on the eve of D-Day there was near chaos at Eisenhower's headquarters. A frenzied check along the track of the buried telephone cable finally revealed that an anti-aircraft battery on the Island, fixing up its camouflage netting, had in all ignorance hammered a stake right through the vital phone line. The Isle of Wight is only a small patch of land, but it can be important on occasions.

THIRTEEN

Into Modern Times

The nineteenth century can compare with the twelfth in one respect, in that church building in both was a major pre-occupation. In the Anglican tradition the first building period 1827-1849 is associated particularly with the fashionable towns and villages. St James's Lind Street, Ryde, and St Thomas's only a few yards away were built in 1827 and 1829. In 1845 Holy Trinity, Dover Street, was consecrated, an elegant building by Thomas Hellyer to suit a fashionable neighbourhood. At Ventnor and Bonchurch new churches were built and in Bembridge the first church was consecrated in 1829 when the parish was taken out of Brading. The second period came between 1858 and 1878 when earlier churches such as St Mary's Cowes had a modern chancel added and St Blasius, Shanklin, was rebuilt. At St Michael, Swanmore, a remarkable tribute to High Anglican ritualism was opened in 1863 but the grandest Victorian church, All Saints, Ryde, designed by George Gilbert Scott, and completed in 1872, was undoubtedly intended to surpass St Thomas's, Newport which had been re-built in 1854-55.

Other denominations were building too. In 1791 the Catholic Relief Act allowed Roman Catholic churches to be built and in the same year, through the generosity of Mrs Elizabeth Heneage, St Thomas of Canterbury in Newport was consecrated. Six years later she provided for the Catholic Church in Cowes. At Ryde it was another Elizabeth, the Dowager Countess of Clare, who was the benefactress. The church dedicated to St Mary, the house and school were built in 1846. Later she paid for the Dominican Priory at Carisbrooke to be built. It began life in December 1866 when Dominican sisters from Stoneyhurst, Lancashire arrived, the first community to return to the Isle of Wight since the Reformation. They were followed in 1888 by a community of Benedictine nuns who settled at Ventnor but moved to Appley in 1922. There they found an Abbey church and cloister already waiting, built by the Community of St Cecile who had lived at Ryde since 1906 but returned to France in 1922. These sisters had been exiled since 1901 and at the same time monks from the Benedictine community of Solesmes took refuge at Appuldurcombe. They later moved to Quarr where the present imposing Church and monastic house now stands. The architect, Dom Paul Bellot, was one of the community, 'a pioneer of 20th century Expressionism', who achieved a wonderful unity of stillness and strength in his brick church consecrated in 1912. All three communities remain today as an integral part of the religious life of the Island.

The most vigorous building programme, however, came from the non-conformists, who, very early in the century, were providing chapels which could seat several hundred worshippers. The Congregationalist, Baptists and Unitarians had survived from the seventeenth century and entered the nineteenth with a resurgence of endeavour. In 1802 Con-

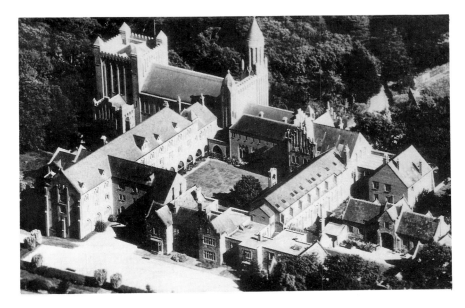

gregationalists built chapels at Cowes and Ryde and two years later a chapel was built in Nodehill, Newport which could seat three hundred. In 1774 the General Baptists built a small chapel in Newport's High Street and the free-thinking Unitarians had their own meeting house and burial ground in Pyle Street. Later they took over the Baptist chapel, adding a Sunday School and new Gothic frontage to it in 1825. West Wight was the province of the Particular Baptist in the eighteenth century and by 1816 they were meeting in a small cottage at Wellow. From this small beginning members went out to found the chapel at Castlehold, Newport in 1809, whose re-building in 1872 has left a fine facade, a temple to Victorian non-conformist self-assurance.

Methodism came to the Island in the eighteenth century and in October 1781 John Wesley wrote in his diary, 'I opened the new preaching-house just finished at Newport in the Isle of Wight.' But the movement grew slowly; there was none of the 'enthusiasm' that marked Methodism in other parts of the country – 'the native Islanders … possess less fire and originality'. At Newport progress was made and as early as 1803 a chapel to seat seven hundred was opened.

'Enthusiasm' had to wait until August 1823 when Mary Toms arrived at East Cowes during Regatta Week and amazed the local people with her vigorous open-air preaching. She was a missionary of the Bible Christian branch of Methodism with a lively message that appealed to the rural labourers. These people were their own church and the democracy involved in organising their meetings came up sharply against the squire and the parson. In Arreton they could hold no cottage meetings, afraid 'that they should lose their work and be turned out of their cottages'. In Shorwell they were 'baffled by the High Church interest.' In Brighstone they met entrenched opposition from Samuel Wilberforce, the rector, who drew up a statement urging farmers to refuse work to labourers who attended Bible Christian meetings. Every farmer signed – except the landlord of the house in which the dissenters met. But the little group of Bible Christians at Bembridge were encouraged by Legh Richmond, the curate at Brading. A committed evangelical himself, his

142

Annals of the Poor and particularly the stories of the *Dairyman's Daughter* made him a bestseller. His housekeeper and his parish clerk at Yaverland were both Methodists and had his support. The first public place of worship opened in Bembridge was a small chapel built by the Bible Christians in 1826. In 1844 the present larger chapel (now a private house) was built; the members borrowed £200, a trusting investment by workers who earned no more than 9s (45p) a week.

Religion and education have been associated since medieval times and the two voluntary bodies that established primary education in the nineteenth century were separately supported by Anglican and non-conformists. In 1812 the British School opened in Nodehill, Newport with non-conformist support and at Ryde Anglican subscriptions founded a National School. Between 1816 and 1821 Newport, East Cowes and Cowes each had its National School where parents were expected to make a small contribution to their children's schooling. At Newport this was one penny a week, to which the management committee added 1s (5p) for each child, raising a fund to provide the poorest children with clothes.

In Lugley Street, Newport, a charitable school for poor girls had been opened in 1761, where they received a basic education and were taught domestic work. By 1880 the school had moved to Crocker Street where the figure of Blue Jenny wearing the distinctive uniform, still identifies the school house, number sixty two.

In the countryside most villages had to wait until the later nineteenth century for general education but some were better endowed. Godshill's grammar school dated to the sixteenth century, Chale had a school in 1784 and Brighstone's small school opened its doors early in the nineteenth century. The typical progress of village education can be followed at Locks Green near Newtown where this tiny hamlet had a Dame School in Bethel Cottage before the Church of England School was opened in 1870. Miss Ward of Northwood House had left a small legacy for the education of the village children and Mr Mew of Porchfield House gave as much stone as could be taken from Quarry Field for the building. The purpose of Victorian education was summed up at Bembridge village school where the 'labourers' children' passed out into the street each day beneath a Gothic doorway inscribed 'Onward and Up-

The gravestone of Elizabeth Wallbridge which can still be seen in Arreton churchyard.

Girls at the 'Blue Jenny' charity school, Newport, taken in the centenary year of its foundation in 1761. The girls were trained to be good servants.

143

New House, Bembridge School was designed by Baillie Scott and built in 1925.

Two Parkhurst boys and an officer. The boys' ages ranged from 7-17 years and most had been sentenced to 7 years transportation.

ward'.

Some children could move on to secondary education in the twentieth century when Sandown Grammar School opened in January 1901. At Newport secondary education evolved from the Pupil Teacher Centre, established in 1897 with voluntary support, to give advanced education to the young assistant teachers in local schools. It was they who moved into the new Technical Institute and Free Library at Nodehill in 1904 and it was their headmistress, Miss Mabel Hinton, who continued as headmistress of the secondary school which opened in 1907. This was a convenient arrangement but when she resigned in 1910 the education committee consciously chose a woman to succeed her. Miss F. J. Monk came from the same mould as the pioneering founders of women's education. She was an inspiring and forceful head teacher for twenty years, establishing a sound foundation for the new Grammar School.

The lack of a Grammar School at Ryde led directly to the foundation of Ryde School. Discussions between local people and W.L. McIsaac, the headmaster of the Upper Grade School at Ryde led to a meeting in December 1920 at which the mayor of Ryde acted as chairman. He emphasized the fact that local boys had to look elsewhere for grammar school education and supported the move to found a school in Ryde. On the 25 April 1921 Ryde Grammar School opened at Hanover House, George Street, with forty six boys and in September the following year the first seven boarders arrived. Its position as a Ryde school was made abundantly clear in 1928 when the Mayor himself helped in the search for larger premises in order to keep the school within the borough. He found Westmont, the present site, and in the summer of that year the boys moved in. In 1932 the name Ryde School was adopted to make clear its independent status.

A little earlier than Ryde School two boarding schools were founded, Upper Chine School came to Shanklin in 1914 when girls from Rockhill House, Folkestone, arrived at what was intended to be a holiday home for foreign students, but the war intervened and Upper Chine became a permanent school. In 1919 a distinctive boarding school opened at Bembridge when John Howard Whitehead began his school with nine boys. He established a curriculum in which art and craft had a major place, a philosophy of education which was much in advance of its time.

A unique aspect of juvenile education began the Island's association with prisons. Prisoners had been kept within its water from 1809 when the hulks *Buffalo* and *Dido* were moored at the entrance to the Medina, crammed with six to seven hundred men, but the new prison at Parkhurst was to be model establishment under the control of the Home Office. The hospital of the redundant Albany Barracks was selected as suitable to be converted into a training prison for boys who were normally kept in the hulks until they were old enough to be transported. The first intake was carefully selected from the *York* hulk at Portsmouth and the boys arrived on Boxing Day 1838. Reading, writing, arithmetic and general subjects were taught, with practical training in farm work, carpentry, bricklaying and house painting. From ninety six boys in 1839 the numbers rose and extra buildings were needed for the six hundred and twenty who were there in 1847. The day began with drill at 7am and work ended at 6.30. The boys wore a military style uniform with the initials PP on the tunic, trousers and hat. The work was hard but the regime

was humane and in the 1840s and 1850s under Governor George Hall many advanced methods of treating juvenile prisoners were introduced. The first boys left from Cowes for Western Australia and New Zealand in 1842 and in the ten years during which the colonies received them fifteen hundred Parkhurst boys were transported, the greater part settling well into their new countries.

In April 1864 the last boys left Parkhurst for more modern institutions. Since 1863 women prisoners had occupied separate accommodation but they went in 1869 and Parkhurst became a prison for male offenders, the first of the three prisons that form the complex still standing in the same area.

The new buildings that were rising all over the Island were brick built; checker-pattern red and blue-black or soft red in the early years of the century, yellow brick after 1860 and an undistinguished red in Edwardian times. Brick was *the* Victorian building material and the brick arch construction the foundation of all their major large works. In the Island the best examples of monumental Victorian brick building are found in the forts that were built in the 1850s and 1860s. These were an expensive response to fears of French aggression at this time, but, as at Carisbrooke in the sixteenth century, they were never required to be used in war in the period of their construction.

There were good strategic reasons for embarking on the string of nineteenth century forts in the Solent. The French navy was already building iron clad warships which required much heavier artillery to pierce the hull. In addition heavily armed warships had to be prevented from penetrating too close to the shore from where they could bombard land targets. The Isle of Wight forts were the first line of defence in protecting Portsmouth dockyard and the two earliest to be built, Fort Victoria and Fort Albert were part of the defences covering the western entrance to the Solent.

Fort Victoria was built on top of the earlier Sconce Point Battery during 1852-53 at a cost of £38,000 but it was never satisfactory as it was too near sea level. Fort Albert was completed in 1856 and by 1870 was as out of date as Fort Victoria. But it had an interesting renewal of life in 1885 when the fort was modified for experimental work on a new torpedo. The Brennan Locomotive Torpedo was the first true guided missile and it was treated as a highly secret weapon in the naval armoury. The Needles Battery was completed in 1863 and Golden Hill Fort, on a site above Freshwater which gave magnificent visibility from the Channel to the Solent, was ready in 1867.

At the east of the Island Bembridge Fort was built between 1862-67, again sited on the downs commanding the eastern approach to Portsmouth. These defensive buildings are usually seen only in terms of their military use but whilst being built they provided employment at a time when jobs were scarce.

One of the problems that faced the Island in the eighteenth century was its isolation from the county hospital in Winchester. Thrown back on their own resources the gentlemen Guardians of the Poor had gradually accepted into workhouse sick wards patients who were not paupers in the strict sense. It had meant that they expanded the medical services far beyond what could be expected in most rural workhouses of that time. By the 1820s a detached hospital had been built, described in 1832 as a 'large hospital' and in 1834 as the 'Upper Hospital', probably on the site of the present day St Mary's hospital. Sick wards remained in the workhouse, gradually deteriorating, until the Local Government board insisted that new wards should be built.

At this time the 'Lower Hospital' or infirmary had twenty-four beds for male patients and twenty-five for female but the Local Government Board inspector had reported that there was no day room for convalescent patients, no bedrooms for the assistant nurses and that the surgery was used as the nurses' sitting room. William Stratton was appointed architect in the summer of 1880 and work began. Progress was slow and patients were only able to move in in the spring of 1883; even then all was not well. The main complaint of the LGB Inspector was that a covered way from the main building would have to be sheltered in the winter. This brought a rare show of defiance from the committee who replied tartly, 'these corridors were built by the advice of Local Gvt. Bd. and the plans were inspected and approved by that Authority...' they were in no position to recommend the committee 'to expend any of the ratepayers money on alterations'. The new wards had cost £6,000 and contained fifty two beds, they had water closets and were lighted by gas. But more revealing of changing attitudes was the decision that all wards and the day room should have pictures hung on the walls.

In 1898 the final phase of building in the workhouse ended with the opening of new receiving wards and imbecile wards. The care of the insane had fallen to the Guardians since the eighteenth century and, as there were no private mad houses in the Island, they had always taken in non-paupers when this was necessary. In 1813 separate accommodation with wards and convalescent rooms was built and in 1822 the workhouse was licensed as a lunatic asylum. When the county asylum at Knowle opened the incurables were sent to the mainland but visiting by their families was virtually impossible and in 1850 the harmless incurables were returned. The problem of caring for the insane was finally resolved when the large asylum at Whitecroft, Gatcombe was opened in 1896, leaving only the imbeciles remaining at the workhouse.

Princess Beatrice inspected the new wards in 1902 and met Elizabeth Gilliard, the oldest woman inmate, then aged 92. For this occasion she had on her bed the quilt made by the Princess's mother many years before. Queen Victoria's visit to the workhouse in 1869 had been made with little notice to the staff. The governor was given only two hours warning before the Queen stepped out of her carriage to see the institution in its every day life and her satisfaction in 'the good order and cleanliness' says much for the management of the old building.

The Poor Law Union continued to act an embryonic local government for most of the century. Guardians were elected local representatives and it was in this capacity that women entered local government. Mrs Frances Bull attended her first meeting on the 8 July 1895, one woman among forty-seven men. She proved to be a model guardian, concerning herself mainly with children's affairs, and she was followed by other women who gave 'invaluable services' to the community. When the corporate life of the Guardians of the Poor ended on the 27 March 1830 the clerk rehearsed the areas of local government for which they had been responsible. They acted as the first registrar for births, marriages and deaths; they had appointed the first district medical officers in 1830; they had collected poor rates and assessed property for rating, and for rural parishes they had acted as Sanitary authorities. In 1890 the Isle of Wight County Council came into being and was the natural successor in local government to the Guardians. They continued to follow government directives on poor law policy until in 1930 the public assistance committees of the County Council took over their remaining powers.

*   *   *

In the everyday life of the Island there was a short period each summer when one town became a glittering social spectacle. During Cowes Week the fashionable world filled every hotel and house, basking in the glory reflected from yachting's inner sanctum, the Royal Yacht Squadron. The origins of the Squadron lie in the early years of the nineteenth century when gentlemen of like interests were forming private clubs. Racing was already popular with those wealthy enough to build and man their own yachts and in 1815 this loose association became a club of gentlemen enthusiasts for salt-water sailing. In 1833 it became the Royal Yacht Squadron and in 1854 the members were able to lease Cowes Castle which was to become their permanent home. The old building was inadequate for their needs and Anthony Salvin the distinguished Victorian architect was asked to prepare plans for restoration and extension. Between 1856-57 the work went ahead and on New Years Day 1858 the light on the battery was lit for the first time.

The golden days of Cowes came at the end of the nineteenth century

The steam yacht Xarifa, *built at Cowes in 1894.*

Members of the Royal Yacht Squadron assembled before Cowes Castle during Cowes Week 1895. The figure wearing the white cap in the foreground is the Emperor of Germany. In the background the pale figures of the ladies can be seen on the lawn.

Morgans of Cowes were the fashionable tailors of the yachting world, and it was they who introduced the tailor-made blue serge lady's costume of the late 19th century.

when the Prince of Wales stood at the centre of social life. He was elected to the Squadron when he was twenty eight and became senior flag officer, in which post he served for nineteen years, only relinquishing it in 1901 when he became king. The Prince was able to persuade the Squadron to relax some of its regulations, not least the prohibition on women entering the Castle precincts. This transformed the staid green-turf surrounding Cowes Castle:

'The Squadron Gardens are thronged, as ever, morning noon and evening' wrote a yachting correspondent in 1901, 'including Miss Langtry, looking very pretty in mauve…'. This small item of news indicates the position of Cowes in the social world. It was a great centre for yacht racing but it was more than that. An editorial in *The Yachting Monthly* sums up Cowes Week just before the First World War, 'as a yachting fixture … it is pre-eminently a fixture in the calendar of society rather than a race meeting; it is indeed the show week of the sport … As an annual gathering … Cowes Week is *the* week of the year, and that in which one may see the finest yachts of the world in one anchorage.'

This was visibly true; moored in the harbour there floated the most beautiful steam yachts, the ultimate expression of 'conspicuous consumption' that could be found in a closed society that delighted in the display of its wealth. The owners of these floating palaces gradually created what were in reality floating country houses. In Sir Thomas Lipton's *Erin* the saloon with its patterned carpet, deep armchairs, display cabinets, tiled fireplace and ornate overmantel could have been a drawing room in any castle or mansion. The Royal Yacht *Victoria and Albert II* took Osborne into the Solent with pretty chintzes. Others adopted a more masculine style with red leather button seats, and all made lavish use of mahogany. Keeping up the yachts during the season was expensive. 'A snug little yawl' of 80 tons employed a crew of nine, captain, mate, five seamen, steward and cook who contributed to end of season expenses totalling just under £1000. This was an average expense for that size of yacht based on the usual assessment of £12 for each ton of the vessel.

148

The people of Cowes, in the main, looked on from the fringe, thankful for the prosperity that even so short a season brought, but they did gain one valuable long term amenity through the generosity of G.R. Stephenson, son of the railway engineer. He celebrated the first occasion on which the new Princess of Wales came to Cowes by giving £500 to purchase the land beyond the Castle, now Prince's Green, as an open space for the town. When the Prince and Princess attended Cowes Town Regatta in 1882 she and her two daughters were noted as wearing costumes supplied by Messrs. J. Redfern of Cowes, a notable supplier of fashionable yachting clothes. In the High Street, was another distinguished tailoring firm John Morgan, tailor to the Royal Yacht Squadron, who was the first to design the blue serge yachting costume for ladies.

At the west of the Island, removed both in distance and style of living from the fashionable world, the Poet Laureate, Alfred Tennyson, had made his home at Freshwater. When Tennyson first came to this western corner in 1850 it was still remote and secluded. The mainland railway stopped at Brockenhurst, after which a horsebus took the traveller on to Lymington, although it could not be guaranteed to arrive in time to catch the boat. This was the situation that faced the Tennyson family when they first came to their new home. The steamer had left and a rowing boat carried them across the eight mile stretch of water to Yarmouth.

Farringford was all that Tennyson wished; an eighteenth century castellated house beneath the downs, Freshwater Bay and Afton Down framed in the drawing room window and towering cliffs only a mile away behind the house. Here they could look forward to a happy family life. Farringford was taken furnished on a three year lease with an option to buy at the end of that time. Tennyson made his study in a small room at the top of the house and he began to take the long walks that made him familiar with the country and coast of west Wight. During this period he was drawing on his surroundings to create the long poem *Maud*, published in 1855, which was to bring him sufficient to buy Farringford outright. The first four *Idylls of the Kings* and *Enoch Arden* came from this happy period when his two boys were growing up and he

149

Seaside cottages with butlers' pantries were still being built in the 20th century; this was built at Cowes.

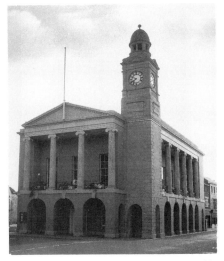

Queen Victoria's jubilee was celebrated in Newport by adding a clock tower to the Town Hall. It has not always been admired but was clearly an improvement on the earlier bracket clock and can be seen today as a handsome addition to the building.

and his family were untroubled by the outside world.

Progress determined that this should not last. From the 1860s Tennyson was a national 'personality' whose individual dress of flowing black cloak and broad brimmed black hat was universally known. He was also a friend of Queen Victoria who admired and found consolation in his works during her long widowhood. There were recurrent rumours of his being granted a baronetcy and this only added to public interest. He was persecuted by unbearable intrusion into his private life during the summer months when strangers might be found hiding up trees or behind hedges, or even peering in through windows to catch a glimpse of the great man. The bridge he built over the sunken lane that separated the house grounds from the wilderness was his own route to avoid obtrusive strangers. In the late 1860s he built himself a new house on Blackdown in Sussex and here he escaped each summer, returning to the Island in the autumn when the last of the visitors and day trippers had left.

It was while making the crossing from Lymington to Yarmouth one evening that Tennyson witnessed the scene that was to produce what is probably his best loved poem. A pilot was leaving an outward bound steamer near the Needles having guided it safely through the Solent and Tennyson was struck by the symbolism of the moment. He scribbled down four verses on the inside of an old envelope and, in 1889 as part of a collection of poems 'Crossing the Bar' entered English literature.

* * *

The end of the nineteenth century brought some considerable improvements in the lives of ordinary people. They were still tied to long hours, hard work and little leisure but compared with their parents and grandparents they were well off. Their traditional diet of potatoes, bread, tea, with a little cheese and bacon was gradually transformed by imported flour and meat from North America and the Empire. While farmers suffered, food prices plummeted and for the first time working people could consider meat as a regular food. The weekly diet of a family living in Newport in the 1890s illustrates how much life had improved. Sunday dinner was always a beef joint, with baked potatoes and suet pudding. With beef at 2s 2.6d (10-15p) lb there was enough for cold meat on Monday and cottage pie on Tuesday, while later in the week stew made from beef cuttings at 4d (2p), rabbit pie or bacon and onion roll all varied the diet. Flour cost 1½d(1p) for 3lb, a good piece of suet and pure pig's lard about 1d. There were no puddings except rice pudding and suet dumplings and no cake except at Christmas. It was all solid stodge but hard work used up the calories. The very poor remained, but front parlours, good food and a reasonable education were more common amongst working people.

People living in the towns were more certain of medical care. The Ryde subscription hospital opened in 1842 and was steadily enlarged throughout the 1860s. At East Cowes the Home for Seamen became the Frank James Hospital in 1904 and in Shanklin the Arthur Webster Memorial Cottage hospital opened the following year. Shanklin also had the Scio Hospital for Children. Like the others it was established through the generosity of an individual, in this case Mrs Scaramanga of West

Hill. It was the only children's hospital in the Island and patients were accepted free of charge.

There were also town dispensaries which were established early in the nineteenth century in the Isle of Wight. The first was opened in Castlehold, Newport, in 1823, not by private charity as was usual but by the Guardians of the Poor. Their doctors attended early in the morning dealing with simple ailments and prescribing medicine for the poor of the town and in neighbouring villages. Six years later a dispensary was opened in Cowes through the initiative of two clergymen, the Rev J.B. Atkinson and the Rev J. Ward. Here the local chemist, Mr Manning, acted as secretary and prepared the medicines from his shop in the High Street. The burden of illness was lightened for the poor who previously had to walk or send to Newport for medicine.

The Ryde dispensary opened in 1842, this time through the efforts of the vicar of Newchurch and a local surgeon, Dr Mark Brown. The doctors gave their services free and out-patients were received on the recommendation of persons who subscribed to the dispensary at a minimum rate of five shillings a year. There were also fund raising events and when particularly expensive medicines were needed subscribers would be asked to bear the cost. This dispensary had to cover a wide area from Bembridge, Brading and St Helens in the east to Wootton in the west. In 1848 the dispensary was in Cross Street, run by Mr John Wavell the chemist but by 1871 it was in Kelso Cottage, Spencer Road. The work expanded at the end of the century when in 1890 418 patients were treated. This led to new premises being opened in 1895 at the junction of Swanmore Road and West Street, including now a house for a resident dispenser.

Life in the countryside changed little. Lord Ernle, Roland Prothero, in his autobiography, *Whippingham to Westminster*, described his home Whippingham rectory in the 1860s as being self contained and self-sufficient. Milk, butter, eggs, poultry, fruit and vegetables they provided themselves and they brewed their own beer– 'I cannot remember the time when I did not have my little silver mug filled with beer at my dinner.' They also made their own soap, pomatum and perfumes. In a rectory household the poor were not forgotten. 'After morning Service, my father came into the servants' hall and carved a sirloin of beef into dinners for the … old people who could not come to church… It was my duty to add the baked potato.' This was a household that would not have been out of place in the seventeenth century.

The farm labourer's wage rose very slightly; it was 14s (70p) in the 1870s and could still be as low as 16s (80p) in the early twentieth century. Carters earned more, as much as 29s (£1.45) at the time of the First World War, but they began work at 5am to prepare the horses. Other labourers arrived at 6.30 or 7am, depending on the season, as their forebears had done in the eighteenth century. A ten or eleven hour day followed with one hour for lunch and a short break for breakfast and tea. Carters and cowmen usually lived in tied cottages, rent free, but labourers rented their cottages which had a large garden in most cases to grow vegetables and keep a pig. Women did the same work as their ancestors, planting beans in February and March, weeding, hoeing, haymaking and gleaning for themselves after the corn was carried. A good gleaner could help the family income considerably and the corn sack was an object of admiration among her neighbours. Illness still presented problems in rural villages. The Parish doctor for Porchfield lived at Newport and in the 1870s he had to walk out to visit his patients, a round journey of fourteen miles.

Only one area of the Island has a history of heavy industry, the water-side works of Cowes and East Cowes where naval, and merchant ship-building had grown up with the communities and where later yacht building would add to the variety of work. There was a fine distinction between the two sides of the river which was nicely shown in a 1937 Directory where both Uffa Fox and Marvins listed boat building and shipbuilding as their East Cowes occupations, whereas in Cowes Uffa Fox was a yacht designer and Marvins had a yacht building yard.

In earlier times the distinction was not so obvious, and it was to Cowes that a new shipbuilding firm came in the opening years of the nineteenth century. The White family came to the Island in 1801 with a history of shipbuilding behind them that went back to the seventeenth century. In Cowes they built Thetis Yard on the Medina and within fifty years were the major firm employing several hundred men. As early as 1846 they established their connection with the lifeboat service when the two brothers John and Robert White, with their neighbour Andrew Lamb patented the Lamb and White Lifeboat. Later the firm was to build over one hundred and thirty lifeboats for the RNLI. Their speciality for building high speed boats for the Navy was to remain the backbone of their production. In 1870 they were invited to build one of the first torpedo boats and later they were among the firms asked to submit designs for destroyers to combat the torpedo threat.

In 1889 the company moved into heavy engineering in Cowes, making boilers and engines, and in 1898 the family firm became a public liability company when the name J. Samuel White was born. During the First World War the company was fully engaged building destroyers as it was in the Second World War when twenty five were built, as well as motor torpedo boats and launches. In 1939 they had also established the Somerton works for manufacturing aircraft components.

One hundred years after Whites arrived, in 1901, a new company came to the Island. S.E. Saunders specialized in designing high speed boats with a light hull and it was this light construction that attracted the pioneers of flying boats. They wanted the least possible weight for the frames and Saunders were able to produce this using two layers of

The White family of shipbuilders came to Cowes in 1801, built Thetis Yard and became the major shipbuilding and repairing firm in the Island, introducing heavy engineering into the economy.

J. SAMUEL WHITE & Co. LTD
Shipbuilders and Engineers
COWES, ISLE OF WIGHT
London Offices · · 8, Duncannon Street, W.C.2

plywood. In 1914 the firm was building seaplanes for the Admiralty, initiating the move into plane making. The Osborne Plywood Works was opened at Folly on the Medina, but the post war depression hit the firm badly and they were in a very low state when Sir Allick Verden-Roe, the founder of the Avro Company, put money into the company which became Saunders-Roe. During the Second World War they continued making seaplanes and in the post war period returned to building civilian seaplanes culminating in the Princess Flying Boat.

Immediately following the war it was not unreasonable to suppose that expanding air transport would continue to use water-based machines. These had been the glory of the long distance routes in the 1930s and BOAC was still thinking in these terms when it embarked on the Princess Flying Boat. She anticipated the large passenger carrying planes of the future with her projected one hundred and one passengers flying non-stop between London and New York. But in 1952 BOAC cancelled the project. So many landing fields had been built during the war and pilots were experienced in using grass and tarmac that it was clear the future of aviation was to be with land operated planes. This was a set back for Saunders-Roe but the company was remarkably versatile. In 1947 they had designed a fighter plane powered by two turbo jet engines and this led on to work on Black Knight, the rocket used for firing the Blue Streak missile. The engines were built at Cowes and tested below the Needles Fort before being sent for trials to Woomera in Australia. Finally Saunders-Roe turned to hovercrafts when they were commissioned to build the first manned machine in 1959 and by 1964 the commercial production of hovercraft had begun.

These two firms are significant in the modern period of Island history because their size and type of work brought mainland industrialization into a rural community. Their contribution to economic well being for hundreds of families could not be matched by older ship and yacht building firms. The weakness of such large scale employment lay, as ever, in its vulnerability to economic depression. Smaller firms with a less costly infrastructure could batten down hatches and wait until the storm passed. These yards and machine works, like the nineteenth century counterparts, could not.

The town was not unused to depression, for within three years of the end of the First World War it felt the chill winds of recession – winds that were to blow right across the Island. In August 1921 a mass meeting was held on the Parade to speak for the 1400 unemployed in the area. The Cowes Unemployment Relief Committee was formed and a deputation sent to meet the Guardians commitee at Newport. The men asked for work or maintenance but the committee was incapable of dealing with such numbers. 327 applications for relief had been received and each had to be examined before help could be given. The workhouse works' committee agreed to put painting and building work in hand and men were hired to help with the potato harvest, but these were palliatives and the Relief Committees in Newport, Cowes and Ryde were occupied in making grants.

The scale allowed was 10s (50p) each for a married man and his wife, with 5s (25p) for each child, all given in kind not money. No single person received any help. The local councils were asked to undertake public works; at East Cowes the footpaths were surfaced and road re-sur-

This advertisement succinctly sums up the output of Saunders Roe. S.E. Saunders came to the Island in 1901 and the company was joined by Allick Verdon-Roe in 1928.

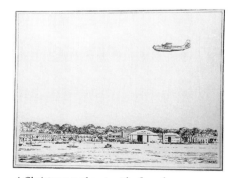

A Christmas card sent out by Saunders Roe showing the Princess flying boat passing their headquarters at East Cowes.

faced. At Cowes bolder ideas were put forward. The Harbour Commissioners were prepared to build a new breakwater and the Guardians supported this but the Ministry of Health refused to sanction the work. Another proposal to build an esplanade at Egypt was approved by the Ministry and went ahead. The inevitable problem of keeping warm in winter arose and extra allowances of 1s (5p) or 2s (10p) in exceptional cases were made when the price of coal in Newport rose above 3s 3d (17p) per cwt. At Christmas an additional weekly allowance of 2s and 1s for each child was granted.

These were grim times throughout the Island and in this period the Union of Agricultural Workers was continually attempting to raise the wages of its members, but reconciliation with the employers on this matter was impossible. In 1924 the Hampshire and Isle of Wight Wages Board was set up and it approved a wage of 30s (£1.50) for a week of fifty or fifty four hours, depending on the season. Far from improving the situation worsened and brought an extra-ordinary proposal from Mr F. Hollis in 1937 advocating a system of family allowances to be paid by the Treasury to the agricultural labourer who had three or more children under school leaving age. This was going back to the eighteenth century scale system and would once again have isolated the labourer as a near pauper. Mr G. Moody was quick to respond that labourers had their self respect and that it was up to farmers to pay proper wages. The motion was unanimously rejected. It was the outbreak of war that brought nationally agreed minimum wage rates and an agreement on hours of work. Farm workers could now expect a minimum of three pounds a week with agreed overtime rates.

A Mark III version of the 'Islander' with a third engine mounted on the tail, designed and built by Britten Norman of Bembridge.

One of the most modern of hovercraft made by the British Hovercraft Corporation at East Cowes. The hovercraft, an AP1-88/200 for the Canadian Coastguard, is to be used on the St Lawrence river for supplying lighthouses and ice-breaking.

The farm labourer, that historic figure who has been the archetypal worker since medieval times has now almost disappeared. There were four hundred and twenty four in 1984 and those who remain are as skilled in mechanical as field work. His place has been taken by members of the service industries which employ seven out of ten workers. In this area tourism continues to fill the role that began in the late eighteenth century, creating summer labour but contributing to winter unemployment – still a chronic problem in Island life. Few large firms remain and only The British Hovercraft Corporation dominates the sea front at East Cowes, a reminder of older firms now gone. A remnant of the aircraft industry can still be found at Bembridge airfield in what must be the most attractive site in the Island. Pilatus Britten Norman remains a testimony to John Britten and Desmond Norman who started in 1953 by modifying training aircraft for agricultural work and then in the 1960s designed the elegant and useful 'Islander'. At Northwood Plessey Radar continues with research work, anticipating the twenty-first century. But this in the tradition of Island life. In July 1897 Marconi set up his wireless telegraph station at Alum Bay and foreshadowed the twentieth century.

So our historical journey beginning with those dinosaurs in their fresh-water lagoon some 110 million years ago ends for now with the research and development of the next generation of radar; and this contrast of old and new sums up the particular blend of tradition and innovation that gives the Island its special character. Cherishing its history but responsive to what is new, it has nurtured the arts and sciences alike: in the 19th century Keats, Tennyson and Swinburne alongside Darwin and Marconi; in the 20th century Louis MacNeice, J.B. Priestley and David Gascoyne alongside the inventors and developers of the hovercraft, rocket technology, and electronics. Whatever the 21st century may bring, we can hope that the Island will keep that gentle pace of life, and unintrusive charm, that has given it this special capacity for refreshing the spirit.

Her Majesty the Queen and His Royal Highness Prince Philip on a recent visit to the Island, continuing a royal link with the Isle of Wight that goes back to the Middle Ages.

Bibliography

UNPUBLISHED THESES

K.R. Andrews: *Economic Aspects of Elizabethan Privateering* (London Ph.D. 1951)

J.D. Jones: *The Isle of Wight 1558-1642* (S'hampton Ph.D. *1978*)

M.J. Jones: *The Administration of the Poor in the Isle of Wight 1771-1836* Southampton M.Phil, 1982)

D.F. Lamb: *The Seaborne Trade of Southampton in the first half of the 17th century* (Southampton M.Phil. 1972)

W.H. Mildon: *Puritanism in Hampshire and the Isle of Wight from the reign of Elizabeth to the Restoration* (London Ph.D. 1934)

D.J. Tomalin: *British biconical urns, their character and chronology, and their relationship with indigenous early Bronze Age ceramics* (Southampton Ph.D. 1983)

J.L. Wiggs: *The Seaborne Trade of Southampton in the second half of the 16 century* (Southampton M.A. 1955)

PRIMARY PRINTED SOURCES

F. Bamford (ed.): *A Royalists's Notebook: the Commonplace book of Sir John Oglander Kt.* (1936)

S.F. Hockey (ed.): *The Cartulary of Carisbrooke Priory* (I.O.W. Records Series, Vol. 2: I.W. Record Office 1981)

S.F. Hockey (ed.): 'Terrier book of Newport (I.W.) 1563' in *Proceedings of the Hampshire Field Club and Archaeological Society* Vol. 19, part 3 (1957)

W.H. Long (ed.): *The Oglander Memoirs: extracts from the MSS. of Sir John Oglander Kt.* (1888)

P.D.D. Russell (ed.): *The Hearth Tax Returns for the Isle of Wight 1664-1674* (Isle of Wight Records Series, Vol. 1: I.W. Record Office 1981)

SECONDARY PRINTED SOURCES

Albin, John: *History of the Isle of Wight* (1795)

Arnold, C.J.: *The Anglo-Saxon Cemeteries of the Isle of Wight* (1982)

Aspinall-Oglander, C.: *Nunwell Symphony* (1945)

Basford, H.V.: *The Vectis Report* (Newport 1980)

Black, Frederick: *An Outline Sketch of the Parliamentary History of the Isle of Wight* (Newport 1929)

Cantwell, A. and Sprack, P.: *The Needles Defences 1525-1956* (Ryde 1986)

Deare, Ian: *The Royal Yacht Squadron 1815-1985* (1985)

du Boulay, E.: *Bembridge past and present* (1911)

Eldridge, R.J.: *Newport, Isle of Wight, in bygone days* (Newport 1952)

Foster, D. Arnold: *At War with the Smugglers* (1936)

Hassall, John: *A tour of the Isle of Wight* (1790)

Hockey, S.F.: *Quarr Abbey and its Lands 1132-1651* (Leicester 1970)

Hockey, S.F.: *Insula Vecta* (1982)

Insole, Allan and Parker, Alan: *Industrial Archaeology in the Isle of Wight* (Newport 1979)

Jones, J.D.: *The Royal Prisoner: Charles I at Carisbrooke* (1965)

Kokeritz, Helge: *The placenames of the Isle of Wight* (Uppsala 1940)

Major, Kenneth J.: *The Mills of the Isle of Wight* (1970)

Moore, Pamela (ed.): *A Guide to the Industrial Archaeology of Hampshire and the Isle of Wight* (Southampton 1984)

Page, William (ed.): *Victoria County history of Hampshire and the Isle of Wight,* Vol. 5 (1912)

Paye, P. and Paye, K.: *Steam on the Isle of Wight* (1979)

Scantlebury, R.E.: *The Catholic Story of the Isle of Wight* (1962)

Shepard, Bill: *Newport Isle of Wight remembered* (1984)

Shurlock, Barry: *Portrait of the Solent* (1983)

Stone, Percy G.: *The Architectural Antiquities of the Isle of Wight* (1891)

Tomalin, David: *Roman Wight: a guide catalogue* (Newport 1987)

Vancouver, Charles: *General View of the Agriculture of Hampshire including the Isle of Wight* (1810)

Venables, Edmund: *A Guide to the Isle of Wight* (1860)

Warner, Richard: *The History of the Isle of Wight* (1795)

Whitehead, John L.: *The Undercliff of the Isle of Wight* (1911)

Winter, C.W.R.: *The ancient town of Yarmouth* (Newport 1981)

Winter, C.W.R.: *The Manor Houses of the Isle of Wight* (Wimborne 1984)

Worsley, Richard: *History of the Isle of Wight* (1781)

JOURNALS

Boynton, Lindsay: 'Billeting: the example of the Isle of Wight', in *English Historical Review*, lxxiv, no. 290, (January 1959)

Coleby, Andrew: 'Communications: military-civilian relations on the Solent 1651-1689', in *The Historical Journal*, 29, 4 (1986)

Jones, J.D.: 'The building of a fort at Sandown, Isle of Wight, 1632-1636', in *Proceedings of the Isle of Wight Natural History and Archaeological Society*, Vol. 6, part 3 (1968)

Jones, J.D.: 'The Isle of Wight and the Revolution of 1688', in *Proceedings of the Isle of Wight Natural History and Archeological Society*, Vol. 5, part 10 (1965)

Kenyon, J.R.: 'An aspect of the 1559 survey of the Isle of Wight', in *Post-Medieval Archaeology*, Vol. 13 (1979)

Wood, L.R.: 'Agricultural Survey', in *Geography*, Vol. 18 (1933)

Index